The UK CompuServe Book

Your Definitive Start-up Guide to CompuServe and the Internet

By the Same Author

The Internet '96 Book
UK 'Internet in a Box' Book
The Daily Telegraph Guide to the Internet
The UK Internet Book, 94 & 95 Editions
The Modem & Communications Guidebook

The UK CompuServe Book

Your Definitive Start-up Guide to CompuServe and the Internet

by

SUE SCHOFIELD

1996

Published 1996 by TekBooks, PO Box 2530, Eastbourne, BN23 5SA, UK.

First printed February 1996

Designed and printed by Galliard (Printers) Ltd, Great Yarmouth
Page Make-Up—Dave Sweetman

Editor: Charles Schofield, Additional research: Dave Pantling

A CIP record for this book is available from the British Library

TekBooks email: tekbooks@compuserve.com
http://ourworld.compuserve.com/homepages/tekbooks

ISBN 1 900643 00 6

Trademarks

Flesch Reading Ease score: Easy.

For Sid, and all the staff at CompuServe UK

"Europe and America are united by Telegraphy. Glory to God in the highest. On earth, peace and goodwill to all men."

The first trans-Atlantic telegraph message sent across the new submarine cable by Cable and Wireless, in 1858.

In 1866 cablegrams cost one pound per word, sent at a speed of sixty letters per minute, with twenty pounds as a minimum for a message. In 1873 the Eastern Telegraph Company transmitted 225,160 words, in 11,258 twenty word messages. By 1872 the cost of sending a message to India was only four pounds...

Source: The Cable and Wireless History CD.

Preface

Welcome to CompuServe!

Around 4 million people of all ages, nationalities, backgrounds and professions have found the CompuServe Information Service to be a valuable tool for both business and personal use. Despite the diversity in membership, our members have a common desire to explore their world through their personal computers, and they look to CompuServe as their link to a vast array of information resources. They use CompuServe to send mail, make travel arrangements, shop, conduct research, obtain hardware and software support, keep up-to-date on world events, play games, and much more. For many, the most important benefit is the ability to share their thoughts on-line with friends across the UK and around the world.

With more than 200,000 members in the United Kingdom, CompuServe is strongly committed to serving this key market. We currently offer more than 60 products developed specifically for the UK, including news and financial services, travel information, entertainment reviews, magazine and computing support forums and a home shopping service. Some of our most popular UK services include the PA News On-line service offering the latest UK and worldwide news; the Hutchinson Unabridged Encyclopedia, which contains more than 34,000 entries; the UK What's On Guide featuring over 5,000 events from around the UK (updated weekly) and the UK Forum where CompuServe members worldwide engage in lively discussions of all things British.

As you move beyond the UK-specific services, you will discover that CompuServe is vast, and teeming with interesting people, activities and resources. Fortunately, it is also well mapped out and easy to navigate, particularly for members using CompuServe Information Manager, the interactive interface for the CompuServe Information Service. A good place to start is in the forums. These are gathering places for members who share a particular interest, hobby or profession. Most members are happy to help a newcomer, and you may have valuable expertise that can help others.

One of the fastest growing areas on CompuServe is our collection of Internet services. We've provided an electronic mail gateway to the Internet since 1989, and currently 8 million messages pass between the Internet and CompuServe members each month. In addition to Internet mail, CompuServe provides access to Usenet newsgroups, the World Wide Web, the ability to download computer files with the File Transfer Protocol (FTP) or to telnet to remote sites.

CompuServe also has its own Web page (http://www.compuserve.com) which provides more information about the service.

One of the challenges of being a CompuServe member is keeping up with the changes, such as new services, products and additions to the ever growing capabilities of CompuServe itself. To supplement the outstanding information in this book, I suggest you check out "What's New" on-line on a weekly basis.

The UK CompuServe Book serves as an excellent guide to the services on CompuServe. It will also take you step by step through the processes of composing and sending electronic mail, downloading files, using forums and exploring the Internet.

You are setting out on an exciting journey into the world of on-line services. Both the UK CompuServe Book and we at CompuServe will do our best to make it a smooth and prosperous one.

Martin Turner
UK General Manager
CompuServe UK

Introduction

Welcome to the UK CompuServe Book

In 1994 the UK Internet Book took a long slow look at the Internet and the oblique process of getting on-line. It decided that there had to be a better way of getting an electronic life than spending the worst part of a day trying to make bad software to talk to a dumb computer. What was needed was a utopian mechanism whereby you could say to the Man In The Shop: 'Plug Me In', and he would reach up to a shelf and pull down a gold and black box. You fed it to your computer, and in return your computer gave you access to a decent slice of mankind's knowledge.

Today, things are easier. You want access to the Internet without spending your free time fighting with software? You can have it. You want a MIDI file of the William Tell Overture to play to your music class? You can have it. You want an update to the screen drivers for your new PC? You can have it. You want access to UK road and traffic reports? It's here too.

You can have all of these things from the combined power of CompuServe and the Internet. Both are just a mouse click away from your modem. There are few caveats, and CompuServe with its unrivalled integration with the Internet has no real competitors. It's easy to use, it's easy to find your way around, and it's easy to get what you want.

In 1995 CompuServe downgraded its prices, upgraded its modems, and casually dropped a new front end onto the Internet. CompuServe UK now signs up five thousand new UK users a week, and the service improves daily. New additions and enhancements to CompuServe Information Manager (CIM) software provide FTP, Telnet and access to the World Wide Web, while the forum services of CompuServe continue to provide that rare and essential quality; managed and adept delivery of personal knowledge and experience.

CompuServe is the definitive professional on-line service for UK users. It has UK forums, UK information providers, UK Weather, UK shopping, UK Internet sites, UK System Operators, UK support, a UK book, UK software, UK design teams, UK support. It has hundreds of thousands of UK members for whom CompuServe represents the best service available, and it's one of the few Internet services where you don't need a PhD in Computer Science to get the software working. Prices are low, support and service are high. And CompuServe evolves faster than your ability to outgrow it. 1996 will be the Year of CompuServe. New services and utilities will make that service easier to use and yet more powerful, and price changes will make a CompuServe account the on-line bargain of the year.

Using this book

As many other authors have found, documenting CompuServe is like painting the Forth Bridge. By the time you've finished, it needs re-doing. So I've adopted a different approach. I've covered the basics you need to get going, and know that your two best friends on CompuServe, the Special/ Find menu option and the computer File Finders will give you a flying start. I've picked out a number of UK sites for you to browse as screen shots and have documented all of the start up procedures you'll need to get going for CompuServe Mail, Forums, Internet use and so on.

If you get stuck with anything GO HELPFORUM for assistance or call the support line on 0800 000 400 from within the UK. Human beings, not Cyborgs, Virtual Celebrities, or computer geeks, will answer your call.

I've stuck rigidly to the use of CIM. There are some wonderful third-party navigation and news handling tools for CompuServe, which will allow you to broaden and evolve your use of the service. But you can't run until you can walk, and CIM is the best way to start exploring CompuServe.

Because CompuServe is so dynamic I have not documented the location of every file and program mentioned in the book. Nor is there a list of every UK World Wide Web site in existence. But pointers to sites which provide fresh information and links to other sites are here, and it's up to you to explore.

If you stay within CompuServe's forums you'll find that the Libraries are constantly being updated with new files. I've included a number of graphical 'walk-throughs' for new users, to enable them to get started on CompuServe and the Internet with a minimum of fuss. There's also a large number of practical tips to make sure you can use the search and find mechanisms of the largest on-line system in the world.

The Internet changes daily, so this book concentrates on getting you up to speed on the basics, rather than trying to turn you into an 'expert'. There are too many Internet experts as it is. The basics are here, in sufficient depth to allow you to get to grips with the navigation and research tools you need. My only regrets are that time and space prevent me from writing ten thousand pages to show you around the multitudinous facilities on CompuServe. It still wouldn't be enough.

Finally, my thanks go to the many anonymous authors of the CompuServe FAQ's included here in some of the Chapters. Most of them are written by the SYSOP's of the forums you will visit, they are the unsung backbone of CompuServe. Electronics and computers bring CompuServe into your office or home, but it is human beings which form, support, and mould that service. Long may it be so.

Bon Voyage

Sue Schofield
February 1996

email: suesco@compuserve.com
Home page: http//ourworld.compuserve.com/homepages/suesco

Thanks to Andrew Salmon, Martin Turner and Alan Scott of CompuServe UK for their assistance with this project.

About the author

Sue Schofield's award winning technology writing has appeared in most of the UK daily newspapers at some time, and in most of the UK's computer magazines. Her UK Internet Book stayed in the Top Ten best-seller lists for eleven months; a record for any computer book. She opened her first email account in 1981 and has been a CompuServe user for about six years. Sue writes the 'Random Access' technology column in Focus Magazine.

Late changes and additions

Updates to the text in this book will be available from the Author's Web site at:
> http://ourworld.compuserve.com/homepages/suesco

Fast startup for new CompuServe members

NEW PRICING FROM FEBRUARY 1ST 1996

CompuServe are removing the communications surcharge from all Mercury and FT nodes across Europe from 1st February. Please GO RATES for up to date pricing information and GO PHONES for updated node information. The pricing information in this book is likely to change without notice and is provided for guidance only.

All users:
Signup Support - 0800 454 260
Pre-sales Support - 0800 000 200
Technical Support & Customer Service - 0800 000 400
Disk Line - 0800 374 971
Online Support - GO FEEDBACK

Which node?
It's recommended you sign up using your nearest CompuServe (CPS) Node. If you want to use GNS or Mercury 5000 local nodes you can change to these later. CPS users, FT users and Mercury 5000 users pay no extra charges from February 1996. GNS users pay an extra £2.75 per hour. These extra charges are known as Communication Surcharges.

PC Windows 3.1 Users - System Requirements

Windows 3.1
4Mb Ram (8MB is better)
Optional CD ROM drive (double speed or higher is better)
 640 x 480 screen resolution, 256 colours is best (run Windows Setup to check)
Optional Sound Blaster or compatible sound card and speakers
Macintosh users - System Requirements

System 7.1 or better, 256 colours (see Monitor Control Panel) MacTCP for use with CompuServe PPP internet access.

4MB Memory (8MB or more is better and is needed for System 7.5) 68030 or better Mac for use with Mosaic, plus 8MB memory for System 7.5 users.

Startup - Windows CompuServe Membership Kit users

You'll need your card printed with the Serial Number and Agreement letters.

1) Insert the CD into your CDROM Drive or insert floppy disk No 1 into drive A:

2) In Windows 3.1 select RUN from the File Manager. Type D:DEMO and click OK or press Enter, or floppy users, type A:SETUP

3) For CD users the demo program will create a "Go CompuServe" icon in Windows. Floppy users will go straight to CIM installation.

4) Follow the onscreen instructions making sure that you select YES when you are asked to copy the sign-up files.

5) When prompted, enter your unique Serial and Agreement numbers. You'll also need your credit card or bank account details at this point.

If you need different format disks please phone CompuServe support on the number above.

Getting going

* First make sure your modem is connected to the correct port on your computer. Use Windows Terminal to check that you can see 'OK' coming back from the modem when you type AT.

* If you have a sound card installed locate the sound volume or Mixer control and make sure the volume is turned down to a reasonable level. The Startup CD uses WAV files for sound. If you don't have a sound card consider adding one, as CompuServe CIM makes increasing use of sound and Multimedia effects.

* Insert the disk into your CD drive, then open File Manager

* Your CD drive will be shown pictorially. Often it will be drive D: although if you have two hard disks, or your hard disk is partitioned, it may be shown with a different letter. Double click the CD icon.

* Look for the file DEMO.EXE. Double click this to start the CD Tour.

Hints for SignUp - ALL Users

The software installed is about 3 megabytes in size. But make sure you have at least 5 megabytes free to allow for downloads and add-on Internet programs.

* Either watch the tour, or go straight to Sign Me Up now.

* Once in Sign Me Up go to Install and Sign Me up. Follow the prompts to add PC sound and SignUP files.

* Select "Sign Me Up" to begin the process. The program will ask for your Agreement Number, Serial Number, country and billing method. Enter these press TAB to move between fields, and double click 'Proceed'.

* You'll be taken to the CompuServe SignUP Screen. Add in your personal name, your evening phone number, and your billing information. Click Proceed after you've double checked the information.

* A second screen will ask if you want to receive the free magazine, be listed in the member directory enabling other CompuServe users to track you down through your Country and name, and whether you wish to receive external promotional sales mailings. A Service Agreement screen appears, click proceed if you want to be contractually bound by this Agreement.

* The SignUP process will take you to a list of access points for CompuServe. At this stage its recommended you pick a CompuServe Node, FT Node, or a Mercury node, unless you wish to pay the extra fees for using GNS. You can easily change your software at a later stage. Choose the fastest basic speed your modem supports. This will be 300, 2400, 9600, 14400 or 28,800. Use a lower speed such as 2400 if you have problems connecting (modem troubleshooting is covered in Chapter 4.) Double Click Proceed.

* On the next screen select Touch Type, unless your phone makes clicking noises when it dials. Most UK phones are now Touch Tone, and make musical tones when dialling. Add in a 9 if you're going through a switchboard, or add 132 here to route via Mercury 132, or whatever the access code is for your long distance carrier. (If you're using BT leave this area blank, unless you're going through a switchboard.) Double Click Proceed.

* Select the COM port to which your modem is connected. For Mac users this will be the Modem Port, the Printer Port or the Comms Toolbox. Most PCs will use COM1 or COM2, although those fitted with a fast serial port such as the Hayes ESP may see a modem on COM3 or COM4. If you're unsure make sure your modem is connected and switched on, then click Auto-Detect. Double Click Proceed.

* The final screen connects to CompuServe to sign you up. If you're a PC user and have selected Auto-Detect in the previous screen, the SignUP process may not happen because the software can't find the modem. A Change Settings box will appear. In this case you'll need to physically select a port to connect. Try COM1, COM2, COM3, COM4 in that order. Your mouse may freeze if you use this method. If in doubt restart Windows and verify which COM port your mouse is plugged into before proceeding.

* If you've entered invalid data into the sign-up screens this will be rejected and the system will disconnect. You'll then be taken back to the screen where the wrong information is entered.

* If you continue to have problems contact UK help on 0800 000 400. Other assistance voice numbers are accessed from the Help Me Icon on the first SignUP Screen.

For on-line CIM support type GO WINCIM, GO MACCIM, GO DOSCIM or GO OS2CIM.

UK services list:
Use Special/GO from the menu bar to bring up a dialogue box to access these services. Use Special/Find UK to get the updated list and add services to your personal Special/Favourite Places menu.

Service	GO Word
AA Roadwatch	[AAROADWATCH]
AA Travel Services	[UKTRAVEL]
Ashmount Research Forum	[ASHMOUNT]
British Books in Print	[BBIP]
British Trade Marks($)	[UKTRADEMARK]
Compaq UK Forum	[CPQUK]
Computer Life UK Forum	[CLIFEUK]
Computer Shopper (UK) Forum	[UKSHOPPER]
Dixons	[DIXONS]
Dogs Forum	[DOGS]
Dun&Bradstreet Internat.($)	[DBINTL]
Dun&Bradstreet UK($)	[DUNBUK]
Election Connection	[ELECTION]
European Co. Reasearch Centre($)	[EUROLIB]
European Forum	[EURFORUM]
European Rail	[RAILWAY]
Executive News Service($)	[ENS]
Global Crises Forum	[CRISIS]
Guardian newspaper	[GUARDIAN]
ICC Directory of UK Comp.($)	[ICCDIR]
IQuest($)	[IQUEST]
Infocheck($)	[INFOCHECK]
Int'l Dun's Mkt Identifier($)	[DBINT]
Interflora	[UKINTERFLORA]
International Trade Forum	[TRADE]

Jaguar(FREE)	[UKJAGUAR]
Jerusalem Post($)	[JERUSALEM]
JordanWatch($)	[JORDANS]
Key British Enterprises($)	[KEYBRIT]
London Film Festival	[FILMONLINE]
Multiple Sclerosis Forum	[MULTSCLER]
NL Computing Forum	[NLCOMP]
NewsGrid	[NEWSGRID]
Northern Ireland News Clips($)	[NIRELAND]
Office World(FREE)	[OFFWORLD]
OnLine Issues Forum	[OLISSUES]
PA Financial News	[CITYNEWS]
PA News	[PAO]
PC Direct UK Forum	[PCDUK]
PC File Finder	[PCFF]
PC Magazine UK Online	[PCUKONLINE]
PC Plus / PC Answers	[PCPLUS]
PC Sports	[PCSPORTS]
PC World	[UKPCWORLD]
PaperChase-MEDLINE($)	[PAPERCHASE]
Past Times	[PASTTIMES]
ProTRADE Forum	[PROTRADE]
Reuters UK News Clips	[UKREUTERS]
Science Museum	[SCMUSEUM]
Selfridges(FREE)	[SELFRIDGES]
Telework Europa Forum	[TWEUROPA]
Tesco	[TESCO]
The Good Pub Guide	[UKPUBS]
The Hutchinson Encyclopedia	[HUTCHINSON]
Travel Britain Online	[TBONLINE]
Travel Forum	[TRAVSIG]
UK Company Information($)	[COUK]
UK Company Library($)	[UKLIB]
UK Entertainment Reviews	[UKREVIEWS]
UK Forum	[UKFORUM]
UK Historical Stock Pricing	[UKPRICE]
UK Information Tech Forum	[UKIT]
UK Newspaper Library($)	[UKPAPERS]
UK Politics Forum	[UKPOLITICS]
UK Professionals Forum	[UKPROF]
UK Recreation Forum	[UKREC]
UK Travel Forum	[UKTF]
UK Vendor A Forum	[UKVENA]
UK What's On Guide	[UKWO]
UKSHAREWARE Forum	[UKSHARE]
United Press Int'l($)	[ENS]
Virgin Megastore	[MEGASTORE]
WH Smith	[WHSMITH]

Contents

vii   **Preface**

ix   **Introduction**

xiii   **CompuServe Fast start for new members**

Section I Welcome

3   **Chapter 1** Welcome to CompuServe

17   **Chapter 2** Getting Started

29   **Chapter 3** All about CIM

43   **Chapter 4** Modems and CompuServe

Section II Using CompuServe

57   **Chapter 5** CompuServe Mail

91   **Chapter 6** CompuServe Forums

113   **Chapter 7** Places to go, things to do

Section III CompuServe & the Internet

137   **Chapter 8** CompuServe and the Internet

153   **Chapter 9** Starting out - setting up

167   **Chapter 10** The World Wide Web

183   **Chapter 11** The Compleat Mosaic

221   **Chapter 12** Network News

237   **Chapter 13** FTP

247   **Chapter 14** Telnet

257   **Chapter 15** Searching the Net

271   **Chapter 16** Epilogue

Section IV Appendices

275   **Appendix 1** CompuServe Rates

279   **Appendix 2** UK & European Access numbers

291   **Appendix 3** CompuServe Forum Index

321   **Appendix 4**   Using the Home Page Wizard

329   **Appendix 5** Glossary of technical and Internet terms

337   **Index**

Section 1

Starting out with CompuServe

1 Welcome to CompuServe

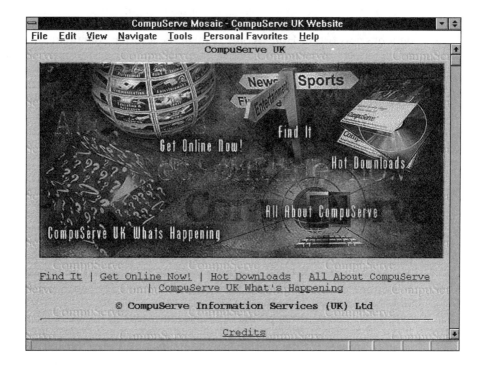

At the time of writing, CompuServe is one of the largest coherent public access systems on the planet. Its conferences and forums cover almost every activity known to man, plus a few that aren't, and it boasts the biggest set of computer file archives of any single system. If you already have access to a computer and modem then you can enter and gain a month's use of this system for less than the price of take-away pizza for one, plus a small contribution to the coffers of your local telephone provider.

CompuServe started life in the depths of the Golden United Life Insurance Company, in Ohio, USA. The insurance company installed a larger DEC mainframe, and started selling time-sharing of data processing to third parties. Golden United adopted the CompuServe name in 1969, and eventually were acquired by HR Block, a large US tax and accounting company. Since then the service has continued to grow, sometimes through acquisitions and mergers.

CompuServe used to run mainly on DEC computers, but now designs its own equipment and software to meet the needs of a growing and dedicated user base. Today CompuServe is the most popular on-line service in the world, and signs up over 7000 new users a week in this country alone.

What's on CompuServe?

The glib answer is 'everything' from Aardvarks to Zebras, and almost everything in between, in a computer-readable form. That information might be a UK railway timetable, a recipe, a computer file, or a note from your manager who's on a business trip to Hong Kong. It might be a forum containing information on any aspect of human behaviour or need, or a live on-line interview with a media personality. It might also be a different view on world events from those in the UK media, or it might be up-to-date medical information. In short CompuServe is a large virtual world of knowledge which contains much of value to anyone with the basic computer skills to access it. In 1996 that means an increasing share of the UK workforce, schoolchildren, and home users.

For corporate users CompuServe acts as a central store of essential marketing, technical and financial information. It also works as an external messaging hub, allowing organizations to send mail and computer data around the world using their internal computer network as the originating system. It also provides a simple, secure and easily managed information resource for managers needing to keep in touch with each other, or with market and financial trends. CompuServe also delivers a central access point for hundreds of external databases such as Reuters News, Dow Jones, and Dun and Bradstreet, making it the number one choice for research for writers and journalists, not to mention the many UK computer magazines and daily papers whose writers stay up to date by using the service.

If it were possible to single out the single most valuable feature of CompuServe, it would be its ability to bring all of this information together into a single cohesive system for the user and his computer. And there's a further benefit. CompuServe is run by professionals and offers good user support, software which works, and a service which is almost glitch free.

CompuServe versus the Others

There's already a plethora of on-line services in the UK. Well known names include Compulink Information Exchange in Surbiton (known as CIX to its denizens), New Prestel run by BT, and the French MiniTel services, which are now accessible from the UK. There are also seventy thousand private bulletin boards in the UK, run from back bedrooms (or worse) and any number of commercial bulletin boards peddling everything from 'artistic' computer-readable pictures, to illicit software. On top of this there's the Internet, providing millions of host computers into which almost anyone can log for almost any purpose. How can CompuServe compete, and why should you choose CompuServe over any of the others?

The answer to the first question is that CompuServe is competitive in both

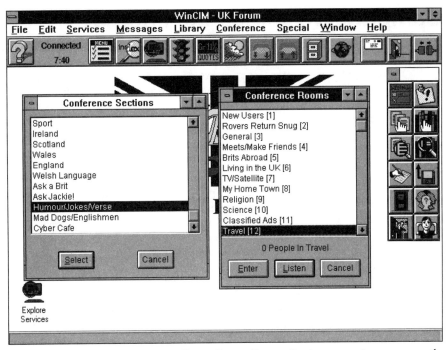

Figure 1.2 *The UK Forum on CompuServe. Forum Sections contain messages, the Library carries files, and there's an on-line live conferencing facility.*

cost and content to other commercial services. New charges introduced from February 1996 make CompuServe as competitive as any other UK service, and cheaper than many.

In answer to the second question, many UK services are highly parochial - the access telephone numbers are local only to a single telephone charge zone, and the information contained within mainly relates to UK regional issues, those within the south-east of Britain taking precedence. In contrast CompuServe offers a truly world-wide view of events and news of all descriptions, and has the advantage of being easily accessed from many local points in UK cities through the packet switched networks of BT and Mercury. Effective from February 1996 CompuServe can be accessed with a local phone call from most parts of the UK via the Mercury network (See Appendices for details). CompuServe can also be directly accessed in many countries of the world, making it a great travelling companion to any lap-top toting wayfarer.

If you already have access to the Internet you can also telnet into CompuServe from anywhere in the world with an Internet connection and telnet client software. CompuServe is well established throughout Europe, and often provides Europe-specific information and guidance in its monthly CompuServe Magazine. Finally CompuServe provides support via Freephone telephone numbers in the UK to make ensure members get started with a minimum of fuss.

CompuServe versus the Internet

Here's the Big Question. Should you get yourself an Internet account, or a CompuServe account? They both appear to cost about the same to run, although you'll often pay more to set-up an Internet account than a CompuServe account with Internet provision. An Internet account will cost between twelve and twenty-five pounds to set-up, and then between ten and fifteen pounds a month minimum charge to run. CompuServe has a minimum charge of around £6.95 per month for five hours use, thereafter it costs £1.95 per hour to use it.

You'll need TCP/IP software to get going on an Internet connection which can add significantly to the cost of setting up an Internet account, unless you use Shareware, for which support and updates can be patchy. For CompuServe you'll need CompuServe Information Manager (CIM - pronounced 'sim'). You can get CIM for free from many special offers, on-line, or via special CompuServe membership kits. New features built in to WinCIM version 2.0 upwards give you access to Internet services such as FTP, Telnet, and Usenet news, and direct access to the World Wide Web. You only need the one free program to access these services although you'll need to use the supplied CompuServe Mosaic browser (or another Web Browser) to get on to the World Wide Web.

CompuServe are also one of the the world's largest Internet Providers. Internet access will be extended in 1996 and the combination of Internet provision and the existing CompuServe file and forum structure make CompuServe unbeatable as the ultimate computer accessory.

In terms of content CompuServe offers huge numbers of files and topics, available through CIM's well developed and easy to use interface. In contrast the Internet offers an even larger number of files and data files but you need TCP/IP compliant software to run Archie searches, more software for gopher searches, and yet more software to handle your mail. As none of the files on the Internet are yet indexed in a common way you'll generally spend a lot longer searching for what you need using the Internet, than you would using CompuServe and its file finders or the inbuilt Forum search engines.

If you need access to specialist discussion forums you'll find that those on CompuServe are indexed, and a single search will find forums of interest. The Internet equivalent News Groups are neither indexed nor generally managed, and finding the information you need is consequently haphazard, although latter-day news readers are making this easier. Another CompuServe search mechanism ('file-finder') will locate data files in matter of seconds from a keyword search.

Support

CompuServe is used by many corporations to provide support for their products. Program file updates, and support forums run by trained technicians are on the system. In contrast the Internet relies mainly on ad hoc support by enthusiasts, who may not always have the right answer, although this situation is also rapidly changing.

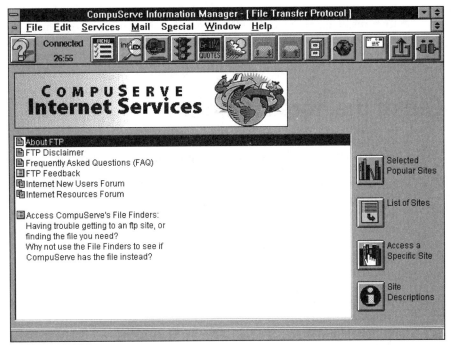

Figure 1.3   *The FTP services from within CIM. CompuServe also offers full TCP/IP Internet access via its CompuServe Internet Dialler, CID.*

If that's not enough, two other points are that CompuServe provides a secure managed environment where you can mail, fax or phone the CompuServe help team if you get stuck. You can also give full CompuServe access to your family without much risk of them being offended by sexual harassment, bad behavior, or bad language. And should you want to explore further then CompuServe also offers full access to Internet mail, Usenet, ftp, telnet and World Wide Web Internet services.

Is CompuServe the best choice?

To be fair it has to be said that all users of dial-up comms, washing machines, cars or any other product have different requirements. The manager of a firm of market analysts may use CompuServe mail for keeping in touch with stock market figures, the computer freak in his bedroom might use the same mail system for interrogating Internet-based list servers. Readers will have to make the their own decisions as to the suitability of CompuServe to match their needs. Extensive use of CompuServe forums or professional databases can also cost more than intensive use of the Internet but the benefits often appear as lower phone bills because data is found so rapidly in comparison.

Recent price changes mean that even if you make extensive use of email you will not incur extra charges, and CompuServe Mail and its in-built ability to transfer eight bit data files is secure, and in widespread use. But if you just want an Internet account without use of forums, databases and so on, CompuServe provide that option too. Internet-only service provision will be increased in 1996 by a number of new options.

Out of the horse's mouth

CompuServe provides excellent research facilities. My CompuServe account is the one I turn to for research, support files, news clippings, financial data, railway timetables, UK road works info, and much more, in preference to current Internet resources I have access to. My own CompuServe bills run at about twenty five pounds (including vat) a month - including the phone bill to my nearest local node in Sussex - but I do make heavy use of the Executive News, on-line databases and other extra-cost forums. In contrast many recreational or email only CompuServe users keep within the minimum charge of around £6.95 per month.

While there is no such thing as a representative set of costs for either the Internet or CompuServe if I had to keep only one account then CompuServe would be the one to stay. This is because as a full time writer and journalist, I cannot get ready access to the many commercial news feeds or the computer support files I need over the Internet. In my case a CompuServe account is vital. A good example is support for the Hewlett Packard DeskWriter printers I use to produce typescripts. In 1994 Apple released System 7.5 for the Mac, which includes QuickDraw GX, a new printing system. A gopher search on the Internet over a long distance phone connection took twenty minutes to tell me that the updated printer driver wasn't around. A search on CompuServe in the HP Peripherals forum (GO HPPER) and the subsequent file download took four minutes - at local call rates.

Other readers will have different ideas about value for money, but I do recommend that you try CompuServe for a couple of months to see if it suits you and your needs. Recreational users may balk at the mention of bills of twenty-five pounds a month, but most non-business users seem to end up staying in or near their monthly subscription. Check out the Rates in the Appendices for a full view of what CompuServe costs.

Flies in the ointment

From the above eulogy you might begin to wonder if CompuServe is really the apian's patella's I make out. Like all on-line services CompuServe has a few quirks. Here's a short list.

1) CompuServe is big
CompuServe is very big, big enough to give new users a sense of agoraphobia. It can take a long time to find your way around, and that puts off many new users.

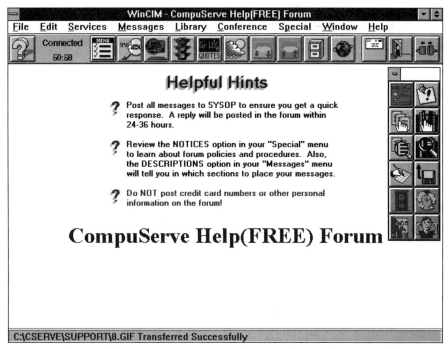

Figure 1.4   *CompuServe offers both on-line and telephone support. The Help forum carries many useful files in the Library, and is a great place for new users to start exploring. GO HELPFORUM to get there.*

You can overcome this by showing a willingness to ask questions. The Practice Forum (GO PRACTICE) helps users both old and new to come to terms with CompuServe, as do the Forum search utilities, and the Filefinder utilities (Go IBM FF and Go MacFF etc.). The HELPFORUM answers many basic queries and keeps a decent library of useful files for newcomers.

2) CompuServe seems run by and for North Americans

That was certainly true when the service started up, but things have come a long way since then. In the last three years CompuServe has concentrated on providing a better and more relevant service to Europeans. CompuServe already has a large number of UK and European services and more arrive by the week. CompuServe UK is supported by real human beings in Bristol, and has a growing support team of helpful people. If you go to any of the major computer exhibitions in the UK you'll meet many of the staff who make CompuServe UK work. All of them, from the General Manager downwards will spend time with you if need assistance, or just want to look around the system.

3) CompuServe is perceived as being expensive

Not since the price reductions at the start of 1995, and the provision of local

Figure 1.5   *There are 450,000 files on CompuServe available for download. You can get support for almost any computer hardware from the Forums.*

call access over Mercury 5000 in 1996. In terms of the services available, CompuServe in the UK is cheaper than any of the other large professional on-line services, and you get Internet provision thrown in for around £6.95 per month.

4) Internet Compliant Binary Mail

Pardon? A binary file is a spreadsheet or wordprocessor file or a picture file and you can mail these between CompuServe users with impunity. But if you want to mail, say a picture of The Queen to your friend in Toronto who has an Internet mail account, then you are going to have a problem. This is because the Internet isn't as advanced as CompuServe, and you'll need to encode your file in a special way to get it from CompuServe over the Internet. (Chapter 5 tells all) And that's all.

On the upside CompuServe offers vital support services from all the major computer suppliers, global electronic messaging for individual and corporates, forums on every topic, as much help as you need to get going, and a decent user interface. There are now over 30 services specifically introduced for UK members such as AA Roadwatch (GO AAROADWATCH), the What's On Guide (GO UKWO) and the Good Pub Guide (GO UKPUBS). You can obtain a full listing of these by entering FIND UK when you are next online. Type GO UK to be taken the a UK browser menu.

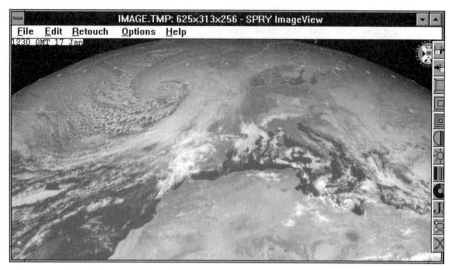

Figure 1.6 *Typical European weather, from CompuServe. GO WEATHER. Weather maps can be downloaded and stored. Italy is just to the right of centre in this picture.*

CompuServe and the Internet

CompuServe has evolved into two services. The first is traditional CompuServe accessed by CIM. The second is full blown TCP/IP Internet Access over a PPP link. (See Section 3.) This uses the same phone nodes as CompuServe but instead lets you use any TCP/IP software over the Internet once you've established your PPP link. In many ways this is an ideal solution as you can choose which of the two choices suits you best.

For the user who needs occasional use of Internet services such as FTP, News or Telnet these are now directly built in to CompuServe and accessed via CIM (GO INTERNET). The World Wide Web can be accessed from within versions of WinCIM from version 2.0 upwards. Charges for all methods of access are the same, giving you absolute freedom of choice in your degree of interaction with the Internet.

Integration of FTP, News and Telnet into CompuServe also means that users of older computers for which little TCP/IP software is being developed can use CompuServe as a managed gateway onto the Internet.

Alternatives to CIM

Not everyone uses CIM to access CompuServe. There are an number of alternate access 'front-end" programs which provide more features, or different facilities to CIM. You get these from the relevant support forum, and, because these programs are developed by private companies you pay the going rate for

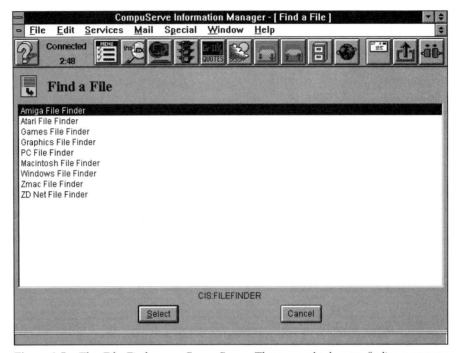

Figure 1.7   *The File Finders on CompuServe. These are the key to finding computer files and provide a keyword search through the file libraries.*

purchasing or using them. This book concentrates entirely on CIM for Windows and Mac users, because CIM offers the easiest way to learn about CompuServe. CIM also comes with free telephone support, which is important for new CompuServe members. Additionally CIM is used by many UK corporates to give CompuServe access to their employees, and must therefore be regarded as the de facto method for getting into CompuServe. Here are the alternatives.

ASCII Terminal access

This is still in widespread use, especially amongst users of older 8 bit micro-computers. You set your terminal software to 7 bits, even parity, 1 data bit and CompuServe will talk to you in ASCII. You can use either VT100 emulation or ANSI emulation, and also log in via the Packet Switch services using this method. I've used ASCII terminal access to check my mail from an Amstrad NC100 portable, and while CIM is preferable (and has a faster user interface) ASCII access is still in use by many people. This method can also be used by many computer speech and voice box attachments so that non-sighted users can work with CompuServe. Use BYE as the command for leaving CompuServe by this method.

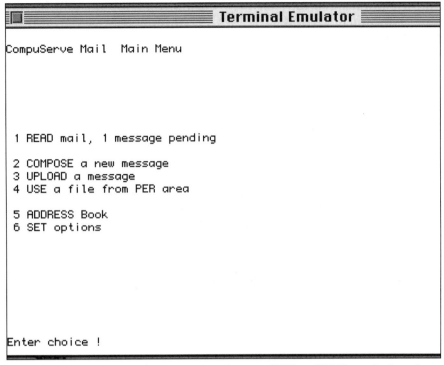

Figure 1.8 *CompuServe also supports use by any ANSI or VT100 terminal emulator. You can use it with any computer which supports this, although the interface is now a little dated. This is a Mac screen.*

OLR's

Navigator and the other programs mentioned here are often described as Off-Line Readers (OLR's) because they do their work with the phone disconnected, once they've grabbed the data they need from CompuServe. OLRs let you browse forums off-line, which is how they save money. CIM is also an OLR, despite some protestations to the contrary, because it too lets you read and write mail and Forum messages off-line. CIM is not as automated as many of the programs listed below as you'll see in the next chapters. But it is free, and you don't have to program it to make it do what you want. This is a plus for some people, a minus for others.

CompuServe Navigator - 'CsNAV' (Windows/MAC)

An alternative to CIM and developed by CompuServe. It's a script driven program which interacts with CompuServe to automate on-line sessions.

Navigator can cut phone and CompuServe bills drastically but it is not as intuitive to use as it might be. However the program is very useful for heavy-duty forum users. It costs around thirty dollars but you'll get an account credit for downloading it. GO NAVIGATOR for more details. The program is supported in the CSNAVSUPPORT forum, and you may want to drop in there before you download the program to see what Navigator is all about. Mac users have to GO ORDER to get the program.

TapCIS (MSDOS)

This is another script driven access tool, and something of a monster with a user interface which can only be described as 'odd'. But TapCIS is fast, and it runs on early DOS computers with only a minimum of memory. Despite protestations in the computer press that DOS is Dead, there's a healthy support forum for the product. GO TAPCIS for more information but remember that TapCIS is not for CompuServe novices.

OzCIS (MSDOS/Windows)

A notorious OLR now in two versions. OzCIS works well but does require a '286 (version 1) or '386 (version 2) computer, and plenty of memory. OzCIS is reputed to be amongst the fastest and whizzy-ist of OLRs, drop by the OZCIS forum for a look. There's also a German language version and a Windows version.

TeePee (MSDOS) WigWam (Windows)

Found also as a CIX variant, TeePee is British (originally TelePathy) and will run on lowly DOS computers. It also (allegedly) runs well under DOS emulation, so Mac and Archimedes users who have machines fitted with PC emulators might find it useful. GO UKCOMMS for more info. TeePee has a sibling called WigWam for Windows, which people either love or hate.

NavCIS (MSDOS/Windows)

A product of Mr John Dvorak's empire. NavCIS also provides off-line use of the File Finders, and formatted email messages. Copious support and suck-it-and-see versions are in the DVORAK forum.

Golden ComPass (OS/2)

A powerful OLR which is data file compatible with TapCIS. It wouldn't install on our OS/2 machine, more to do with the machine than with Golden Compass, but there is full support in the GCPSUPPORT forum.

AutoPilot (Amiga)

Who said the Amiga was dead? AutoPilot uses ARexx scripts and so can be configured to do almost anything with CompuServe. Trial versions are also available from the AMIGAVEND forum.

QuickCIS (Atari ST)

Found in the ATARIPRO forum libraries. This program is free and useful. Copious support in the ATARIPRO forum

... And then there's CIM

CIM is available in four versions for DOS, OS/2, Windows and Mac. Support is from CIMSUPPORT, PCSUPPORT, WCIMSUPPORT and MCIMSUPPORT forums respectively. All versions of CIM are effectively free, and are broadly similar in operation. New releases arrive as Windows versions first, which does cause some grumbles from users of other machines. Mac users always seem to be at the back of the queue when CIM software gets handed out, but being funny creative types, carp the least. They are safe in the knowledge that CIM was first developed on a Macintosh.

CIM Add ons

There are a number of bolt-on utilities for CIM. Perhaps the most useful is AboveSpell, an add on spell check program. GO ASPELL for detials. Or do I mean details?

StockTracker creates tracking portfolios from ticker symbols used on CompuServe. You can use it to log price changes and export them to your favourite spreadsheet for processing. GO STOCKTRADER for details.

Quicken Quotes does broadly similar things and is available in Mac and Windows versions. GO INTUIT.

ACT! Mobile link maintains synchronized contact databases over CompuServe. GO SYMWIN

Voice Email for WinCIM sends speech, music, or any audio file as mail to CompuServe Mail users. GO VOICEMAIL.

2 Getting started

You can start your first CompuServe session once you've got hold of an access kit, a temporary ID and either a credit or charge card for payment, or a direct billing option such as Direct Debit. The first stage involves setting up your modem and computer software to interact with each other at an intimate level. Once that's done you need to get your modem to interact with the telephone network and eventually, CompuServe's computers in Ohio, USA. If you don't have start-up software you can call CompuServe UK who will either send it to you via the post or tell you how to get on-line over a modem.

CompuServe access points

Despite some observations to the contrary, Britain is not yet part of the USA, and so there is some electronic subterfuge needed to hook your computer in say, Lower Dicker, into the Ohio USA computers.

There are several ways of doing it:

* By a dial-up link into a CompuServe Access Node (CPS node)
Pros: Fast and cheap access if you live within 35 miles of one. (Anything over 35 miles is currently classed as a long distance call by BT). CPS nodes support modem speeds of either 9600, 14,400 or 28,800 bits per second.
    Cons: Not everyone lives near a CPS node

* By a link connected through the Mercury 5000 or FT packet switching system
Pros: Cheaper than dialing long distance
    Cons: Slower than a CPS node

* By a link connected through the BT Global Networking System (GNS)
Pros: Cheaper than dialing long distance
    Cons: Slower than a CPS node and you'll pay an extra charge per hour for access. (Communications surcharge). But you can use GNS from anywhere in the world.

* By telnetting in over the Internet
Pros: Reduces call costs to zero if you have a direct Internet network account.
    Cons: You'll need special TCP/IP software, and access to an Internet account. The speed of the link will be dependent on the amount of traffic on your Internet Provider's link, not on CompuServe. Also, not everyone has direct access to the Internet, and you'll still need an account.

Which one is for you?

You can save a lot of money by juggling figures and working out which of the various access options is the best for you. If you live in London then the cheapest (and fastest) way to connect is from the London CPS nodes. You'll also get to download files at 28,800 bps thus cutting down on your phone bills.
    The next best option is to look for the nearest Mercury node, and then compare the distance to the nearest GNS point and do a bit of mental arithmetic to select your best connection option. Don't forget that Mercury access nodes don't incur a surcharge after February 1996. Finally, there's the option of using GNS or France Telecom nodes. These incur an additional cost- the 'Communications Surcharge', so you should be aware of this if you use them.

Example

In my case I live in Sussex. My nearest local call is a GNS Dialplus node but I'll pay an extra charge per hour to use it. So I use the Crawley CPS node at 14400 bits per second, as the faster throughput reduces my phone bills. Crawley is further away, but I get faster access - and I don't pay the surcharge for use of GNS. I get some further compensation by using an alternative carrier to BT for the long-distance call. From February 1996 I'll be able to use a Mercury

Example   19

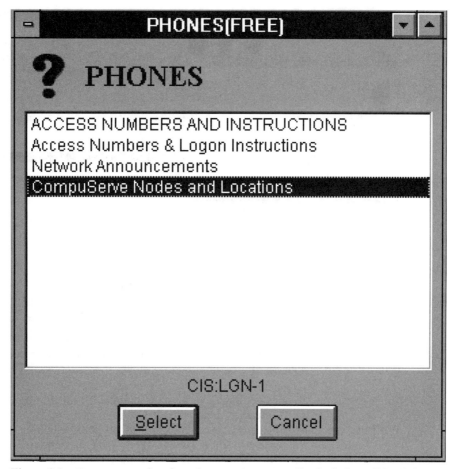

Figure 2.2 *Get an up to date list of connection points ('nodes') from GO PHONES.*
You can list nodes in all countries or just Europe.

node without incurring a surcharge, so I'll use that for all mail, and possibly
go to a faster CPS node in London for file transfers.

Up until the 5th February 1995 you would also pay extra to use the faster
access speeds at CPS nodes. Charge rates were higher for users connected at
9600 bps and 14400 bps, which helped to make the decision about which
node to use a little easier. In those Olden Tymes CompuServe users would
dial in at 2400 bps to lurk in forums, disconnect and re-dial a CPS node at
14,400 bps to download files. But CompuServe now charges the same rate for
what ever speed you choose to connect at, simplifying the entire business. All
CPS nodes will provide 28,800 bps connections in 1996.

As with all information systems using dial-up modems for public access
you'll find that the CPS nodes, especially the faster 14,400 and 28,800 nodes
are very popular and carry a lot of traffic. This sometimes causes problems

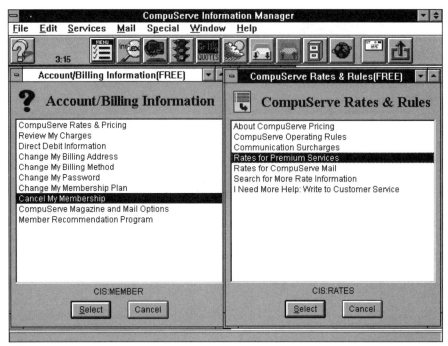

Figure 2.3   *Your personal admin center on CompuServe. GO BILLING for membership details, GO RATES for prices.*

for users as phone lines get engaged, and the bandwidth on the signal line to the modems from CompuServe get clogged with traffic. In the UK these problems are most prevalent at weekends and at off-peak telephone charging times, and you will notice a slight slowdown in your modem connection if you try to compete with 80,000 other UK users all trying to log in at one minute past six PM cheap rate on a Friday night.

There are two solutions, the first is to try and stay away from those 18:01 time slots, the second is to shift your off-peak access to early mornings. Standard rate BT charging starts at 08:00 hours, and many users can find time in between their shower and breakfast to log in and grab their mail before then. There's no real solution if you're a heavy on-line forum browser and your only free time is in the early evenings, but CompuServe are aware that nodes get clogged and are throwing money and technology at the problem. Most other UK service providers currently have the same problems, and CompuServe are updating all their nodes in 1996. However, if you're a business user you will almost always get a connection during UK business hours without re-dialling.

Call discounts

You can make large savings on your phone bill by asking your telephone provider for details of discount schemes. BT have Option 15 (amongst others)

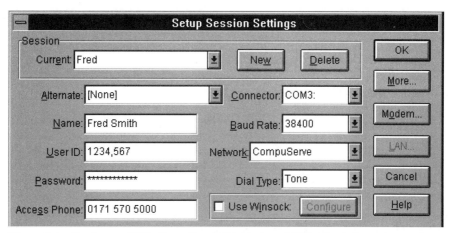

Figure 2.4   *Setting up CIM. Go to Special/Settings and fill in the dialogue box...*

which gives a good discount once you're over a certain number of calls, and also Family and Friends, which gives 5% discount off calls to any five predetermined numbers. You nominate your favourite CPS node for an automatic 5% saving. Call 1500 to ask BT Sales Offices about discounts. Mercury and other carriers provide similar schemes so do check.

Finally, call rates at weekends are very low in the UK, so the weekend is the favourite time for rummaging around CompuServe. UK users also have the option of using alternate carriers such as the Mercury 132 service. You can use a modem with this service by putting 132 <comma> in your dial number for your modem to autodial when it makes a connection to CompuServe. You can do the same if you have a Mercury PIN number. You can also use a Mercury Smart Socket on your line to provide PIN's and 132 routing automatically.

Your money and CompuServe

CompuServe doesn't work if you don't have any money. You'll find this out when you try and sign up. You'll therefore either need a credit card, or a bank account/direct debit mandate to get on to the system, and once you're on you'll clock up charges on a per minute basis. You pay about £1.95 per hour for basic use, plus your phone bill, plus any charges incurred by using GNS, FT, plus VAT on the total. You'll also pay an extra fee for accessing 'extended' services marked with a + or $ or $$ dollar signs.

Price Plans

CompuServe now have two Price Plans. The old Alternate Price Plan has gone, the Standard Price Plan now offers five hours on-line time for £6.95 per month. Extra hours are charged at £1.95 per hour, approx.

The Super Value Plan offers 20 hours free, for £16.30 per month. Extra hours are charged at £1.25 per hour, approx. These prices may change by the time we go to print.

GO CHOICES to swap between plans.
GO BILLING to alter your account details.

Remember Communications Surcharges if you use GNS nodes. FT and Mercury nodes (from February 1996) and CPS nodes are free of surcharges.

And remember, prices change all the time. So far they've gone down over the last year by a significant amount. Keep an eye on the What's New menu in CIM for details, or GO RATES for full information about prices. Values given here are for guidance only and are subject to change.

Setting up your software

Once you have decided which will be your 'local' node you can set up your software to store the number, and your login details.

a) CIM users
If you are using CIM then the program will handle all of the login to CompuServe automatically for you. For this to happen you have to tell CIM which network you are using. In the UK this will be a CompuServe Node, or Mercury or GNS, or France Telecom node. Select the correct option in the list available in the Special/Connection option of CIM.

b) Terminal users
CIM isn't available for all computers. In particular UK users of older Atari, Amiga, BBC and other machines will find that their use of CompuServe will mainly be through ASCII terminal emulation software ('comms' software) - although there are third party navigation utilities for many non PC or Mac computers. Some Internetters who telnet into CompuServe will also use the terminal services of CompuServe. Once you've got the hang of this it's not too difficult, but you can see why CIM was invented.

Terminal users can still go via any of the access methods and nodes, but they will need to follow the instructions at the top of the list of Access Numbers in the Appendices to login through the packet switch services. Users of terminal software should also remember that the terminal software you use to access CompuServe needs to be set to 7 bits, even parity, one stop bit. Terminal use can also get expensive, as it's often slower than using CIM until you find your way around.

c) Telnet users
Telnet users will need a terminal emulation package which can use the CompuServe B+ or XMODEM protocols if they want to download files from CompuServe over the Internet. Most Shareware and commercial emulation packages don't allow this, as they expect to see data coming in through a serial

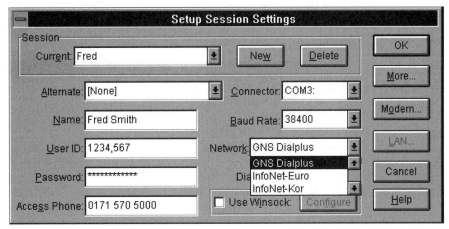

Figure 2.5   *Select the network type if you're not going to use CompuServe nodes.*

port, not an Ethernet or SLIP/PPP connection, but there are an increasing number of packet drivers becoming available. Try the Internet Resources (GO INETRES) forum for details of new fixes.

PC Windows users will find that they can use WinCIM and a utility called ComT (in the Internet/Access CompuServe library) - once they have acquired all the other software they need for TCP/IP working.

Mac users are recommended to get hold of a copy of VersaTerm which works well with CompuServe over Telnet although as a commercial product it costs money. The cheaper and later versions of Microphone also work in this way. Other users will need to talk to experts or dealers, or the crews of the Internet Forums on CompuServe, as terminal emulation software is evolving all the time, and not all of it will permit file transfers over the Internet. In general you'll need a terminal emulator with 'TCP/IP compliant XMODEM, ZMODEM or CompuServe B+ transfer protocols' to make this method work. It's envisaged that later versions of CIM will work over telnet connections.

Getting started with CIM

C.I.M. (inexplicably pronounced SIM by its American authors) is CompuServe Information Manager. It's a set of dedicated communications, file and text handling software which interfaces your computer to the host systems on CompuServe. Before the heady days of CIM, CompuServe users logged into the service with an ASCII terminal and fought with a command line interface and the horrors of a hostile menu system. Today, users of DOS, Windows, OS/2 and Mac users get the benefit of CIM, while everyone else still gets to fight with ASCII.

You get hold of CIM by either downloading it from the service via your ASCII interface, by having it thrust at you as part of some special offer or by buying it as part of a CompuServe Start-Up pack. (Call the Disk Hotline on 0800 374 971 if you don't have the correct disks for your computer.) You'll

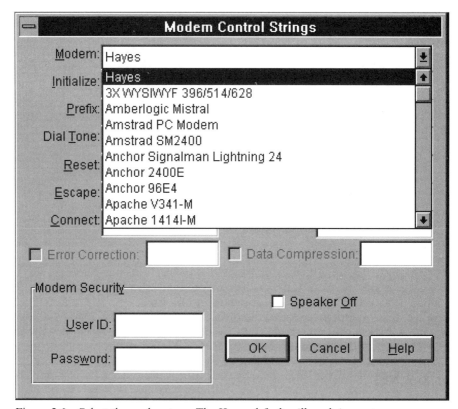

Figure 2.6   *Select the modem type. The Hayes default will work in most cases.*

also need a start-up ID before you can do anything on the system:

The CIM startup CD contains all you need to get started for PCs and Macs equipped with a CD drive. If you don't have a CD drive, your options are to fit one, (about a hundred pounds) or to send for the software on disk, or to download it from CompuServe. Of these options fitting a CD is the best one, although the most expensive, as you'll then be able to use the monthly CompuServe CDs to reduce your file downloading costs for CompuServe.

You'll need Sign Me UP details which are:

Agreement Number
Serial Number

Late changes

Once CIM is installed you can alter the setup of your account by going to the Special menu option. From there go to General (Mac) or Session Settings (PC) to set up your account. If you're an existing CIM user you'll need to run through the following to alter an existing setup:

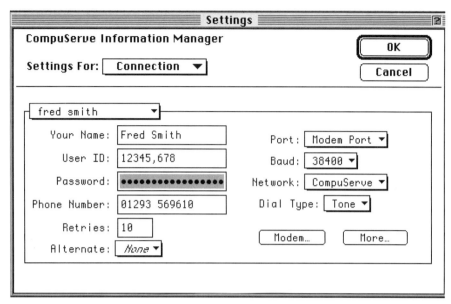

Figure 2.7   *Setting up Mac CIM is similar. Use the modem port in preference to the printer port.*

* Check your name in the Your Name Box

* Check your User ID in the User ID box

* Check your password in the password box.

* Put the phone number of the node you are going to use in the Phone number box.

    If the node you are going to use is a Mercury, GNS or France Telecom node, go to the Network box and select either GNS Dialplus, FT, or Mercury. If the node is a CompuServe (CPS) node make sure that CompuServe is selected.

* Select the Port (Mac) or Connector (PC) your modem is plugged into. On a PC this could be COM1, COM2, COM3, or COM4. On a Mac it will be either the Printer port or the Modem port. (If you are using an internal modem on a portable Mac you'll need to go to the PowerBook Setup control panel and set 'internal'.)

* Set Dial Type to tone if your phone makes beeps when you dial. Set it to pulse if your phone clicks when you dial.

* Set redial attempts to 5, initially.

* Mac users are presented with a choice of languages when they click on the More button. Set the language you need. Windows users should make sure

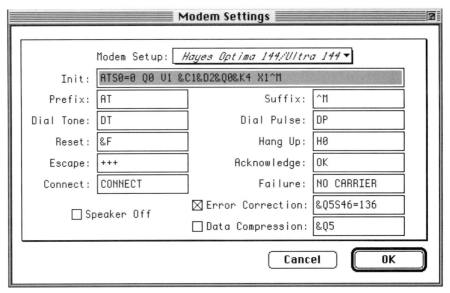

Figure 2.8 *Modem settings in Mac CIM. De-select error correction and data compression options if you have problems logging in.*

that they have the correct UK settings in Control Panel/International. Enable Carrier Detect should be set on (cross), HMI time-out should be set at about 30.

* Finally, click Modem to set your modem type. If your modem isn't listed try using the Hayes setting. If this doesn't work you'll need to modify this basic setting to suit your modem. (See Chapter 4 for help)

And that's it. What should happen when you click on any connect option in CIM is that your computer should tell the modem to dial out and connect automatically to CompuServe. If this doesn't happen it's almost always because of modem problems, which need to be painstakingly worked through.

Disconnecting your on-line sessions

There are four basics of using any on-line service; dialing up, logging in, logging out, and disconnecting. The last two operations, and their distance in space and time from the first two, dictate the length of your CompuServe bill in pages, and the weight of your phone bill in kilos. You MUST ensure that you disconnect cleanly from CompuServe to ensure that your billing is as accurate as possible. To do this use the File/Disconnect option or click on the Toolbar disconnect icon. Don't disconnect by pouring coffee into the modem, or throwing it about in a tantrum. CIM will disconnect rapidly from the service if you tell it to. You can upset the billing procedures if you switch off your modem during a session, or reboot your computer during a session. If

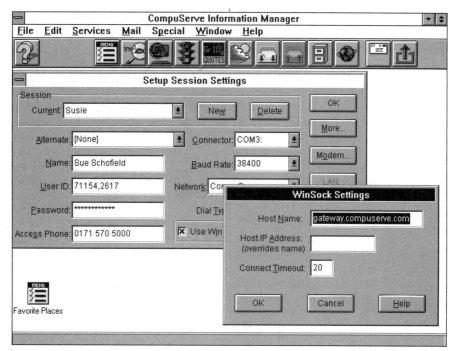

Figure 2.9   *WinCIM users - leave the Winsock Box de-selected for normal use. The CompuServe Internet Dialler will automatically call W,insock when it needs it.*

this does happen you're recommended to log back in, and out again to ensure CompuServe has logged you off.

Generally speaking CompuServe errs on the side of the customer, but you can GO BILLING at any time to check your account charges. If you don't agree with them, phone CompuServe support on 0800 000 400 and ask them to check. You'll get an account credit if there's any doubt at all on your on-line charges.

Hang it all

Getting your modem to disconnect on command is also the key to minimizing phone charges. If you don't have your modem set up properly, the modem will stay connected to the line even though CompuServe has logged you out and dropped the line at the remote end. You can check for this by watching the CD (Carrier Detect) light on the modem. If this goes out, and the OL (On Line) light stays on then your modem isn't disconnecting cleanly. In some cases this could add an extra charge unit to your phone bill.

The remedies are buried deep in your modem handbook, but the basics are that modems should watch for +++ATH0 (ATH ZERO) as the hang up command. The modem should also drop the line if the cable to the computer toggles the DTR pin at the modem, but this feature is often disabled at the modem. The TR (terminal ready) light on the modem tracks DTR and can be used to see if CIM is toggling this pin.

If either ATH0 or the DTR disconnect isn't working, your modem will still hang up at some point after the CompuServe modem has disconnected. This delay is governed by a modem setting which looks for Carrier Loss and then disconnects. Check this option in your modem's manual and lower the waiting time if you're having trouble getting your modem to disconnect. However, the ATH0 method is entirely preferable and you should try and make sure this works. Some modems use ATH as the hang up command, just to complicate matters.

Forgetting you're on-line

It does happen. You decide to write mail on-line, and then lose your concentration and do something else, leaving your modem on-line to CompuServe. One of two things should happen - either CIM will flash a warning after some minutes with no data transfer, or your modem will time out and disconnect.

There are several ways you can remind yourself that you're still on-line, such as leaving your modem's speaker enabled all the time, (Special/Connection/modem) which will make sure that your neighbour bangs on the wall every five minutes, or positioning the modem where you can see the lights. However at some stage you'll walk away from CIM and forget you're on-line. It happens to everyone. CompuServe will disconnect you, after fifteen minutes or so, after trying to warn you with a pleasantly ridiculous screen message.

3 All about CIM

CompuServe Information Manager (CIM) is the key to making a start with CompuServe. It provides an easy to use set of 'front-end' software which will make using CompuServe less fraught for new users.

CIM is updated regularly. The version used for this book is Version 2.0 for Windows, and version 2.4.2 for Macs. If you have an earlier version you can use the CD to upgrade an existing version without the cost of down loading from CompuServe. You can also order the disks from CompuServe UK on 0800 374 971.

Check which version of CIM you have. For Windows users the info is in Help/About. Mac users should click on the Apple Logo/About. Upgrade if possible as you'll get the benefits of faster operation.

Upgrading an earlier version of CIM

Installing a new version of CIM on top of an old version will upgrade it. All old files are saved to disk and the new version will run directly after the upgrade.

Windows 3.1 CD users can use File Manager to locate the file D:\UPGRADE.EXE on the CD assuming that your CD drive appears as D:. Windows 95 users can use the Explorer if they can find it or the Find option from the Start Button, if they can't. Double click UPGRADE.EXE and then install WinCIM into your existing CompuServe Directory. This will normally be C:\CSERVE. You won't need the Signup files if you're upgrading older versions.

Mac Users should locate the ENGLISH folder on the CD, and then double click the CIM 2.4.2 Archive Installer. Again, you don't need the Signup files. The Installer will work over an AppleTalk network, so you can set the CD up for sharing and update multiple Macs from one CD server.

CD upgrades come thick and fast from CompuServe, so that these instructions may differ. Generally speaking, all install methods will enable you to upgrade your existing CIM set up, without losing the data and email files you already have on your hard disk.

CIM walkabout

If you want to try your first mail message and test your set up, do the following:

* Click on Mail/Create Mail

* Put Sue Schofield in the Name Box, and 100113,2132 in the address box

* Put 'Witty Message' in the subject box

* Type a suitably intelligent and polite message in the text area. They normally go along the lines of 'Oi, mush! Is my email working?'.

* Click Out-basket. This puts mail in your out-basket on the hard disk for sending at a later time.

* Play around with CIM a little more, and then click Mail/Send-Receive all mail. On the Windows version of CIM click the box marked 'Disconnect when done'.

* Make sure that your modem disconnects after the call. If it doesn't after thirty seconds or so go to File/Disconnect. If you still can't disconnect after a minute or so you have a real problem indicated by the CD light on the modem remaining lit. Switch your modem off by hand to make it drop the line. Then go to modem troubleshooting in Chapter 4.

You'll eventually get a response from the author if you've done everything correctly; if you haven't you'll get a warning message from CIM. The most common problem, (after setting up your modem incorrectly) is getting your password wrong in the CIM Settings dialogue - so make sure this is correct if you get login error messages.

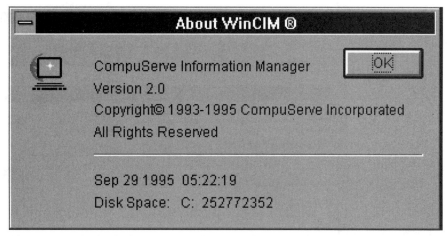

Figure 3.2   *Check which version you have. Windows versions from 2.0 carry significant improvements. You can get free disks from the Disk Freephone number.*

Passwords on CompuServe are formed of two random words and a separator, which might be a space or another character, as in: BRUSH*ZOOMER or CAT:OSCAR. Make sure you use the correct separator for the password. In these examples it's an asterisk (*) and a colon (:). Spaces are used too, so be careful about noting the correct separator.

Advanced CIM Setup

CIM offers a lot for the tinkerer to play with. You can set-up multiple dial-up connections by clicking on the Session (PC) or Connection (Mac) box. Your original settings get copied when you click New, making the facility useful for setting up connections to different nodes or even different countries.

Once you have got your basic set up working you should take time out to fully configure CIM. The set-up options are accessed from the Special/ Preferences menu and will be covered fully as we go through CompuServe. For now go to the Session Settings/Preferences (PC)/Mail dialogue box and select (cross):

PC:
* Delete Retrieved Mail
* File Outgoing Messages
* Always Retrieve (Postage Due Messages)

Mac:
* File Outgoing Mail
* Prompt for Unsent Mail
* Auto delete Retrieved Mail
* Receive (Postage Due Message Handling)

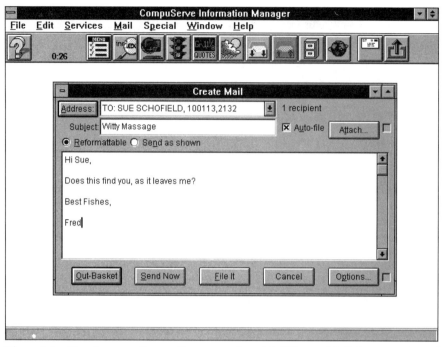

Figure 3.3   *Creating your first mail message, from Mail/Create Mail. Later versions of CIM pull down an address book for you to fill in. Click Outbasket to store the mail for sending at a later time, or SEND to send now.*

These settings will ensure that you get all the mail sent to you, rather than leaving it held on the host machines As you become more proficient with CIM you can decide what you want these settings to be but you won't lose mail during your learning time. You can also set up CIM forum handling at this stage, but it isn't so vital.

CIM in Depth

As mentioned earlier, CIM is updated frequently to work with upgraded operating systems such as Windows 95 or Mac System 7.5. Consequently the version you have may be older or newer than the versions used for this book.

The versions for the different operating systems vary in their abilities too, for instance the Mac version downloads Library files in a slightly different fashion to the Windows versions. However all are sufficiently similar for users to find their way around. As with all computer software it takes a while to find your way, and the best way with CIM is to disconnect your modem and then play with the settings. That way there's less danger of you running up your overdraft on-line.

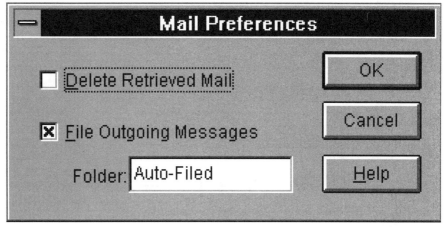

Figure 3.4   *Set your Prefs to configure CIM. This setting, in Preferences/Mail, ensures you won't lose mail during your early trials. Mail will stay on CompuServe. Eventually you must check the Delete Field or your mail will appear never to be collected.*

Left to right with CIM

1) FILE Options
FILE/New
Opens a text editor window for you to scribble in. On the Mac version CIM uses any old built-in editor, in Windows you get Notepad.

FILE/Open
Opens an existing file via a dialogue box for file selection.

FILE/Save/Save As
Work as normal for putting files onto disk. These options are useful for grabbing text from CompuServe messages into text files.

FILE/Print/Print Setup (Page Setup on the Mac)
The usual options for making sure your printer is set-up correctly, and for printing files.

FILE/Connect (Windows only)
Dials out and logs you in to CompuServe, without actually going anywhere. Normally you'll double-click an icon to go where you want, and CIM will automatically dial and take you there.

FILE/Disconnect
Drops the line after carefully logging you out of CompuServe. If you just pull the plug CompuServe can go on charging you for the time elapsed until it discovers you're not there.

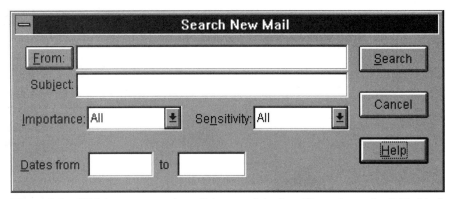

Figure 3.5 *CIM lets you search mail in your Inbasket. If you leave the fields blank CIM will search mail on CompuServe for matches.*

FILE/Run
Runs another program under Windows.

FILE/Quit (Exit in the Mac version)
Closes down CIM after logging you out and disconnecting.

Extra options in Mac Versions
FILE/Decompress/Decompressed Retrieved
Will de-SIT those compressed archives you've downloaded.

FILE/Credenza
Provides access to In-Basket, Out Basket and Mail etc.

File/Revert to saved
Abandons changes to text files and goes back to the last saved revision.

FILE/Leave
Takes you back to the on-line desktop ('front') when in a forum or within another on-line service. Useful for a quick getaway from some of the more tedious forums.

EDIT Option (Macs only)
Provides the full range of Mac Clipboard options (cut, paste, select all, etc.)

SERVICES
Services provides a customizable menu of places to go, things to do within CompuServe. The Favourite Places customizable menu lives here, as does What's New, CB Simulator and Executive News. The Services area is often customized in specialized versions of CIM, such as those supplied to on-line support groups such as Novell.
    The Browse Option brings up a window of Icons which provide a list of services and forums. Thus the 'Computers' Browse option takes you to a full display of computer-related topics, from where you may rummage further.

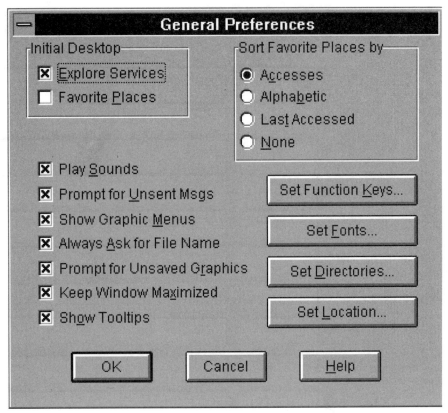

Figure 3.6 *Setting the rest of the Prefs. Leave 'Show Graphic Menus' on to get the latest graphic menus. Turn this option off to speed up the service.*

The Browse option is good for newbies as it gives a good idea of the scope of services available, without the user having to join any of them.

Later versions of WinCIM from 2.0 onwards, offer a link to the CompuServe Mosaic World Wide Web Browser under the Services menu, but the two most useful standard items are the Go and Find options.

SERVICES/Find

The Find option will search forums for the keyword you type into the dialogue box. If you're off-line CIM will then dial-up and rummage.

Use the Find option to search for say, topics relating to Motor-cycling, (Find motorcycle) Tropical fish, (Find Guppy) Sanskrit Texts (Find Sanskrit) etc. The Find dialogue is great for tracking down generic areas on CompuServe. Once you're there you can ADD the forum to the Favorite Places menu or you can go back another time with the GO command. If your search brings up a number of different forums the Favourite Places dialogue is brought up automatically so you can add the forums. Try a 'FIND books' or 'FIND UK' for your first shot.

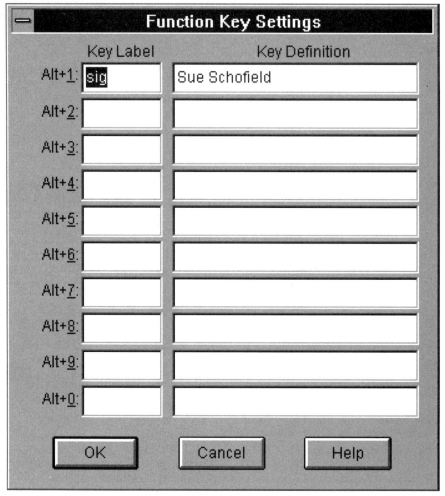

Figure 3.7   *Set the Function Keys up to hold your signature, or to run text macros. This option doesn't appear in Mac CIM, to date.*

SERVICES/Go

The GO option takes you straight to the forum of interest. It's very much the 'key' keyword in CompuServe. GO BILLING, GO MOTORCYCLES, GO PRACTICE are commands which take you into new forums. You can use keyboard shortcuts with the GO command to speed up CIM usage. Type CTRL G (Windows) or Splodge G (Mac) to pull up the GO dialogue. (The Mac Splodge Key is the one with the Apple logo on it, right of the Option Key.) And if you don't know where to GO - use either FIND to find it, or GO INDEX to go to an index of all the forums which you can plagiarize with the FILE/SAVE AS command. There's a copy of the Index in the Appendices to save your phone bill, but you'll need to grab a new Index at some point as it's always being updated.

Neat GO's
Try GO IBMFF to access the File finder for PC files, or GO MACFF to access the Mac File finder. Both of these options will locate a file by its name, creator or keyword, in half the time it takes to rummage around the Internet with Gopher. GO MEMBER is where you'll find all the Admin stuff to do with your account, GO WEATHER for novelty satellite views of your area, GO CISSOFT for the latest versions of CIM. GO UKFORUM for topics featuring this green and pleasant land. GO INETRES for Internet TCP/IP software for use with CompuServe's Internet Provision.

* You can also type a URL (WWW address) into the GO Box. If you have WinCIM 2.0 or later installed try adding

http://ourworld.compuserve.com/homepages/suesco/

into the GO box and hitting Enter.

4) MAIL
The CompuServe Mail service gets a chapter to itself, sufficient to say here's where the menu versions of the mail icons live. Check out Special first as it's where many of the Mail settings are.

5) SPECIAL
What's special about SPECIAL? SPECIAL is where you set your Preferences for the way CIM operates. The settings are saved for the future and also become current for your current session. You'll need to be off-line to muck about with the SPECIAL Options, that is, your modem should not be connected to CompuServe.

SPECIAL/Session Settings
CIM won't connect to CompuServe if you get these wrong. See the screen-shots for a full layout and set your version of CIM up with your details. The Current Session Box carries the settings for one connection setting.

Use the New option to add another set of sessions settings, for instance, if you travel and want to add different phone numbers for CompuServe, you might set up three new sessions for Scunthorpe, Invercockieleekie, and Pratts Bottom. If you want to extensively use CompuServe's Internet access then you'll use a slightly different configuration here unless you're a Mac user. (See Section 3 for details).

You can also set up a new session for your partner if he/she/it has a CompuServe account - leave out the password and said partner will be prompted for it at connect time, before the modem dials out.

The option of leaving the password out is useful for corporate users. In the UK it's common for multi-million pound concerns like merchant banks to have only one modem in the company. This lives in the safe behind the IT Manager's desk, and permission to use it has to made a week in advance, written in your own blood. If you haven't died of old age by the time you get to use the modem you can simply select your own Session Settings and then enter the password when CIM asks for it. Your CompuServe security remains

Figure 3.8   *Use Services/GO to go directly to a Forum, or a Web page.*

intact during your time out from CompuServe use, as the password is not stored on your machine.

The Delete button deletes sets of session settings, while the Current and Alternate options let you set which Set gets used first (Current) and which Set gets tried (Alternate) if the Current setting doesn't connect.

Connector
It means 'Port'. On a PC a Port is where you plug something in and it refuses to work. For modems this is often either COM1: or COM2:. If you have a go-faster serial port card in your PC this might be COM3:. You can check by exit-ing to DOS and using the MSD program in the Windows Directory to locate and identify the port. Often the port you think has a modem attached to it has a mouse attached and vice versa.

On a Mac you'll be offered the Modem Port, or the Printer Port. Both accept modems but your Printer Port will often have a Printer or a network attached to it. If you're using an internal modem on a portable Mac go to Control Panels and select PowerBook Setup, then click Internal Modem. You won't be able to use the external port at the same time, but your internal modem will now run. Similar complexities exist for Laptop PCs with internal modems, so check your documentation first.

Baud Rate
Baud means speed. No it doesn't, Baud is a 'unit of telegraphic transfer rate' named after Mr Baudot, as in Baud Rate. Here it means 'the maximum speed at which you can transfer data from CompuServe, all other things being equal'. Chapter 4 which deals with modems, explains all. Until you've read it bear in mind that the speed you set here is limited by your modem. For a start-up setting try 2400, 9600, 14400, or 28800, depending on what is says on the box your modem came in. Some modems have speed buffering which lets you set a faster speed than the real connect speed, but for the moment try the above suggestion. Then jump to the Modem option to do the final configuration once you've got CIM working.

Network
The computers which comprise the CompuServe system live in Ohio, over the Pond. To get to them you either use a direct phone connection to a

Figure 3.9   *Use Services/FIND to find topics of interest. This is one of the most powerful CIM features. Once you've found a topic you can add it to your Favorite Places menu where it is stored.*

CompuServe node, or you use the packet switch (PSS) networks of the telecom provider in your country. In the UK PSS networks are provided by Mercury or by BT (GNS Dialplus) or France Telecom amongst others. Your choice of network will be decided by the location of the nearest node to you. If you live in London you'll use one of the London nodes, if you live in Northern Ireland you might well use one of the GNS nodes. The operator of the node is shown against the phone number in the list in the Appendices (GO PHONES for an update). Remember that if you use a PSS node other than Mercury then the charges levied by the operator of the PSS node will be reverse-charged to your CompuServe bill as the dreaded 'Communications Surcharge'. Select the Network type in the Network option to enable you to log in.

The PSS network options will be vital if you travel abroad as they give access to CompuServe from almost any country in the world. You'll find a GNS Dialplus node almost everywhere, often linked to the local Packet Switch network provided by a different telecom supplier. If you want advice on international use of GNS call the BT Dialplus sales office on 0800 282 444 for information. The CompuServe GO PHONES area also provides Packet Switch node numbers but the GNS Dialplus people often have up more to date information.

Packet Switch nodes are useful if you live in a rural area - often it will be cheaper to use a PSS node, than to dial long distance. However keep a check on BT and Mercury direct dial phone rates - they're falling all the time, and PSS access to CompuServe looks increasingly expensive in comparison.

Redial attempts
Set to 3 unless you want more dial attempts.

Modem
Set your modem type here. If you want life to be as complicated as possible you can go to Chapter 4 to find out about initialization strings and so on. If you have problems then set 'Hayes generic'. If you still have problems then

de-select Error Correction and Data Compression. If you still have problems then it's Chapter 4, your modem handbook, and a long night. If you still have problems after that then CompuServe Helpline staff on 0800 000 444 will sort you out over the phone. Before you call have to hand the make of machine, the make of modem, and the operating system of your computer, plus the version of CIM you are using.

More
This is where you put extra logon parameters for extra access features and so-on. You'll be told about these by CompuServe Admin if you have anything other than a standard account.

The HMI Time-out is important because it decrees what happens when your computer loses synchronization with CompuServe's machines. The setting is best left at 30 - if you increase it your computer could spend a lot of time listening to an inactive connection, at your expense. HMI is Host/Micro Interface, the language CIM uses to talk to the big boxes in Ohio.

Deselect the Enable Carrier Detect Option if you can't connect to CompuServe. Some old modems don't support this option, but most all new ones do.

Additionally on Macs, the More dialogue box lets you set the character Set (Latin-1 if you're English, ASCII if you're American) and your country preferences. Set these to English, especially if you're a Scot, a Welshman, or an Irishman, because the other choices are limited to Spanish, French, and German. And if you are anything other than English bear in mind that CompuServe Sysops originally objected to Welsh language submissions in the UK forums in August 1995 - presumably because Welsh is all Greek to the Sysops of the conference. If you have the use of a native non-English UK language then this scribbler exhorts you to use it on CompuServe. Otherwise we'll all be metamorphosed into Americans come the Millennium. GO UKFORUM for more, including Irish, Scots and Welsh topics.

Connection
Shows the last connection, total elapsed time and so on. Useful for checking your CompuServe bills.

Winsock (Windows only)
If you have installed the older CompuServe Netlauncher or the newer WinCIM 2.0 this option will appear in your WinCIM configuration. (Net-Launcher is now part of WinCIM 2.0.) You'll select this box to enable the CompuServe Internet dialler, and then be able to use any TCP/IP Internet software such as Mosaic over the CompuServe PPP Internet link. See Chapter 8 for details. You DON'T need this option to use the internal Internet services within CompuServe, such as FTP, USENET and TELNET. All are explained more fully in Section 3. Mac Users will need the MacTCP option explained in the Appendices.

Preferences ('Settings' on a Mac)
The Preferences options mainly set the visual appearances of CIM, but there are important options for Mail and CB simulator users. The Mail options

Figure 3.10 *The Special/Connection Info box keeps track of your connect time on CompuServe, and can be used to check your billing.*

have already been covered, Forum, News and other options will be covered as we go along. One useful (or useless) option is the Ribbon, called a Toolbar in every other computer book. The Ribbon is where you put all of those indigestible icons which duplicate the menu commands and make CIM look like the control desk of the Starship Enterprise. The ribbon does mean you can click a 'Disconnect' Icon instead of typing CTRL-D, but it eats screen display space.

The Turn Graphic Menus On option is also important - if you turn it off CompuServe won't try to upload new images to your computer. By the same token, if this option is deselected you won't be able to use the graphical FTP and Telnet clients on CompuServe. Leave this option on, for the time being. Once CIM has uploaded new images (usually updated Graphic Menus) your computer stores then on disk, and CIM won't need to re-send them.

Rebuild Cabinet Indexes (Windows Only)

This option will attempt to rebuild the database indexes on your hard disk, after you've inadvertently shut your PC down without exiting Windows, and perhaps damaged some files. There's no direct equivalent command on a Mac, except to delete all the .CACHE files in the relevant Mail and Filing Cabinet folders. Do this if MacCim reports it can't find files due to 'Disk Errors'.

Forum Databases (Windows only)

This option will let you delete stored message files accumulated from various forums. It's useful if you find your PC disk is getting full. Its also useful for getting rid of obscure forum information at one fell swoop, instead of deleting individual messages.

Finally...

CIM is an organic product. Organic, not in the sense that it's carbon based, but in that it's a constantly evolving piece of software. The version you have, or have had in the past or might have in the future could well bear no relation to the version this book was written with. New updates are published regularly and readers are urged to keep up to date with software releases if possible. The benefits are enhanced features and a friendlier interface, and new releases are paraded in the What's New Menu, updated weekly.

CIM is also evolving as the de-facto easy to use Internet interface and new versions reflect this increasing sophistication.

4 Modems and CompuServe

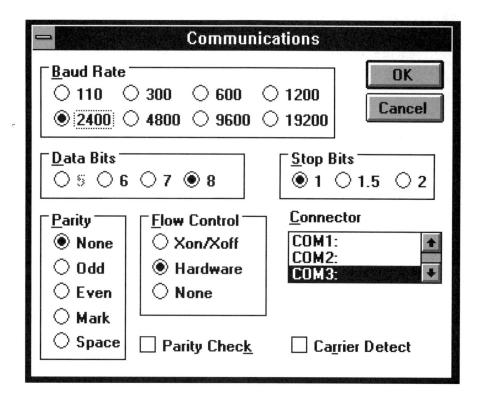

Most of CompuServe's UK users will connect to CompuServe via a modem. In the UK modems are available in all shapes and sizes, and range from desktop mains powered modems, internal modems which live inside your computer, through to 'pocket' or portable battery powered modems and PCMCIA 'credit card' modems. In general the speed of modem you buy will affect the amount of money you pay to your Telecom supplier for access to CompuServe or anywhere else, and the general rule of thumb is to buy the fastest modem you can afford.

External desktop modems and pocket modems tend to cost the same for similar specifications; internal PC and Mac modems are often cheaper, unless you're buying a proprietary internal modem for a laptop computer, when prices seem to double. Most current modems also offer a fax transmit/receive capability which is useful, although you can save a few pounds by buying cheaper (and soon-to-be obsolete) data-only modems. In many cases the portable battery-powered modem will be good bet; they come with a mains adaptor, offer fax capability, and unlike internal modems, don't need the attention of a toolkit when you upgrade your computer. Desktop modems are always tied to a mains power supply, which might become a burden when you upgrade your computer, or decide that you can't live without a laptop.

Modem speeds

Modem speeds are designated by numbers which at first sight mean nothing. They still mean nothing after spending money on computer magazines, so here's a quick guide:

Speeds:

V21	300 bits per second mode. Obsolete
V22	1200 bits per second mode.
V22 bis	2400 bits per second. Cheap, ideal for low volume electronic mail
V23	1200/75 Split rate mode. Obsolete except for car dealers networks.
V32	9600 bits per second. Now found in V32 bis modems
V32 bis	14,400 bits per second.

V34   28,800 bits per second mode. Many services and PC's can't handle data at V34 speeds. The current fast standard modem for CompuServe and most other systems.

V34 bis   Coming soon. Should handle data at 32 kbps but not all providers will use it.

Bell 103   Obsolete USA standard still found in modems for compatibility reasons

Bell 212a   Ditto

Additionally there are a few fax standards:

V21, V27 ter, V29, and V17 (fax modems should be V29 for speed, where possible)

and a couple of data compression and error correction standards:

V42, MNP 1-10, V42 bis.

('bis' means first revision, as in the Second Implementation, 'ter' means second revision as in Third Implementation.)

Generally speaking, today's modems are much better than the modems of even three years ago, and the fastest V34 modems carry all of the above data,

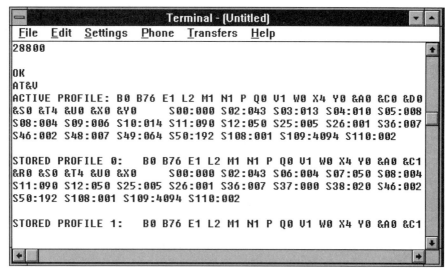

```
═                    Terminal - [Untitled]              ▼ ▲
 File  Edit  Settings  Phone  Transfers  Help
28800                                                       ↑

OK
AT&U
ACTIVE PROFILE: B0 B76 E1 L2 M1 N1 P Q0 U1 W0 X4 Y0 &A0 &C0 &D0
&S0 &T4 &U0 &X0 &Y0      S00:000 S02:043 S03:013 S04:010 S05:008
S08:004 S09:006 S10:014 S11:090 S12:050 S25:005 S26:001 S36:007
S46:002 S48:007 S49:064 S50:192 S108:001 S109:4094 S110:002

STORED PROFILE 0:    B0 B76 E1 L2 M1 N1 P Q0 U1 W0 X4 Y0 &A0 &C1
&R0 &S0 &T4 &U0 &X0      S00:000 S02:043 S06:004 S07:050 S08:004
S11:090 S12:050 S25:005 S26:001 S36:007 S37:000 S38:020 S46:002
S50:192 S108:001 S109:4094 S110:002

STORED PROFILE 1:    B0 B76 E1 L2 M1 N1 P Q0 U1 W0 X4 Y0 &A0 &C1
                                                            ↓
◄□                                                        □►
```

Figure 4.2   *Setting up a modem in Windows Terminal. The hardest part is identifying the comms port on a PC.*

fax and error correction modes. Modems are also referred to by their top speed, so a modem that has V21, V22, V22 bis, V32, and V32 bis capability is often called a 14,400 modem, despite the fact it can work at the other speeds. The other common modem is the older V22 bis modem, which has a top connection speed of 2400 bits per second.

Compression

This top speed capability is something of a misnomer, as modems with data compression can squeeze more data down a phone line than the top speed implies. A 14,400 modem, fitted with V42 bis data compression can, under ideal circumstances, compress data by up to four times to give a maximum throughput of 4 x 14,400 = 57,600 bits per second. Some advanced V42 bis schemes, such as those fitted to the Hayes Optima 144 + Fax and the Optima 288/V34+fax modems can give up to eight times compression - but only if the receiving computer has a matching modem, and only if both computers are fast enough to handle the data stream and then only if the data is highly compressible.

Get it correct

To make matters even more complex, some modems are not fitted with error correction or data compression but use external software to implement this. Examples include modems containing the Rockwell Protocol Interface (RPI) scheme such as the Pace Mobifax, the WhiteBox series and others. This is not a problem when using CompuServe, as the service does not implement compulsory data compression or error correction. However, you'll get faster throughput with a fully equipped modem although you'll a little pay more for the modem in the first place.

Readers contemplating buying an RPI modem for use with CompuServe's PPP Internet provision (or any other SLIP/PPP setup) should be aware that RPI modems have to rely on the inherent end-to-end error correction of the TCP/IP protocol that the Internet uses - because they lack internal error checking. Any error on an RPI set-up means that the remote server has to be warned of the error and then correct it, which can take time over a link to the other side of the world. In contrast a modem using the V42 bis scheme will error correct with the remote modem at the CompuServe access point, without requesting any re-transmission from the remote computer.

In the first case not only does the RPI modem add extra load to the Internet connection, it can't error correct start-up procedures which don't use TCP/IP. This is apparent when login scripting is in use (such as within ConfigPPP on Macs) and can and does lead to some log-ins being either protracted or failing altogether. Neither does CIM support the obscure requirements of RPI modems and readers are therefore fore-warned about using RPI modems with CompuServe's Internet access, or with CIM for these reasons. Paying the extra for inbuilt error-correction will save your phone bill - and your temper. However, if you are on an extremely tight budget, CIM will allow you to connect with an RPI modem, at least.

Buying checklist

To simplify matters you should choose a modem which has:

* A top speed of either 14,400, or preferably 28.8k bits per second

* Inbuilt fax capability if you need it.

* Inherent data compression and error checking

* Battery power if you have a battery powered computer, or may buy one in the future.

* UK service and support if you live in the UK

* A BABT APPROVALS sticker, to make sure your modem is up to scratch technically and that you won't commit an offence by using it in the UK.

Unless you are on a very tight budget it's recommended that you buy a 28,800 bps modem as the higher speed will pay for itself in saved phone bills in the first year of operation. However, CompuServe functions quite well with a slower 2400 modem, as long as you don't want to download any large files or collect vast quantities of forum messages - and you don't mind the larger

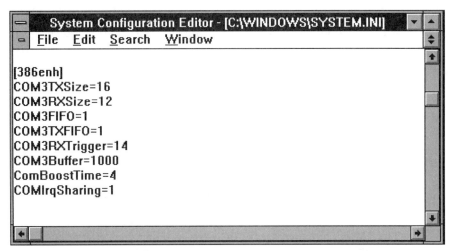

Figure 4.3 *If you're a Windows 3.1 user you can enhance performance by using a 16550A comms port. You'll need to alter SYS.INI to make Windows get the best from the new card.*

phone bill. You may find that your old 2400 bps modem will do quite nicely for grabbing your email, but you'll certainly need something faster for any real use of CompuServe forums, file transfer systems or Internet Web usage. For instance this book was written on a Mac laptop fitted with an internal 2400 bps modem. That was fine for sending and receiving email, but file transfers took a long time and hogged the phone. I used an external 28.8 battery modem to get forum messages and files, leaving the internal modem in place for travelling and email work.

The INIT string

Modems sometimes need an 'initialization string' to configure them to make them work with a particular service. If you use CIM then you'll find initialization strings for many modems in the Setup Session Settings/Modem screen. In general, modems use the Hayes AT Command Set to accept commands such as 'Dial a number', or 'Hang up the Line' from your computer. Normally you only have to tell CIM what make and model modem you have and it will set up the INIT string for you.

The dial command is ATD followed by the number.

The Hang Up command is AT, followed by H or H0. (H Zero)

Modems differ in the way they use the Hayes set, and more often than not you'll need to spend some time setting up CIM to work with your particular modem. ATD for dial and ATH or ATH0 for hang up are fairly universal, but the more you pay for a modem the more difficult it will be to set-up as it will have more features. For a CompuServe link you should set:

Auto Answer Off (S0=0)
Quiet mode Off   (Q0)
Verbose codes On (V1)
Carrier Detect On (&C1)
Hard Handshake On   (&D1)

as a get-you-going setup. The codes in bracket are for most Hayes 'compatible' modems.
You put the codes into the 'Initialize' box in CIM as:

AT S0=0 Q0 V1 &C1 &D1 ^M

The ^M is computer speak for carriage return and is entered with the Caret key (Shift 6) on many computers, and the capital M key (Shift M).

Serial ports

PC users with Windows 3.1 will need an enhanced serial port or 16550A UART card to get the best from a modem at these speeds. (Dos users may not.) If you don't yet have one it's still wise to buy a 288 modem and run it at 38400, because one day you'll upgrade your computer and your new one will be fitted with a fast serial port.

If you're a Mac user then you can ignore problems with serial ports as 68030 and better Macs can run at 57600 bps with no trouble. If you have an older 68000 or 68020 Mac you should still be able to run at 38400, and Mac Classics, SE's and so forth make great CompuServe mail and Forum terminals. AppleTalk networks can sometimes cause problems with fast downloads on Macs, but the CompuServe CIS B+ protocol will minimize errors if these occur. Try turning AppleTalk OFF in the Chooser if you hit problems with slow downloads.

Speed buffering and error correction

Modern modems are able to connect at many different speeds, depending on the complexity of the modem at the far end of the line. If you set your modem to 14,400 and then dial a CompuServe connection which can only provide a 9600 bps link, your modem should 'speed buffer' the link, so that you can leave your computer set to 14,400 bps, but the connection runs at 9600 bps.

Most UK modems will speed buffer automatically, that is, they have a default setting which leaves speed buffering in place when you take the modem out of the box and switch on. But many cheap USA sourced modems don't have this feature, or don't have it enabled. This causes problems when you set

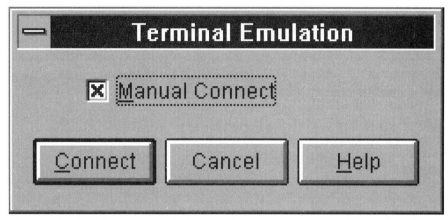

Figure 4.4   *CIM has a Terminal Emulator built in. If Manual connect is selected CIM WON'T dial out. Use it for testing your modem.*

your computer to 14,400 bps and then find that it won't connect at 9600 bps. The only solution is to grin and bear the lower speed and set your computer to 9600 or 2400 bps depending on the node speed, or fight with the modem manual and turn speed buffering on. The command to do this varies widely.

In general you should try your modem out of the box first, and only get involved in the black art of modem configuration if you have a problem. You should also avoid the temptation to buy USA sourced modems for use in the UK as service, help, and odd power supplies can be a problem. (This statement doesn't apply to American modems specifically designed and built in the USA for use with European or UK telephone networks which posses a BABT Approvals sticker).

As a start, set your modem to the speed of the node you're about to access, then increase the speed to the next higher to check out your modem's speed buffering capability. If you can connect you can leave your computer permanently set to the higher speed.

Some of the cheap 2400 modems which don't have speed buffering include the Global Village Bronze series for Mac PowerBooks, and some low price Viva pocket modems from the USA. In general if a modem has the higher speeds of 9600 and 14,400 bps then it will include speed buffering. If you don't have speed buffering don't worry, CompuServe will still work, as long as you set the 'BAUD RATE' setting in CIM to match the actual speed of the modem, often 2400.

CIS B+ protocol

Finally, you'll get error correction thrown in for free if you use the CIM software. This embodies something called the CompuServe B+ protocol for transmission of data packets between your CIM equipped computer and CompuServe. In simple terms this means that there's no major disadvantage in running your computer at the node speed of 2400, 9600, 14,400 or 28,800 bits per second. But speed buffering does save you from having to change the speed in your software every time you change nodes. (Use the Setup Session options to allocate a new connection if you need to do this more than once) CIM will take care of things automatically if you use Internet software which can make use of data compression.

Modem troubleshooting

As you'll realize from the above, modems offer endless opportunity for things to go wrong. Once your modem is set up it will function without problems for years, but getting to that happy stage can take hours.

PCs & modems

Problem: Don't know which COM port the modem is on.

Use the Windows Terminal program if you have it to track the modem down. Set it to 8 bits, 1 stop bit, no parity, 2400 bits per second. Otherwise use substitution to find the correct port. Often a mouse is on COM1 and the modem on COM2, but settings vary widely. If you have a terminal emulation program such as Windows Terminal, you should be able to get the lights on your modem to flash when you type AT <enter>. You should also see OK as a response when you type AT <enter>. Remember that serial ports on PCs have prongs (pins) whilst VGA and printer ports have (sockets.) Macs have lables...

Found the correct port but the modem doesn't answer

If the modem lights flash, but you don't get OK, reset the modem with

AT&F <enter>
ATZ <enter>

You should now see OK.

If you don't, and your modem lights flash, then you have the right COM port, but either the interrupt settings on your PC are wrong, or you have the wrong cable, or you have a clash with another piece of hardware in your PC such as a mouse. The only way to track these conflicts down is with a 'clean boot' disk and some expertise. Try your modem dealer or a knowledgeable friend.

Some PC's are fitted with fast UART chips in their COM ports and owners spend endless time discussing how to fine tune their comms. CompuServe users don't need to worry about such things, as CompuServe won't yet drive your PC at anything like top speed.

UART serial ports and Windows

Windows 3.1 isn't very good at comms, as you'll find out if you use it to drive a fast modem with a non-error corrected file transfer protocol such as

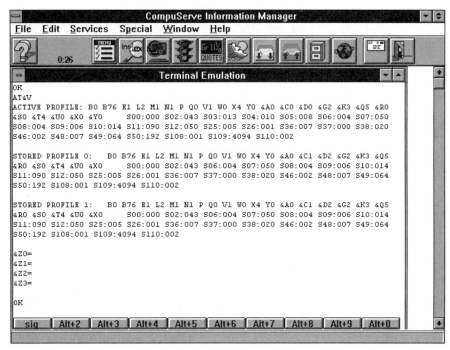

Figure 4.5 *Using the CIM Terminal to check out a modem. This is the View command,*
AT&V. Mac CIM has similar features.

ZMODEM. CompuServe uses an error-checking protocol, but for each error
corrected, time is lost, and phone bills increase. If you have a 16550A UART
chip in your serial port you can set Windows 3.1 up to use it. Back up all
your *.INI files first. Then use the SYSEDIT utility or Notepad to open the
SYSTEM.INI file in your Windows Directory.

Then look for the section headed :

[386Enh]

Add the lines:

COM3Irq=4
COM3Base=03E8
COM3fifo=1

into this section, assuming that your serial port is COM 3, is set up to use
INT4, and has an address of 03E8. Restart Windows to make it work. See
Fig. 4.3.

Microsoft provide a program called MSD.EXE in the Windows directory
which will tell you which port lives at which address. The INT setting is set-

up by a jumper on the board, and you'll often have to hunt for an IRQ which is free, or sacrifice one from a serial port which isn't in use. Your dealer should be able to help, in case of crisis, or if all of this is pure gobbledygook.

Windows 95 works without problems with existing versions of CIM. You'll still have to find out which port your modem is installed on, if the Setup program didn't find it during installation.

Macs and modems

Macs don't suffer from the terrible internal design of the average PC and users consequently report fewer problems with dial-up comms. However Macs are sensitive about the cable between the Mac and the modem, which in all cases should be a 'hard-handshake' cable with at least eight wires between the modem and the computer. Earlier three-wire cables are not suitable. Most Mac modems now come with a proper cable but if you are having problems then suspect this first. Other problems are related to INIT conflicts (hold the Shift key down and reboot to test without the Extensions being loaded) and a general lack of support in the UK for Mac computers. However Mac dealers are often more helpful than their PC counterparts, and a local dealer is worth his weight in gold. If you've bought mail order at rock bottom prices you might find it hard to get lengthy support.

Network modems

CIS can use the INT14 method of connecting through a network modem. Set the Connector in Setup Sessions Settings to INT14 then click on the LAN button to select a port allocation.

If you're connecting over the Internet via dial-up then select the Winsock option in the Connector box. This will call up your Internet dialer and access software.

Mac users can select any item in the Comms Toolbox to give access via net modems, trick ports, or other devices.

Travelling abroad

There are a couple of barriers to connecting to CompuServe whilst in foreign climes. The plug on your modem's phone lead won't go into the wall socket, and the power supply of your desktop modem won't fit the power sockets. You may also find it hard to get batteries in some countries, while others will regard your modem and laptop as military hardware, and will impound it.

There are a few ways around these problems. First buy a battery powered modem. Then either get hold of the relevant phone lead adaptor - available in many European supermarkets or from the TeleAdapt company - or use an acoustic coupler to connect your modem to the phone handset. Modern couplers such as the TeleAdapt Telefast work in conjunction with a modem to give relatively fast speeds and can be used with some cellular services. We used a Telefast Executive Kit - a small case containing adaptors, leads, a phone handset and so on, to connect our modem up whilst abroad. You can get full details from TeleAdapt from the Managing Director Gordon Brown who is 100111.2713@compuserve.com. It's best to do this before you go abroad as TeleAdapt can advise you on which adaptors you'll need for your journey. Check also with TeleAdapt about modem hostile countries.

One final pitfall is that the small modular socket on your modem will be wired in one of two (opposite) ways, depending on the model, and country of origin. You may also need a Reversing Coupler to make adapters and acoustic couplers work with your modem. TeleAdapt will advise on 0181 421 4444.

Finally, before you leave make sure you have a copy of the access numbers for your trip. GO PHONES will provide you with a list, and there's also a short summary in the back of this book.

Section 2

Email and Forums

5 CompuServe mail

Quick Start 1 - Sending mail

To send CompuServe mail you Create a message (Mail/Create Mail) and the either Send it straight away by connecting to CompuServe, or place it in the Outbasket on your hard disk for sending later. If you use the Outbasket you can close down CIM and turn off your computer, and your outgoing mail will still be stored there when you turn back on. You Send mail from the Outbasket with the Mail/Outbasket option. There's a 'Disconnect When Sent' option which will drop the line when your mail has been successfully despatched. Don't trust it for unattended use as all modems can detect when a room is unoccupied. Then they refuse to disconnect.

Quick Start 2 - Receiving mail

Mail is received to the Inbasket on your hard disk. It's stored there until you delete it, or have a disk crash, whichever comes first. The (Inbasket stores mail messages, the Filing Cabinet stores files.) You open old mail and resend or edit it from the Mail/Inbasket. You can also read mail on-line without retrieving it to your Inbasket, or delete it without reading it. See the Screenshots for examples. You can sort mail in your Inbasket in ascending or descending order in a variety of ways. 'Sort by Created date' keeps the last messages at the top of the list. As your Inbasket fills up your computer will take longer to sort it.

Messages can be Deleted, Printed, faxed if you have a fax modem. You can save to File or Forward by email to another email user or Forward by Fax or Telex using CompuServe Mail. You'll need to Open the Messages to do any of these things, by double clicking them.

CompuServe mail

CompuServe Mail is CompuServe's electronic mail service. It gives you the opportunity to communicate not only with any CompuServe Information Service member, but also with most users of the Internet, MCIMail, AT&TMail 400, Western Union 400, Advantis, Uniscource arCom, British Telecom Messaging Services, Nifty-Serve, Deutsche Bundespost, Infonet, Sprint Mail, NetWare MHS Local Area Network, Lotus cc:Mail or Notes.

Many UK external mail systems use the Mail hubs within CompuServe to distribute their mail. It's often more cost effective for short term projects, and the service can be more reliable than some temporary ad hoc corporate email gateways.

You can also communicate with anyone around the world who has a postal address, Group 3 fax machine (it must be available via direct dial) or any telex machine. When you send faxes or telexes, you'll get notification telling you whether the message could be delivered and the time of delivery.

You can also send all types of computer files through CompuServe Mail. Besides text messages, you can upload and send binary files, such as spreadsheets, graphics, worksheets and word processor documents in their native format to any CompuServe member. You also have the ability to download any of your mail messages and file them on your hard disk into the 'Filing Cabinet". If you send a "receipt requested" message, you will find a notification in your mailbox when the message has been retrieved by the recipient. CompuServe Mail also has an electronic address book to store the names and mailing addresses of the people to whom you send messages.

From early 1996 CompuServe will add more options to Mail, including and Email-to-fax facility, email to pager facility and other services. GO MAILHELP for details.

For information on CompuServe Mail prices, GO MAILRATES. For help using CompuServe Mail, GO MAILHELP.

Using electronic mail

Electronic mail ('email') is a highly useful means of transferring information over local or trans-national distances. It takes the form of text or binary

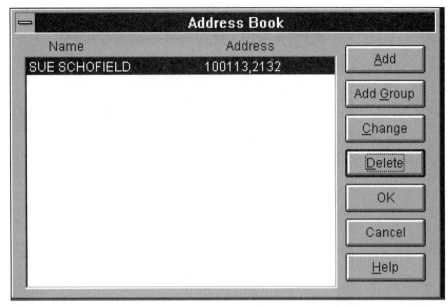

Figure 5.2   *The Address Book in CIM. This is where you add new addresses, and create groups of addresses. It's called up automatically when you Create mail.*

messages, sent to another email user anywhere on the planet. CompuServe mail is secure and fast - messages can be sent to another CompuServe user within minutes. Email is now the preferred method of global text transfer and supersedes Telex and even fax for many purposes. Email is cheap too. A mail sent to a user on the other side of the world costs no more than a local phone call, and a small fee. Compare this with the cost of long distance sending faxes and the benefits are obvious. CompuServe offers the most flexible email service available. You can send ordinary text messages, faxes, and even postal messages to international destinations from the comfort of your computer, as well as binary computer files.

Using CompuServe mail addresses

You get an electronic mail address when you join CompuServe. It looks like 123456,1234 and also comprises your Membership Number. Other members mail you from inside CompuServe by using 123456,1234 as your address.

As numbers are less than convenient as mnemonics, from February 1996 you'll also have the option of registering a Username as an alias to your address. The number will still work, but instead of being 123456,1234 you'll be FREDSMITH@COMPUSERVE.COM. Except that the convention is to write it in lower case as in fredsmith@compuserve.com. As a final complication, the Internet standard of email addressing declares that if you mail a CompuServe user from outside of CompuServe then you would use either:

Figure 5.3 *GO Mailcenter for all your mail needs. You can register your textual address (as in fredsmith@compuserve.com) from here.*

123456.1234@compuserve.com - (the comma has changed to a full stop)

or perhaps more easily:

fredsmith@compuserve.com.

Some CompuServe addresses will also have CSI in front of them, such as:

fredsmith@csi.compuserve.com

and members may well select a nickname for themselves, just to make contacting them by email as hard as possible:

wongo@compuserve.com
GO MAILCENTER to see a full range of mail options when you've signed up.

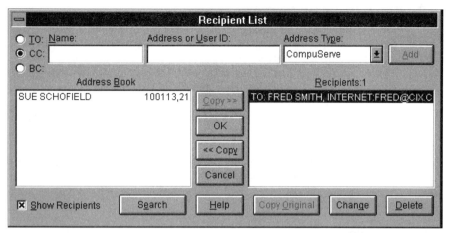

Figure 5.4 *Using the Address Book to Add addresses from incoming mail, allocate INTERNET:, FAX:, CC:Mail or other addresses from here, too. You then paste them into the Recipient list to send to.*

CompuServe mail advantages

CompuServe Mail has a number of advantages and a few disadvantages over standard Internet mail. The Internet is a seven bit system and so 8 bit files such as those your PC or Mac generates have to be converted to transfer them between users (more on this later). CompuServe Mail uses 8 bits so that you can send binary files to other CompuServe users with impunity. This is a very large advantage and has been seized on by millions of users across the world who can mail pictures, spreadsheets and even entire books to each other with impunity. However, Internet usage is climbing astronomically and CompuServe mail needs a separate add-on program to make binary files travel over the Internet to non-CompuServe recipients. Normal text mail isn't affected - CompuServe users can both send and receive mail to and from any Internet user with ease. It's just that the Internet hasn't yet caught up with the 8 bit world, so CompuServe users need a little more technology to use it. It's likely that the next versions of CIM will include all the conversion routines necessary for automatic Internet file transmission and reception.

Mail caveats

There are a few caveats to using email for all your correspondence; the intended recipient may be on holiday or otherwise unavailable for weeks or months, and you won't know if your message has been read (CompuServe users can ask for a receipt). Secondly, very large files don't travel well over email, and anything over say a couple of megabytes is either going to have to be broken down into smaller segments, or sent by floppy disk and 'snail-mail' (the Postal system.) Also if you send mail to systems outside of CompuServe, notably to those on the Internet, there's no guarantee that your mail will or can be delivered, or that your message won't be intercepted by the wrong person, or that your mail is at all secure. Despite these annoyances email is highly useful for short-ish messages (of less than a megabyte or so) sent to anywhere in the world, and the vast bulk of CompuServe mail messages are less than a megabyte bytes in length and delivered in minutes. Because CompuServe mail is more secure than Internet mail, or mail sent through many other UK systems, it is ideal where a greater than normal degree of security is needed, such as for corporate or professional mail use.

CompuServe mail never seems to get lost - accordingly the design and research team for this book were assigned CompuServe accounts, so that mail and binary files were always delivered, and were delivered in minutes at that. We used the Receipt system (Create Mail/Message Options) to keep tabs on when files were collected.

Occasionally, CompuServe slows down and mail is delivered in hours rather than minutes, but this is very infrequent, and in some years of operation, I've never had to complain.

Bounced mail

On the other hand sending mail to Internet addresses is pretty much of an ad hoc affair, although most of the mail gets through most of the time. But it can take anything up to two days for mail to arrive, although the vast majority is delivered worldwide in a few hours. The biggest problems are caused by faulty addresses, and much mail is bounced (returned to sender if possible) because of this.

Bounced mail will be returned to you with a message telling you why. Reasons vary from 'Host Unknown', where routing services can't find the part of the address after the @ sign, to 'User Unknown', where routing finds the bit of the address after the @ sign but can't find the user there. 'Service Unavailable' occurs where both user and host are found but the host computer there is not accepting mail. And 'Can't Send' happens because of network, or 'administrative' problems.

CompuServe mail features

CompuServe Mail provides you with the ability to send messages to up to 50 recipients at a time. If you need to send the same message to more than fifty recipients, you will need to send the message to groups of 50 recipients. You can Create Groups in the Address Book found under the Mail menu.

Message size limits

When sending messages to other CompuServe members, messages as ASCII, text, or binary may be up to 2 Mb (2 million characters) in length.

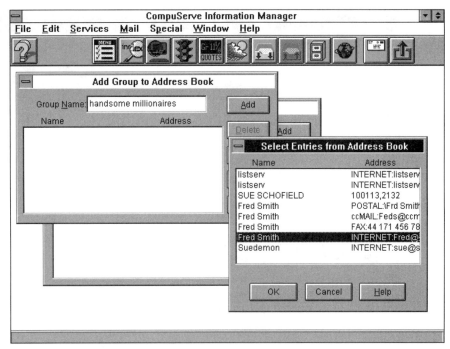

Figure 5.5   *Adding a Group to your Address book. Mail sent to the Group goes to all the Group members.*

Messages to and from X400 gateways, (e.g. Western Union 400, AT&T Mail 400 or Sprint Mail) may also be up to 2 Mb in length. Messages to and from the Internet may be up to 2 Mb in length, although some systems connected to the Internet may not be able to handle messages of this size. Many have a 32 or 64Kb limit on message size. The maximum size for CompuServe fax messages is 50,000 characters (1,000 lines) while messages sent to and received from Telex are limited to 50,000 characters. Postal letters can be up to 219 lines long (4 USA Letter length pages). These limits do change occasionally as CompuServe updates its service.

Storage limits

ASCII messages stored in the (remote) mailbox for CompuServe Mail are automatically deleted 90 days after being sent.

BINARY files which cannot be read on-line are deleted after 30 days. To renew these periods of access before a message is deleted, read the message and select Option 6 (Save in mailbox) at the CompuServe Mail Action Menu.

ASCII messages also may be stored in your PERsonal File Area by selecting Option 2, File in PER Area, at the CompuServe Mail Action Menu. Files

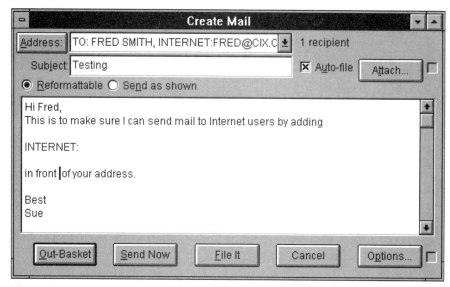

Figure 5.6   *Sending mail to Internet users by adding INTERNET: in front of the Address. WinCIM adds in the prefix for you. Autofile saves a copy in your Filing Cabinet.*

remain in your PER area for one month (or six months if you have the Executive Service Option) or until you delete the file. (Note that BINARY messages cannot be transferred to your Personal File Area from CompuServe Mail). This item is useful for backing up small amounts of data if you're away from home, especially if you think your laptop is going to be zapped by the airport X-Ray system on the way back.

Your CompuServe Mail mailbox can hold up to 100 messages at a time. Once this limit has been reached, anyone attempting to send a message to you will receive a return message stating that your mailbox is full. To make space in your mailbox, you need to retrieve and/or delete existing messages. CompuServe staff do not have access to individual mailboxes, so it is not possible for them to remove mail messages from a full mailbox on your behalf.

Using CIM for CompuServe mail

CIM provides all you need for email. It has an address book, editor and a mechanism for finding CompuServe member's names. Mail can be sent to anyone with an email address on any other system in the world which can accept external mail - that is mail from outside of its own computers. Additionally CIM can send files to other CompuServe users directly, and soon to anyone in the world.

The starting point is the Mail menu option, but first make sure CIM is set up to work the way you want with the Preferences option.

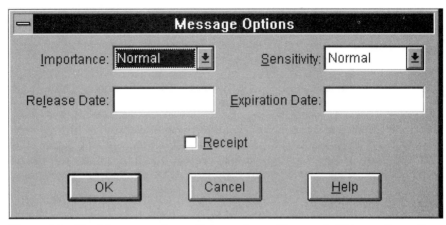

Figure 5.7   *The Message options will be used to add more facilities to CompuServe Mail, such as faxing important email to you. Some corporate mail systems can also handle these flags.*

Mail preferences

The Mail Preferences dialog displays your current Mail options and preferences so that you can review or modify them. You get there by choosing Preferences from the Special menu on any CIM desktop, and then choosing Mail from the Preferences submenu. To have Mail messages automatically deleted from your on-line mailbox after you read them or retrieve them to your hard disk's In-Basket, mark Delete Retrieved Mail and then select OK. (Newcomers may want to leave this option unchecked so as not to loose any mail during early sessions.) To have copies of all outgoing Mail messages automatically saved to a Filing Cabinet folder, mark File Outgoing Messages and type the name of the folder or directory to store them in.

Creating and sending mail

The Create/Send Mail command lets you compose and address a CompuServe Mail message. Create/Send Mail takes you to a Recipient List dialog where you can assign recipient and carbon copy information using your Address Book; from there you access a Create Mail dialog where you compose the text of your message. If you change the folder associated with File Outgoing Messages, message copies previously saved will remain in the old folder, while message copies subsequently saved will go to the new folder. The Recipient List dialog assigns names and addresses to a CompuServe Mail message that you are creating.

Each recipient must have a valid address format.

TO: identifies a primary recipient. Every message must have at least one primary recipient.

CC: identifies a carbon copy recipient. CC recipients are shown as recipients in the message distribution list if you elect to send it along. (The Show Recipients checkbox at the bottom of the Recipient List dialog controls whether recipients will see any message distribution list.)

BC: identifies a blind copy recipient. BC recipients are not shown in any corresponding message distribution list.

If a recipient is already in your Address Book, simply highlight the entry in the Address Book window and then click on the >>Copy button. If a recipient is not in your Address Book, provide the appropriate information in the boxes below Name, Address or User ID, and Address Type, and then click on the Add button.

Address Type: Reflects the address type for the current recipient. If you are typing an address in the box below Address or User ID, specify the address type, such as MCI Mail or Internet, from the list menu. If you provide a name and address in the boxes below Name and Address or User ID, or if you are editing recipient information there, you will need to click on the Add button to actually add the person to your recipient list.

* To remove an entry in the Recipients window,
highlight the entry and then click on the Delete button.

* To add an entry in the Recipients window to your Address Book, highlight the entry and then click on the Copy button.

* To modify an entry in the Recipients window, highlight the entry and then click on the Change button. Clicking on the Change button copies the entry to the Name and Address or User ID boxes at the top of the dialog, where you can edit the entry.

* To include a distribution list of all TO and CC recipients with your message, mark the Show Recipients checkbox.

* If you are forwarding or replying to a message and want the new message to be sent to each original message recipient, mark the Copy Original checkbox.

* If you want to learn the address of someone who is not currently in your Address Book, you can click on the Search button, and then search for member information on CompuServe. Once there, you can add a member's address directly to the Recipient List dialog.

Message options

The Message Options dialog gives you some options for your outgoing CompuServe Mail messages. You get there by selecting Options, at the Create Mail dialog.

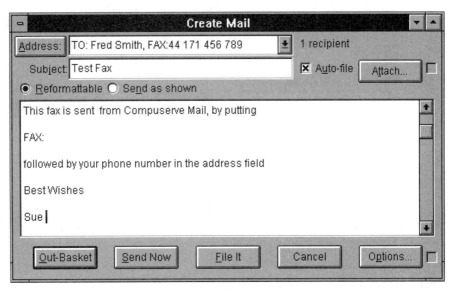

Figure 5.8   *Sending a FAX from CIM. Add FAX: and the country code. You can store Fax addresses in the Address book.*

* If you want to receive a confirmation message when your recipient reads your message, mark Receipt.

* Select the importance level for your message from the Importance pop-up menu. Some external systems will deliver messages of high importance first.

* Select the sensitivity level for your message from the Sensitivity pop-up menu if the external service you are sending mail to can use this feature.

* Type the date on which you want CompuServe to send the message in the box beside Release Date. Unless you specify a different date in the box beside Release Date, the current date is the normal release date.

* If you want the message to be removed from the recipient's mailbox on a particular date, type the date in the box beside Expiration Date. To make your options take effect, select OK.

Test your mail

If you want to test your mail you can send a text mail to the Author at 100113,2132. If you don't get a reply inside a reasonable time do make sure that you've entered the address numbers properly and separated them with a comma. You can also check that the author exists in the Directory to further test your skills, with the Mail/Member Directory option.

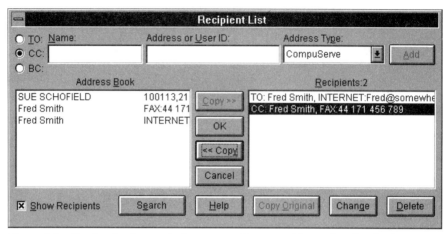

Figure 5.9   *Sending 'carbon copies', one to an Internet address, the other by fax.*

Sending and receiving mail

There are two ways of sending and receiving your mail. The Get New Mail Option will connect to CompuServe and list available waiting mail. You can then manually select the message(s) you want to download to your Inbasket on your hard disk, and delete messages you don't want. This option can be handy to avoid unwanted or unsolicited mail.

The second option is Send/Receive All Mail. If you select the Disconnect When Done option CIM will dial in and collect all waiting mail to your Inbasket, and send all waiting mail in the Outbasket on your hard disk. Generally speaking the Send/Receive mail option is the most used as it provides a fast means of grabbing your mail.

How often should I check my mail?

It depends on the amount and importance of your incoming mail, and the need to respond. Many CompuServe users log in once a week to check mail, others log in once a year or once a day. If you use mail for important work then the sooner you receive your mail the faster you can react. We logged in three times a day during this project to stay updated, perhaps a good minimum for a busy project. Many users log in once a day around lunchtime, to give themselves time to respond to mail. Remember that mail from other CompuServe users gets to you within minutes, not hours, and that a fast response can often clinch a deal. Also remember that if you publish your email address in any form, people will expect you to be contactable by email. If you don't check and respond to your mail you'll get a reputation for un-reliability. If you have more than one account, say an account on any other system, you're going to find it tedious to have to dial

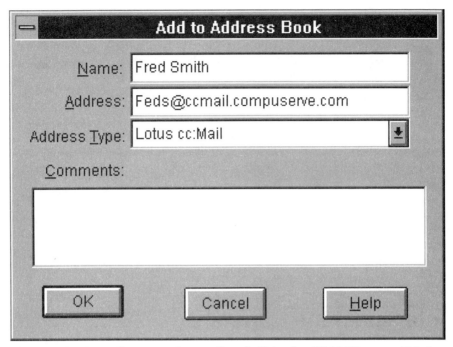

Figure 5.10 *CompuServe provides excellent facilities for CC:MAIL users. This is a CC:MAIL user stored in the Address Book.*

into both accounts to collect your mail. Generally speaking, unless you have good reason to publish more than one email address it's best to stick with just one.

Mail enclosures

A mail enclosure is something you enclose as an email message, using the Send File option within CIM. It takes the form of a binary file, which is a useful way of sending real data around the world. A binary file can be a spreadsheet file, a graphic file, digitized photograph, or a complete software application. CompuServe users can send binary files to each other with the Mail/Send File Option. This option allows you to navigate around your computer's hard disk to select a file for transmission.

For transmission or reception over the Internet, binary 8-bit data files are encoded into a 7-bit representation of their hexadecimal codes, and then fired over the Internet as email. At the receiving end the ASCII text is decoded back into binary, and the result is a reconstruction of the original file. At the moment CIM can't handle this directly so a separate mail program must be used over a CompuServe Internet Connection, or an add-on encoder used to encode the file for transmission as a text file.

This is a great inconvenience for CompuServe users, but CompuServe are up-dating their systems to provide MIME compliant email, and a MIME version of CIM will arrive very shortly. This will allow CompuServe users full binary transfer and reception over the Internet from within CIM without the need for add-on programs.

In the meantime the actual program tool you need to achieve this small miracle varies depending on which computer and which mail software you are using. PC and Amiga owners can use variants of UUencode and UUdecode email software, whilst Mac users often use BinHex 4, a single utility which provides both encoding and decoding functions. However, most of the better stand-alone Internet email programs such as Eudora will handle encode/decode functions automatically for you, and at both ends too. All you have to do is set up a document with the address of the recipient in it, add a few lines of text to say what's happening, and click on the 'attachment' or 'enclosure' button. The program then picks up the data file and does the rest. Bear in mind that you can't do this from within CompuServe, but must use a direct Internet connection unless you are using an add on program for use with CIM. See the Internet Resources forum (GO INETRES) for the utilities you need for you machine.

Inter-machine transfers

Once you get the hang of the need for converting files for transfer you can use this method for transferring data files from DOS to Macs, and vice versa. You might, for instance, want to transfer Word for Mac files into Word for Windows. You just code them into ASCII or RTF, ship them over the net as email or a file enclosure, and your Windows-owning colleague on the other side of the desk can load them straight into his PC. However, at this time, these encode/decode routines leave a lot of confusion in their wake, and the best way to send binary files around is between CompuServe members.

Internet mail encoding standards

There are some emergent 'standards' for attaching these binary files to mail as enclosures to be sent over the Internet. One of them is MIME – Multipurpose Internet Mail Extension, and there are others fighting for dominance. MIME is perhaps the one you'll hear most about, as the business community are now investing in MIME-compliant email systems. MIME is also becoming the default PC standard, and as such is finding its way into email encryption. MIME decoders are available for all computer types - and the Internet Resources Forum on CompuServe has the software for your machine.

Things are more complicated than they should be in the UK, mainly because there are thousands of bulletin board systems in this country which sprang into being before Internet usage became widespread. Many of these systems use mutually exclusive methods to transfer files between subscribers, and you cannot (at the time of writing) use your newly found Internet mail skills to

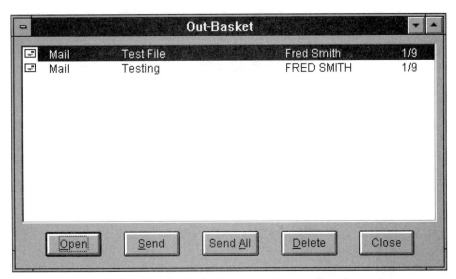

Figure 5.11 *Mail placed in the Outbasket stays there until you're ready to connect. You can Open mail for editing.*

directly send a binary file to many UK BBS's – except as a binary-coded ASCII mail message as MIME, UUCode or BinHex. All three coding systems are mutually exclusive, by the way. You'll need the correct decoder software to retrieve the binary file for each of the file types, although some utilities can handle two or more encoding methods. Check out the Internet Resources forum for details as new file encoders are being written by the minute.

If you do decide to send binary files to another non-CompuServe user you should check first by Email whether the recipient prefers MIME, BinHex or UUCODE files. You'll be startled to find that many users won't know what you mean. Also users of other UK services such as CIX will have decided to standardize on one utility or the other, (CIX uses UUCODE in its standard 'Front-End' program at present). As MIME will almost certainly emerge as the de facto standard you should at least equip yourself with a good MIME program, until the next release of CIM.

Luckily, many corporates can send binary mail to CompuServe via a variety of electronic mail hubs, so if your company uses external electronic mail there's every chance that you can get binary files routed via CompuServe in this manner. You won't be able to do this with the hundreds of other UK-centric dial-up systems which use their own internal mail 'standards', so you'll have to use UUencode, BinHex, MIME or its equivalent.

At the moment the Binary file enclosure represents a real stumbling block for many CompuServe users wishing to transport files by email over the Internet. If you do have a requirement to send file enclosures to non-CompuServe users first mail the intended recipient to ensure they are equipped to receive it with MIME, UUCODE or Binhex. If not you won't be able to get your file to them regardless of what you do.

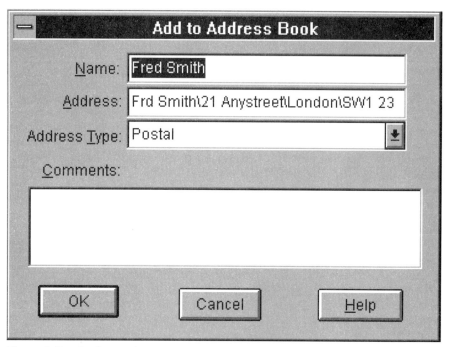

Figure 5.12 *Sending mail to a postal address anywhere in the world from CIM. Use \ to separate address lines. Mac Users get a dinky address box to fill in.*

Common errors with word processor file enclosures

Because it's so easy to mail files around with CompuServe, many users don't give a thought as to how the recipient is going to deal with them. The most common mistake is to assume that the person at the other end uses the same equipment and word-processing software as you do. In most cases this won't be true, and in most cases it's users of Microsoft Word 6 who think that they can attach Word files with impunity - and it's up to the rest of us to go out and buy a copy of Word to read them. This is a common fault in the UK, where large corporations send out general press releases as Word 6 binaries. You can avoid Word 6 binary-itis by sending all mail wherever possible as text.

You only need to send a WP file as a binary if text formatting, graphics and pagination needs to be retained. If you do this the recipient will need the same application program you used to create the file, unless they have file translation facilities on their machine. If you don't know what system the recipient is using then you must email them first and ask. If you can't do that then the only WP format that most everyone can read is called RTF, (Rich

Figure 5.13 *Send a File enclosure to another CompuServe member. Click Send File from the Mail menu, add a recipient, then browse for the file. You can send Binary, GIF or text files this way.*

Text Format) so use that to save your file, and then send it as a binary enclosure. (RTF doesn't retain graphics in files.) If you're sending text for publishing in a newspaper or magazine, leave out all formatting and send it as plain text, unless you have a previous agreement with the recipient.

Things are slightly more difficult for spreadsheet users, as spreadsheets won't recalculate if you send them as text. Your only recourse here is to mail the recipient and ask what format they can read, the most common being the XLS format, from Microsoft Excel and the WK1 format from Lotus.

Despite Bill Gate's omnipotence, not everyone yet uses Microsoft applications and mailing large binary files around that could so easily be sent as plain text just tends to make normally placid CompuServe users extremely irate - especially if they can't read the two megabytes of data they've just downloaded and need in a hurry. Check first before you mail off a binary WP file, and work on the basis that everyone uses a different word processor to you.

Binary files and security

The other common error is to mail security information out with your binary. A large UK modem company recently sent out a binary Word 6 press release which unambiguously showed the name of the server where the file was held, the directory, the time and date of its creation, and the name of the laser printer last used. This may not often matter, but anyone who takes their site security seriously would blanch at the thought of this information being shipped out to two hundred computer journalists. Moral - be careful with those binary files - and use plain text where possible for WP documents - unless you need to preserve the formatting.

File compression

Users of bulletin boards, dial-up services and the Internet will be well aware that most computer files can be compressed down into around a half of their original size or less, by the use of file compression programs such as PKZip, PKArc, Stuffit, Compact Pro and the like.

There are many reasons for compressing files, the most obvious being the need to fit more files in a given area – be that a local hard disk or a network server. File compression utilities are also useful for adding two or more files into a single bundle for transmission over modems or for adding encryption or password protection to files. Some compression programs also allow large compressed files to be filed to disk in segments for reconstitution at a later date (multi-file segmenting) and this option is also used to mail binaries to the Internet where many mail and news systems limit file sizes to 64 or even 32Kb. Most compression programs also have an option to create self-extracting archives. These let users decompress files without access to the original program, but can add about ten per cent or more to the size of the compressed archive.

PC file compressors

The most common format for compressed PC files is PKZip. These compressed files have a suffix of ZIP and you'll need PKUnzip (or a PKUnzip-compliant clone utility) to decompress these files. You'll find such an animal in most of the CompuServe libraries which distribute PC files, and there are Windows and Dos versions of the utility around. As with most things to do with personal computers there are no real standards for file compression, and CompuServe users tend supply files compressed with different utilities. Many older files are compressed using PKArc, a few using the Unix TAR scheme.

Filenames tend to indicate the compression scheme in use FILENAME.ZIP, FILENAME.ARC AND FILENAME .TAR are all self explanatory. Self-extracting PC files are often 'executable' and have an EXE suffix, as in FILENAME.EXE. A common scheme is LHA which produces files with an LZH suffix, as in FILENAME.LZH. At the moment WinCim doesn't automatically decompress files for you - although the Mac version will if it can find a decompressor program stored on your hard drive.

File compressors are vital if you want to send two or more files at the same time to the same recipient or group. You bundle all the files up into a packet, and they travel as a single file to the recipient. Furthermore the files are compressed so that they travel faster, and take up less on-line time. Compressed files also take up less space on hard disks, but with the advent of compression built in to operating systems (DBLSPACE for PC's and AutoDoubler etc for Macs) this is less of a concern than it used to be.

Mac file compressors

Mac users will come across several compression utilities. Probably the most common is Stuffit, which produces files with a suffix of SIT. Slightly less

Figure 5.14 *You CANNOT do this. Sending a file directly to an Internet user. This needs a MIME or UUCode encoder to turn a binary file into ASCII until the next CIM update which should do this automatically. So...*

common, is Compactor (suffix is CPT), and many sites are starting to carry files with an LZH suffix, which means they are compressed with the Mac version of LHA, titled MacLHA. A Mac program called Zipit produces some compatibility with ZIP files generated on PCs. Self-extracting Mac Archives often have a suffix of SEA.

Many Mac libraries carry files in 'disk image' form. This is a scheme where a bit image of a floppy disk is compressed into a single file, and the corresponding de-compressor is used to re-create the disk image. This process either creates a floppy disk with the original information on it, or mounts an image of the virtual floppy onto the desktop. DiskCopy is the utility to do the former, MountImage to do the latter and disk image files often carry the suffix 'image'. MountImage is sometimes the more useful of the two, as it allows users of pre-SuperDrive Macs to mount an image of a 1.44 megabyte disk on the desktop of a Mac which can only read 800 kB floppies. You'll find image files used to carry copies of Apple installer disks, for instance.

UNIX compressors

As if that wasn't enough, the UNIX fraternity often decide that an additional compression process is needed to compress the compressed files while they live on the server, and many Internet servers now use a GNU-ZIP variant to do this. The result is that you'll need yet another process to unlock your data. These files have a GZ (Gzip) or TAR (Tape Archive) suffix and you'll need a program called Gzip or similar to turn the file into binary, Binhex or UUencode format. (The Chapter on FTP has more details.)

Machine independent compression

There are a number of machine-independent compression schemes around. LHA is used on both Amiga and PC files, and is creeping across to the Mac platform, and both ZOO and TAR files are starting to catch on, although the older ARC utility is slowly fading away. You can find decompression utilities for all of these files with the File Finder for your machine or in almost every Forum Library, so getting hold of them should not be a problem.

Viruses

In all cases CompuServe users should have an anti-virus utility to hand to check downloaded files. While files stored on CompuServe are virus checked before they arrive in libraries, a second line of defence is always wise. You can't catch a virus from text files, although you can from binary files.

You can catch file and disk destroying routines from WP files which carry macros, as in the famous Word 6 Prank macro. If you have any doubts about viruses in files then the Sysop of the forum you're working with will be able to answer any queries. But get your own virus checker sorted out first. Use the File Finders to check 'virus'. Files on the Internet (outside of CompuServe's care) are almost never checked for viruses by the operator of the server where they live, and Internet users must have good virus checking utilities as a matter of course. Mac users seem to suffer less than PC users, but viruses are endemic on the Internet.

Keep regular backups of your hard disk data too, as anti-virus programs can't restore damaged hard disk files, or restore erased disks.

Graphics files

Graphics files are stored on CompuServe in various formats, the most common being GIF (Graphics Interchange Format) files, the most uncommon being Mac 'picts'. Other formats abound, and you'll generally need the right sort of file viewer on your computer to view and manipulate graphics files. GIF files will go straight into most graphics programs on most types of computer, and so are consequently the lingua franca of CompuServe users. Full installations of CIM from CD ROM come with 'ImageView' which lets users view, crop, and manipulate many graphics files in various formats. Most computers can view GIF files with ease, so if you don't know which format to save your graphics files in for transfer to other users, use GIF first.

TIFF files, on the other hand, come in a dozen different types and are not guaranteed to cross computer boundaries smoothly. There are also JPEG files, Windows Bitmap files (BMPs) and TGA files (TARGA). TARGA files are slowly being replaced by JPEG files.

As mentioned, you'll need a graphics viewer of some sort to see these files on your PC or Mac. Graphics Workshop is a good all-rounder for the PC, and Graphics Convertor is arguably the best all-round Shareware graphics

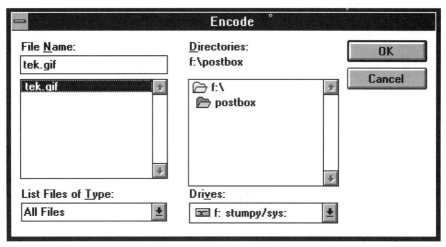

Figure 5.15 *Sending a binary GIF file over the Internet. (1) Log into the InetRes forum and Search the Libraries for a MIME or UUcoder.*

program for the Mac, or any other platform. Both are readily available on CompuServe.

CompuServe are slowly moving towards a new graphic standard called Portable Network Graphics (PNG). Details are in the Graphic Support Forum GRAPHSUP.

Graphics file transfers

Once you've grabbed a graphic file from CompuServe you may want to share it around a little. Your friends will all have their own ideas about what constitutes a computer so you'll need to learn ways of sharing these files around. The trick is to bring the file into a common disk format, and then convert it into a common file format. Mac, Amiga and Atari machines have utilities that let them save files in MS-DOS formats – but if all else fails (and you have a modem) you can upload the file from the alien computer to your CompuServe Personal File area and then download it to your computer for conversion.

Most of the Mac's graphics translator programs will work with most graphics files on MS-DOS disks. For instance, if you have a Windows BMP file on a PC floppy disk then Apple File Exchange will read it into the Mac without error. It can then be translated with Graphic Convertor or similar. But Mac users often run into problems with PC TIFF and EPS files. TIFF files have many inherent formatting differences, including black and white, grey scale, 24-bit, 4-bit and 8-bit images. TIFF also supports the use of multiple types of data compression – and to complicate matters further, two byte-ordering schemes are supported (Intel and Motorola), as indicated by the internal TIFF file header. So don't be surprised if you have problems loading transferred TIFFs into your computer - be it a Mac or a PC.

PC based Encapsulated PostScript Files (EPS) come as either plain ASCII files, or binary files with a header that describes both the PostScript commands and the preview (TIFF or Metafile) section of the file. Again, not all EPS files will translate easily between computers or platforms, so if you have a choice, go for GIF. If you really need to handle PostScript file over CompuServe make sure you run a few trials first. Many EPS files need to be pasted or inserted into an already open PostScript document, and large files will defeat the small clipboards available on Windows based PC's. PostScript files are text files, and can be sent as straight email, a tip worth trying. However because they are text they also compress readily, and large PostScript files are best sent compressed as ZIP files or similar for maximum economy.

Email encryption and decryption

Mail over the Internet isn't as private as you might think, although mail sent between CompuServe users is highly secure. There have been numerous instances of non-CompuServe mail being intercepted, and there are endless rumours that the FBI, the Inland Revenue, the CIA, and Jeremy Beadle all have secret hooks into private Internet mail. To get over these fears many mail programs now provide encryption of text. The most basic encryption routine is something called ROT13. ROT stands for Rotation, and all the letters of the alphabet are rotated thirteen places forward in a ROT13 message. ROT13 is therefore hardly an encryption at all, as a five-year-old can decrypt ROT13 messages in a matter of minutes. So ROT13 is used to protect the endings of jokes in public mailings, or to keep sexually explicit material from the eyes of those who don't want to read it. It's most often used in Usenet messages.

There are other more serious encryption schemes around such as PGP (Pretty Good Privacy). But do you really need to encrypt your mail messages? The first thing to realize is that few people use encryption so you have to make sure that the recipient uses the same scheme. At the moment this is difficult if you use an Amiga and the recipient uses a BBC Micro or a NeXT Workstation. The second thing is that your CompuServe mailbox is highly secure - to the extent that CompuServe support staff normally have no access to it, so you may not need to encrypt your CompuServe messages - unless they go outside the system over the Internet.

Internet Email security

If you do have commercially sensitive information to send over the Internet then you should look at some method of password-protecting it, at least. One easy way is to password-protect word processor or spreadsheet files in the application program, or to bundle files through a compressor program such as PKZip for the PC, Stuffit for the Mac, or LHA for the Amiga. These programs will produce a collection of files (called an archive) which can be password-protected and sent over the 'Net after being converted to ASCII in

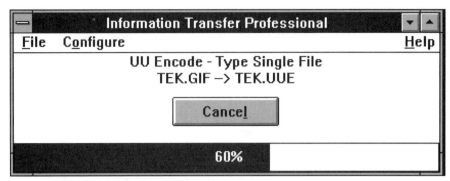

Figure 5.16 *(2) Use it to turn the binary file into a text file. (TEK.GIF into TEK.UUE). UUE is the UU Encoded file and is now all text.*

the normal way. However the security of these programs can be broken in minutes, and they only serve to prevent ad hoc lurkers seeing your mail. A determined effort can break compression program passwords easily.

Similarly you shouldn't mail your credit card details around, nor post messages which say 'I live at such and such address and my hobby is collecting rare diamonds' (or Macintosh computers) otherwise you'll be receiving mail from burglars asking you when you're going on your holidays. Unfortunately, they don't always ask.

The subject of mailing credit card numbers around is a thorny one. Again you're OK on CompuServe but as the Internet continues to lean more towards Mammon than Academia there will be more commercial transactions carried out over it. At the moment many of the Internet transactions between vendors and customers require a credit card number, and generally speaking the Internet is not a safe place to leave credit card details suspended in Cyberspace. Many commercial vendors will dispute this but there are an increasing number of programs around called Packet Sniffers. The sole purpose of these is to track IP packets travelling over a network, and log their contents to disk. Packet Sniffers generate huge amounts of logged data, and it takes a while to write algorithms to sort that data into human-readable form, but it can be done, and the format of credit card data is easy to distinguish from plain text traffic. So the answer is – at least be wary when mailing your credit card number around outside of CompuServe There is a slim chance that it might be intercepted and misused.

Pretty Good Privacy

Phil Zimmerman's PGP (Pretty Good Privacy) program lets users encrypt mail or documents. It's caused political havoc in most countries its been used, simply because it works so well. PGP can protect files or entire hard disks from snoops, and it's a great tool for everyone who wants to hide data. This includes the UK government, your doctor, and your neighbourhood crack dealer.

PGP works by using two encrypt/decrypt keys. One is made public, so that anyone can encrypt mail to send to you for decoding, the other is your private and secret decoder. The private key is needed to decrypt a message coded with the public key. Additionally PGP can create or verify digital signatures to ensure that email or files really did come from a verifiable source. In short PGP scares the lumps out of Governments because it's so powerful.

Whilst it's probable that PGP encrypted files can be broken (research indicates it would take twenty 66Mhz 486 PC's over twenty years to decrypt a file) it's not generally thought that PGP encrypted files can be broken in anything like a reasonable time. Notably your average government office does not have twenty 486 PCs available to decode suspect files, although covert government departments do have larger toys to play with.

If you want to try PGP it's freely available on CompuServe, although the PC versions of the program are as hostile as they come (there's now a Windows version in the EFF forum.) Look out too, for email messages posted in newsgroups showing PGP public keys as part of the signature. Then ask yourself whether these people really send mail they want kept secret, or if they're just playing techno-geeks.

If you want more info on this topic then the Electronic Frontier Foundation carry a well maintained file library in the EFF forum.

Mail lists

A mail-list is something you join, and in the course of a few hours or days, you receive endless messages covering the sphere of interest you enquired about. Some of the mail-lists are quite informative. You can have the White House mail you with the President's agenda for the day. Other lists cover national or regional issues, or aspects of human sexuality.

Mail-lists vary in content and interest. Many mail-lists contain stuff other people have mailed in. You post a message to the list server, and everyone else on the list gets a copy, whether they like it or not. They are called Reflector Lists. Other mail-lists are assembled by the list owner, who then sends out single-topic mail. Mail-List Digests are simply large files containing all the stuff mailed to the server by members. You get a huge mail-message or file containing hundreds of messages at a time. In both cases mail-lists can be moderated, that is, have offensive or off-topic stuff edited out by the list moderator. While moderating mail (and Usenet groups) might seem like censorship, many aspects of Internet mail and messaging benefit from a small amount of control. On the other hand, too much control makes the moderator seem like a totalitarian ogre to his victims, and there's often a very fine line between the two extremes.

Mail-lists can be fun, especially if you can find one which hits your particular interest spot on, but it's often harder to get off one than to get on. To sign on to many lists you simply send a mail message saying 'Subscribe me' or some such, and you'll be on the list. To leave, you send a message saying 'Resign'

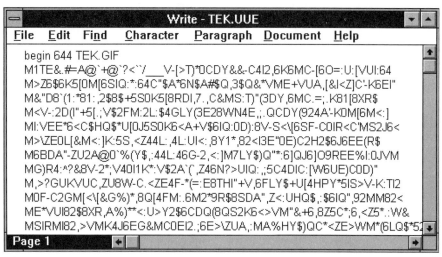

Figure 5.17   *(3) Use CIM Send File to send the TEK.UU file as TEXT.*

or 'Unsubscribe' or similar. Often it gets ignored. Many mail-lists now have 'intelligent' software that lets you pick and choose which topics you want to receive from the lists, and in what order or format, and the White House system is a good example. See the next Section for more information on using mail-lists.

Finding the unfindable

CompuServe users can track each other down with the Directory facility, and access to this is built into CIM in the mail section, or can be accessed directly by GO DIRECTORY. (This is NOT the Help Directory WinCIM installs on your hard disk). However some users may decide that they will be ex-directory, so a search won't find them. The other method on CompuServe is to search the Forum Membership lists. If you're looking for another UK user you might for instance search the UK Forum profiles for a surname. This method can often work well if you know the likely interests of who you're searching for. Join the Forum of choice, then go to Special/ Search Membership. You can search for a user name or a membership number.

You can often track down academic or corporate Internet users with WHOIS - as long as there's a WHOIS server running at their institution and they are logged to it. You can do it by sending email to mailserv@internic.net or any of the other whois servers with the command 'whois xxx'. European users can subscribe to the RIPE Whois databases, but few do. It's often better to get hold of non-academic email addresses by phoning the people concerned or by sending them a fax.

How to send a FAX via CompuServe mail

CompuServe Mail provides you with the ability to send text messages to Group 3 facsimile (Fax) machines around the world. This feature is highly useful, as it doesn't involve you fighting with trans-world telephone charges. You use the Create Message option, and put FAX: in the address box, followed by the international phone number.

If you wanted to fax home to London 0171 123 456 you'd put:

FAX: 44 171 123 456

as the number. (Note the deletion of the leading 0 in the phone number and the addition of the UK International Code.)

Faxes are delivered swiftly, often in less than ten minutes and each page of the message is numbered. A Fax header sheet contains your numerical CompuServe address. There's a maximum size for fax messages of 100,000 characters (1,000 lines).

If you are using CompuServe Information Manager (CIM) software:

1) Select Create Mail from the Mail pull-down menu and a Recipient List dialog box will appear. There will be the option to fill in the Name and Address (in this case, fax number) of the intended recipient(s)

The name of the recipient should be typed in the "Name" field.

The "Address" field should begin with the notation "FAX:", followed by the fax phone number, including country code plus the fax number.

After entering the Name and Address information this can be added to the recipient list (up to 50 recipients at a time). You can store the address for future use if you copy it to your Address Book in CIM.
2) Store the fax mail in your Outbasket for transmission at a later date, or click Send to send it immediately. You'll get warning messages if the country code or address format is wrong, advice on the charge if it's correct.

Confirmation

You will automatically receive a confirmation through CompuServe Mail when your fax message has been delivered. CompuServe Mail will attempt to send fax messages up to five times. If the message cannot be delivered in first attempts, it will be returned. CompuServe is not responsible for fax messages not delivered because of incorrect phone numbers.

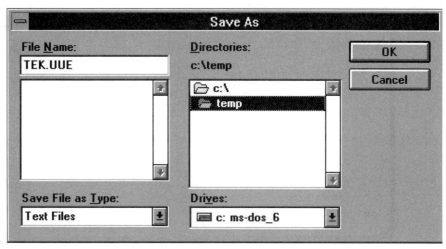

Figure 5.18 *(4) To decode an incoming message, save it as a text file with the File/Save command, using UUE as the suffix, for a UU coded file.*

There are extra charges for using CompuServe Fax. Go MAILHELP and MAILRATES for details. Charges for sending faxes within Europe are around $0.90 per 1000 characters.

Sample report text:

Re: Test Fax

Message 951224180201 100113.2132 EHQ69-1, sent 13:02 EST 24-Dec-95, was delivered at 13:06 EST 24-Dec-95 to:

FAX:44-1323470450 sue (CSID: 44 01323 470 450).
Two FAX pages were transmitted.
Transmission succeeded on the first attempt.

A report from a two page test fax sent to the UK. It cost $2.70 in December 1995, and was delivered in four minutes.

CompuServe postal mail

CompuServe Mail allows you to send personalized, professional, laser printed letters around the world to any postal address.
Each line can be a maximum of 80 characters wide. Any lines longer than this will be truncated. Maximum number of lines per letter is 219 (or 4 pages)

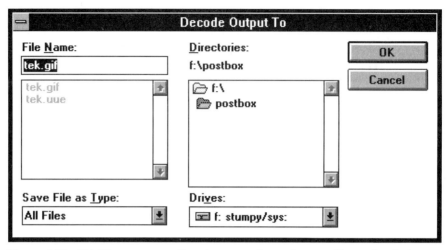

Figure 5.19 *(5) Then set your Decoder to work on the text file to decode it as a Binary. Later versions of CIM will handle Internet binary mail automatically.*

Any additional lines will be truncated. Of the 4 pages, the first page is 39 lines long (not including the addresses). Pages 2 through 4 are 60 lines long each. A distribution list of all receivers will automatically be appended to the letter if your options are SET to 'SHOW recipients [YES]'. For more information on the SET command, and the SHOW RECIPIENTS option, type HELP SET at the CompuServe Mail Main Menu. (GO ASCIIMAIL if you are using a CompuServe Information Manager (CIM) program.)

All letters must be in pure ASCII (text) format. This includes:

– Alphabet: A-Z, a-z
– Digits: 0-9
– Spaces
– Punctuation: !@#$%&*()_+=-:;"<>,.?'/
– Special Characters:
+ Page Feed: Ctrl-L
+ Carriage Return: Ctrl-M
+ Tab: Ctrl-I
– Tabs will be interpreted based on regular placement every eight characters (1,9,17,25,33,41,49 etc.)

– All other characters are illegal and will be removed.
Both the recipient and returnee's addresses automatically will be printed on the first page of the letter. Letters are laser printed on 8½ x 11 inch white paper. Letters are placed in white envelopes with two windows - one for the recipient's address and one for the sender's address.

Please note that the instructions for creating and addressing postal mail are different for the various versions of the CompuServe Information Manager.

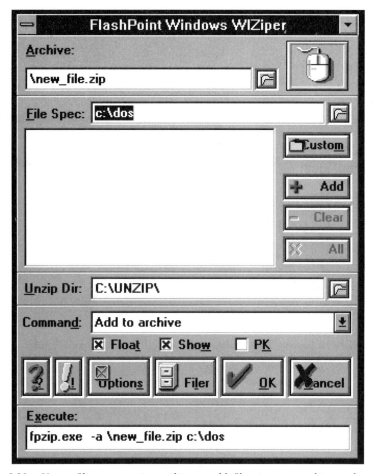

Figure 5.20   *Use a file compression utility to add files into an archive and compress them. This is Zip Navigator. Mac CIM will de-compress archives automatically if you have the correct utility on your disk.*

If you are using DOSCIM:

Select the "Address Book" option off the "Mail" pull-down menu. From the dialog box presented, select "New". In the "Address Entry" dialog box select "Postal", and you will then see all the appropriate postal mail address fields you need to complete.

After completing the address information select "OK" and then "Save". When you want to use this information, you can choose it from the "Address Book" presented to you when you select to "Create Mail" or "Send File".

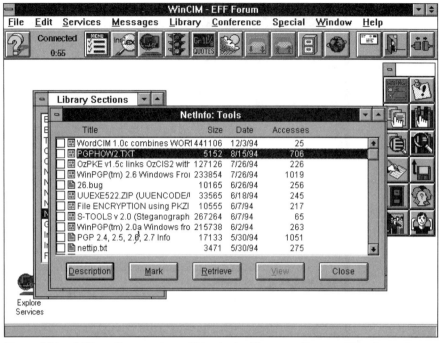

Figure 5.21   *PGP mail encryption utilities in the Electronic Frontier Foundation Forum.*

If you are using WinCIM & MacCIM:

Select the "Address Book" option from the "Mail" pull-down menu. From the dialog box presented, select "Add". In the address entry dialog box select "Postal" from the "Format" selection. At this point you will then see all the appropriate postal mail address requirements.

Telex

CompuServe Mail provides you with the ability to send and receive messages to and from any Telex I or Telex II machine in the world. The cost of sending messages to Telex machines in the U.S. is $1.15 per 300 characters. The cost of sending Telex to any other worldwide location is determined by the country of destination and the length of the message. A list of country codes and rates is available by typing HELP TELEX INTERNATIONAL. To find the exact cost of sending a message, you may compose your message and enter the address information (details below). Then when CompuServe Mail displays the address for your verification, the exact cost will bedisplayed.

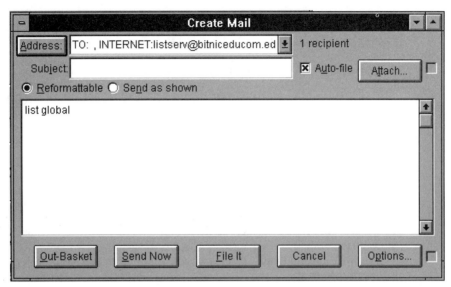

Figure 5.22 *Subscribing to a Listserv. This one is listserv@bitnic.educom.edu. Send 'list global' for a complete list of what's available. You get a very large file back.*

Sending telexes

The command used to send a message to a Telex I or II machine is:

Send to (Name or User ID): TLX: (machine no.) (answerback):

Send to (Name or User ID): TLX: 1234567 ABCDEF

where the machine number is "1234567" and the answerback is "ABCDEF."

Telex information

Telex messages up to 50,000 characters in length may be sent.

The answerback is optional, but if used it must be correct AND complete for the Telex to be delivered. If you are not certain of the correct AND complete answerback, please omit it! Some telex machines include part or all of the machine number in the answerback. If this is true for the telex machine you are transmitting to, you must include this information as part of your answerback in order for your transmission to be successful.

A distribution list of all receivers will automatically be appended to the telex if your options are SET to 'SHOW recipients [YES]'. For more information on the SET command, and the SHOW RECIPIENTS option, type HELP SET at the CompuServe Mail Main Menu.

For example:
If the answerback for telex machine 987654 is 987654 AB CDE, the command used to send a message would look like this:

Send to (Name or User ID): TLX: 987654 987654 AB CDE

CompuServe is not responsible for Telexes returned as "undeliverable" due to incorrect answerbacks. Answerbacks are optional, but can be very helpful in verifying the machine number.

TELEXes sent to MCI Mail subscribers require a special prefix before the TELEX number. The prefix is 650.

TELEXes sent to destinations within the continental U.S. are domestic TELEXes. TELEXes sent to destinations outside of the continental U.S. (regardless of point of origin) are international TELEXes, and the TELEX machine number must be preceded with a 3-digit Country Code. (Type HELP TELEX INTERNATIONAL at the CompuServe Mail Main Menu for a list of country codes.)

You will automatically receive a confirmation when your Telex message has been delivered.

Receiving telexes

CompuServe Mail allows a message to be sent from a Telex I or II machine to your mailbox. Telexes up to 50,000 characters in length may be received. The information the Telex user needs to send a message to your CompuServe mailbox is:

* Your User ID

* The machine number to send the message to - 3762848 - which has the answerback of COMPUSERVE

The sender must specify on the first non-blank line of the message a "TO: " followed by your User ID to inform CompuServe Mail where to deliver the message. If a subject is desired, the sender can also add a "RE:" after the "TO:" line in the message. The format would appear as follows:

TO: 70001,1234   (This is Required)

RE: TEST MESSAGE (This is optional message subject)
This is the information you requested...

The "TO:" line must be formatted as indicated in the example above. A colon (:) must follow the "TO." Nothing can follow the User ID, unless the message is to be delivered to more than one mailbox.

NOTE: When sending a Telex message from some countries, a prefix may be necessary before the CompuServe machine number. A list of prefixes is available by typing HELP TELEX PREFIXES. The sender also can specify that the message be delivered to more than one mailbox by appending additional User ID's separated by semicolons on the "TO:" line. It also is possible to have multiple "TO:" lines specified in the message. For example:

TO: 70001,1234; 71110,111
TO: 70000,1
RE: INFORMATION YOU REQUESTED

More information is available for Telex. To reach these "sub-topics," from the CompuServe Mail menu, type HELP TELEX, followed by the sub-topic (INTERNATIONAL or PREFIXES).

6 CompuServe forums

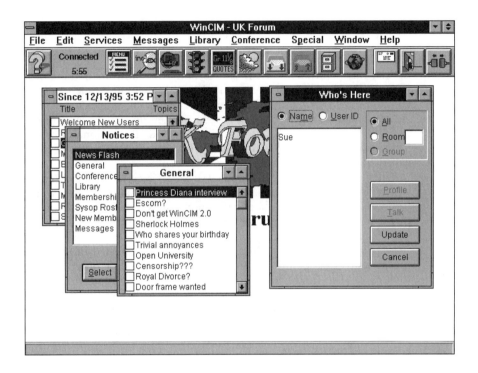

A Forum is where people meet, tell jokes, gossip and exchange files, and occasionally chat in real time to each other. CompuServe Forums provide a convenient way to swap information (Messages), store and access files of interest to others (Libraries) and interact in real time (Conference Rooms). Topics are maintained and regulated by the Forum operator, often assisted by a team of sub-operators.

Topics

Forums ideally contain information related to just one topic, like Pet Care, Windows 95, Vegetarian Motor Bikers. Each Forum is divided into sub-topics, so the fictional Vegetarian Motorbikers Forum might have sub-topics of Veggie Bikers Meetings, Tattoos For All, and Acne - Your Problems. In reality messages in Forums, like all areas of human communication, tend to drift off-topic; a

Pet Care Forum (such as PetOne) contains messages from people bleating on about computers, which is a common problem with a computer based medium. But by and large Forums can be terrifically useful once you've got the hang of them. They form the core of CompuServe's interest for many people and are an essential part of getting the best from your CompuServe account.

Finding a forum

There are two ways to find a Forum that interests you. The first is to use the Special/Find Option in CIM, the second is to download the Forum Index (GO INDEX), load it into your WP, and search it. Generally the Find command will bring up three or four items of interest, but beware the Americanization of the English language when you do a search. For instance a 'Find Vet' command will bring up the UK Professional Forum 'Ask A Vetinary' and also the USA Military Forums. (USA ex-servicemen are also called Vets. - as in Veteran.)

When you sign up for CompuServe you'll receive a New Members guide which lists all the Forums. This will serve as a handy reference, as will the Index in the back of this book. If you choose GO FORUMS you'll get a list of Forums categorized by type, so you can browse through nested options to get where you want to be.

Use the Find option to locate topics you're interested in, as it's generally quick, and often points towards places you wouldn't otherwise thought of looking in. The Find command also lets you place 'found' Forums (hits) into your Favorite Places menu for later use, which is even more convenient, except that after a year or two's use your Favourite places menu then contains the complete list of CompuServe Forums.

Once you have found the Forum you want, go to it with the CTRL G command (That's the Apple Key plus G for Mac owners.).

Forums in depth

Forums (fora) have three main sections. These are:

Message Sections where you read or leave (post) public messages for others to read and comment on. The message sections are superb for computer support, socializing and getting answers to almost any problem. Generally speaking you'll always get an answer to a question in about 24 hours, even the most obscure question on almost any subject will have generated at least four responses inside a week.

Perhaps a good example is the question left in the UK Wales topic from a chap who had once found the single place in Wales which makes its own whisky. He wanted a bottle sent to his new home in Holland and left a question asking if anyone could help. Within three days he'd got not only travel directions to the door of the distillery, but the full postal address and the phone number. This might be a trivial example, but the power of the CompuServe Forums to

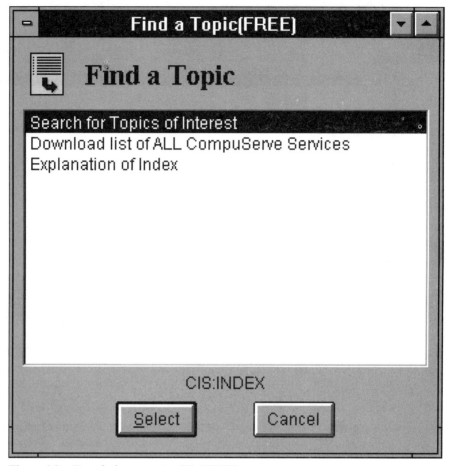

Figure 6.2   *First find your topic. GO INDEX to rummage.*

come up with the right answers is unsurpassed on almost any other system. This includes the international Usenet system, of which more later.

To send a message to a Forum you create a new Forum message in CIM while disconnected, with Mail/Create Forum message. Address it to ALL or the SYSOP if it's for public consumption, then go on-line, join the forum and upload the message.

File Libraries contain binary and textual computer files for downloading. These cover every possible theme from digitized home photos to support files from leading computer suppliers. You can upload your own files for 'publication' in the libraries, or simply browse and download files as you need them.

The File Libraries are linked to several search mechanisms. The first level is the FF structure, as in IBMFF - where FF means File Finder. Simply type GO IBMFF, GO MACFF, GO PCFF, GO GRAPHFF (Graphics) GO ATARIFF or GO AMIGAFF to enter the search mechanism for your particular

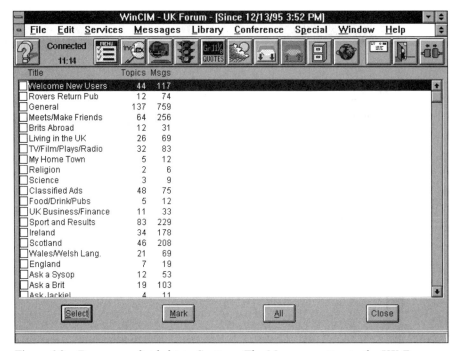

Figure 6.3   *Forums are divided into Sections. The Message section in the UK Forum.*

needs. If you've joined the ZiffNet (ZD) computer information service you have additional File Finders in GO ZNT:ZNTFF and GO ZNT:ZMAC.

You can search for files by keyword or file-name or author. You might for example want an upgraded driver for your Hewlett Packard DeskJet printer. You'd GO IBMFF and type 'DeskJet' as a keyword. You'll get a list of files found, together with the library they are in and a short description ('abstract') of the file contents. There's is a second search mechanism in each Forum library section, but the FF mechanisms seem to be much more useful when searching, as they search all Forums for your keyword.

Each Forum may also contain a **Conference Room**. These are places to which you may repair for a on-line natter with others. They're a great form of entertainment, but UK phone charges tend to keep usage to a minimum on this side of the Pond.

Not all topics conform to these structures - some of the support Forums contain only file sections, and the free Forums do not tend to have conference rooms. But by and large this is the structure you'll find in most of the Forums that you'll use.

Finding it

Navigating around CompuServe is the single biggest obstacle for new users so here's a tip is worth its weight in gold phone bills - use the Find command to navigate your way around for your first few sessions. You'll get a feel for

Figure 6.4   *You can Search the Messages for a keyword or subject.*

how CompuServe works, and you'll start to build up your own small corner of CompuServe by adding your 'hits' to your Favourite places menu. See the screenshots for examples.

Bear in mind that the File Finders only track down computer related files. If you want a file of good British pubs you would need to search the relevant Forum Library for it. (GO UKFORUM)

Off-line help and searches

The full versions of WinCIM come with the CompuServe Directory. This is a Windows Help file which lives on your hard disk. You use it to search for a topic or subject and the Directory will give you the GO address for any hits it comes up with. All this happens off-line so you're not running up your phone bill doing searches.

If you subscribe to or purchase the CompuServe CD-ROM magazines you'll also find versions of the File Finders on many of the CDs. You use the File Finder off-line, locate the file you need, and CIM will then dial up and go get it. When you see this in action you'll realize that this is the one application for which computers were designed and marvel at the degree of integration between the CD player, CIM and several large computers on the other side of the world. The CD's cost about five pounds and represent extremely good value for money. You can buy them one at a time, or subscribe for a regular supply.

A complete list of all CompuServe Forums and their contents is stored in a file called FORUMS.LST. This exists in formats for all machines so do a search for the version you require. It always lives in the PRACTICE Forum, currently as a PC ARC file for which you need a decompressor for your computer (see Chapter Five). Once de-Arced you get a large ASCII file containing intimate details of CompuServe's insides.

Figure 6.5 *The Library section in the UK forum. This carries files and is where you download data from.*

Finally, if or rather when, you get completely baffled by CompuServe you can always GO HELPFORUM and leave a message. Most likely you'll find that someone else has left the same question earlier and the answer is already there. Failing that, there's Customer Support on the 0800 000 400 Freephone number if you need help in a hurry.

Joining a forum

You can get into a Forum in two ways - either as a Visitor, or as a Full Member. You'll pay the same fees regardless of which method you choose, but Visitors don't get all the rights that full members do. This distinction is more to do with CompuServe's' internal accounting methods than anything else, so you might as well always join as a full member. But first you must decide what your name is.

When you join a Forum you'll be offered a dialogue box in which to enter your name. The great temptation is to enter some witty and entertaining

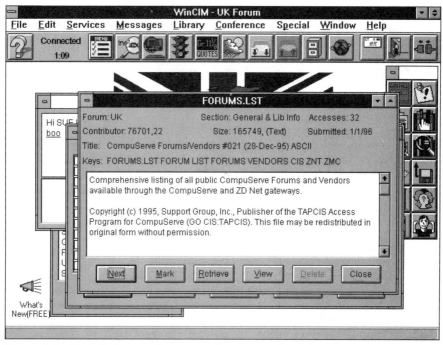

Figure 6.6   *Each file has an Abstract - a description of the file.*

nickname like Wozzo, or Plim, but do this and your first messages will be jumped on by a Sysop who will sternly, but fairly tell you that real names, and full names at that, are required, at least for new members. When the members of a Forum have got used to you - you might then consider using a nickname, but first timers should use their real name, or at least the one their account is held in. This can cause problems if you share a computer with a work mate and use the same account - and the same Forum name - as many corporate bodies do. But at least forewarned is forearmed.

Do make sure that you sign your forum messages (at first) with your full name too. After a short while people will get to recognize Fred Smith (Wozzo) and you can default to your nickname. You can also add details of your social life in the Interests Field when you join a Forum. This allows other Forum members to take a peek at your profile while you're conferencing, or loitering with intent around the file section.

Posting a message

To leave a message decide who you want to read or action it.

* Address it to ALL if you want anyone to read or reply.

* Address it to the SYSOP if you want to flag the message for the Sysop's

(system operator) attention. This is the most common practice, but can be confusing, because a message addressed to SYSOP can and will be read and replied to by non-Sysops, i.e. anyone. Leaving a message to Sysop simply flags it as a Waiting Message to Sysops when they log in. Sometimes new users won't reply to a message flagged 'To Sysop' as they think it's private. It isn't.

* Address your message to SYSOP/ALL. This avoids any confusion. Anyone can and will reply.

Try to avoid posting the same message in multiple forum sections, too. This just makes people irate when they pay good money to read the same message four times.

Leaving a forum

Once in a Forum, you are inside a small discrete area of CompuServe. You can't directly do non-Forum tasks like getting files from other areas or checking your email from within. You'll need to Leave it (go back to the Top area where you came in) with the Leave command. This takes you out of the Forum and back to the level where you can check your mail, navigate to other Forums, and so on. Think of Forums as being one level down in CompuServe; you need to go 'up' to get back to daylight. The Leave command is symbolized by a chap going through a doorway on the CIM Toolbar, or there's a File/Leave option in the menus.

Resigning a forum

Erm, you can't. Once you've 'joined' you stay joined until an automatic system decides that you're unjoined because you haven't dropped by for a while. Don't worry about this. You don't pay any charges just for being a member of a Forum, just a charge when you actually leave the Top area and go into a Forum on-line.

Newsflashes & notices

When you rejoin (or join) a Forum you'll get a Newsflash detailing Forum changes, the colour of the Sysop's new socks, news of new files and so on. Newsflashes can get very tedious after a while, because all Forums always have something new to announce. You can turn off the automatic gathering of news flashes in the Forum/CB Settings section of CIM - do this and the Newsflash icon will simply flash at you when you enter a Forum.

Forum Notices contain a great deal of admin information which most people don't ever read. You get at them by setting the Special/ Notices option in WinCim once you're in Forum. They contain really interesting stuff like the names of the Sysops, new member details, and admin messages. Forum

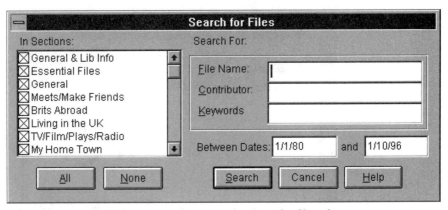

Figure 6.7   *Use the Library/Search command to hunt for files of interest.*

notices are especially useful if you suffer from insomnia. Case-hardened CompuServe freaks save these Notices to disk with the File Save option. It sure beats reading them.

In with both feet

Sooner or later you're going to leave your first message in a Forum. What you almost certainly will have done is to browse the existing messages, and seen what the inmates are up to. You'll notice that Forums are 'topicalized'; for instance the UK Forum contains, amongst other things, separate topics for Wales, Ireland and Scotland. Within these topics messages are 'threaded' around a single message subject, such as Irish Mist, Scots heather, and English eccentricities. Each message subject will have an initial message, and a number of replies. You can jump in at any stage and leave a reply, or start a new message.

This message threading can get a bit confusing and the easy way to avoid getting lost in threads is to remember to REPLY to an initial message or another REPLY - and to CREATE a new subject. Replies get woven into the existing thread, new messages get a new thread of their own as the startup message.

CIM does a neat trick of mapping threads graphically on Windows and Macs so you can see who replied to what, and watch how the thread develops. Sometimes the thread Map is more interesting than the messages, so either way you'll always get good entertainment value from Forum messages.

Forum virgins

Almost all Forum members are extremely tolerant of Newbies jumping in with both feet and making utter idiots of themselves the first few times around. We all do it, including computer journalists, many of whom go on

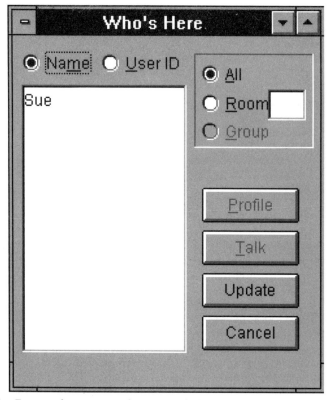

Figure 6.8 *Forums also carry conferences and chat facilities. The Who's Here screen lists other members already in the forum.*

making utter idiots of themselves in the National Press and getting paid for it. Almost all Sysops will send you guiding emails, couched in the most polite and friendly terms if you do make the odd boob when on-line. Contrast this with the Internet newsgroups, where putting an apostrophe out of place results in aspersions being cast upon your ancestors or your synapse count, and you'll realize why CompuServe Forums are so successful.

There is also very little sexism, ageism, or any other 'isms' in CompuServe forums, so feel free to dive in and introduce yourself. But do remember that the best part of having something to say, is having something to say, and that whatever you do place in a forum can be read by 3 million other people.

Introducing - You!

Generally speaking, new members often join a new Forum and a leave a message to 'ALL' to say 'Hi I'm a new member'. Generally speaking they'll get a warm response and lot of goodwill from existing members. But as with all aspects of human nature goodwill does not always apply and the best advice

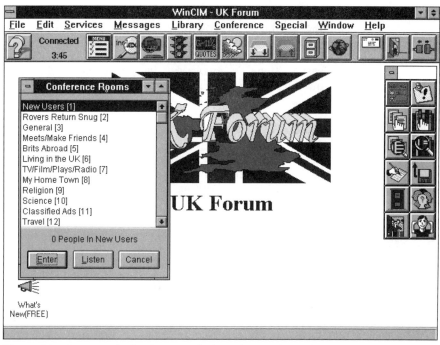

Figure 6.9 *You can check who is in which conference from the Conference screen. This one shows there are no users in the New Users room.*

is to have a look around a new Forum before leaving a message. Almost all the time new members will be greeted with open arms, because of a) genuine goodwill and b) CompuServe Sysops don't like turning away good money.

Off-line messaging

You can either read messages on-line with the charges mounting up, or off-line with the phone disconnected. To read messages on-line, simply click and browse your way around. To read them off-line, mark the box with a click at either the Section level to retrieve all messages in that section, or from within a section to mark a thread. The second of these two options is the one you'll use most - as it's cheaper. Messages are placed in your Filing Cabinet under the Forum heading, from where you can read then at your leisure off-line.

You can also Reply to or Create messages or admire the Map off-line. Just follow the Toolbar buttons and your replies or new posting will be placed in the Out Basket for transmission the next time you connect to CompuServe and the Forum.

To post those messages back into the Forum you have to actually join the Forum again on-line. This is the biggest problem with CIM. It won't log into the Forum and post your messages automatically. Other programs such as

TapCis and Navigator will - but they cost real money. As you get more proficient with CompuServe and CIM you may want to move up to one of these alternatives- especially if you do a lot of forum work. But CIM suffices for many people. Using the Favourite Places menu will take you straight into a Forum, at least, as long as you've Added the Forum to the menu. (Do it every time you join a new Forum).

Waiting messages

If you have Forum messages addressed to you there will be a Waiting Messages icon flashing when you join the Forum. The messages will be in their correct place in the thread, but the Waiting Messages icon will take you straight there.

Scroll off!

One of the most useful automatic facilities of the Forums is Auto Scroll Off, or Message Forwarding as it's known. You might, as I have done, leave a message in the Toshiba Forum asking about 256 colour video drivers, and then forget to call back and pick up the replies. Limited space in the Forums means that messages are removed in a first-in first-out queue, and if your message has generated replies which you've not had time to collect, the messages will be automatically placed in your email for you to download. This is a unique feature of CompuServe, doesn't happen on other UK services and is entirely useful.

Message etiquette

You'll either have it or you won't. If you don't you'll wonder why you receive dismissive - or no - replies to your messages. If you have it people will be courteous and polite in their responses to you.

There are only a few tips; DON'T USE UPPER CASE FOR SHOUTING; because it makes you look like you haven't discovered the Caps Lock key; don't use profanities; avoid religious arguments to avoid fatwahs; don't rubbish other peoples racial or social outlooks because they don't agree with yours, and don't copy the other guy's entire message into your own to emphasize a point ('quoting') . Keep your message signatures short (called a 'sig') and don't correct other people's spelink and gramer like what I do.

But also don't take unnecessary stick - my favourite screen shot is one of a Sysop who took me to task for not using my full name in a message. It says 'We don't like messages using nicknames here - The Sysop'. Perhaps he was new, too. I've left it out to preserve his modesty.

Avoid too the Flame War. These occur when two or more people disagree. The first generates a message containing a contentious subject. The respondent replies that, not only did the originator have his higher brain functions

Figure 6.10   *The Notice Board. Has the Sysop got new socks? Find out from here.*

switched off when he composed the message, but he ought to be strung up to a tree and have his soggy bits fed to the rats for even thinking of posting it. The originator responds in kind, and a Flame War develops. Most Sysops stamp on this kind of thing if it develops, but Flame Wars do spring into life quite frequently. The most contentious topics is 'my computer is better than yours', oddly enough. Nyah Nyah Nyah.

Finally, be polite. It pays dividends. Realize that a million or so Europeans use CompuServe and that one day you're going to turn up to a job interview and the guy behind the desk is going to say 'Hey, you're not the Fred Smith who left that flame about rats and soggy bits, are you? That was me you were slagging off.' It does happen.

Forums and files

The forums store computer files in the Library areas. These are divided up into similar sections to the Message Area so if there's a Vegetarian Bikers message section, there will often be a Library Section with the same title. Files are stored latest first and are dated so you'll find the latest version of a file near the top of the list.

Again, the best way to find a file of interest is to use the File Finders, or to do a Special/Find to isolate the Forum of interest. But you'll often discover yourself browsing the libraries just for the fun of it, because they are updated so often.

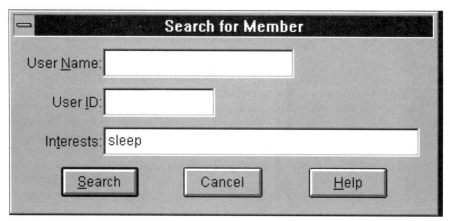

Figure 6.11   *Looking for Mr. Goodbar. Ten UK Forum members list sleep as their main interest. Who can they be?*

These regular updates also mean that files get moved around, so do familiarize yourself with the search mechanisms.

Library searches

There's another search mechanism in the Library menu which appears when you join a forum. This lets you search for a file within the forum itself or just a section, by either keyword, filename or author. Unfortunately I've had mixed results with this; mixed in the sense that I either get no hits, even if the file is there, or I get no hits because I don't realize that the file is actually spelt F-LE_NME.X2@ or it's been moved, or renamed. The system supports wildcards - so if you want to find a GIF file you could search for *.GIF (all the GIFs). Again, this doesn't always seem to work for me, perhaps being left-handed gets in the way. Other options are self-explanatory, including various options to search between dates and so on. But the File Finders from outside the Forums still seem to be the best way of looking for data files on CompuServe.

Downloading files

Once you've got used to the odd way computer people designate their filenames you'll want to download something. You can either go and get it immediately with the Retrieve Option; mark it for batch retrieval with the Mark option or View it (text and graphics files) with the View option. If you click on a file title you'll be offered a short Abstract describing the file. Do this first to make sure it's the one you want.

Other than that, which way you'll grab your files will depend on personal

Figure 6.12   *Files in the My Home Town Library Section. Double clicking one will bring up a short dialogue about the file so you can decide if you want it before you download.*

preference. Often it's best to mark all the files you want and then Leave the Forum. You'll be asked if you want to download the marked files before you go. You can use that option (say 'No') to leave marked files on the service while you go and borrow a faster modem for the download. When you log back in and re-join the forum you can click on Retrieve Marked to get the files. The disconnection in the middle of the process doesn't cause any problems (as long as you log off in the normal fashion.)

The other neat option is 'Disconnect When Done' which appears if you want to download more than file. You can leave CompuServe downloading while you go and buy that new hard disk you'll need to cope with all the files you've grabbed. CIM will disconnect automatically when it has finished. See previous notes about modems disobeying disconnect orders, and don't leave your modem alone in a room. It will get lonely and phone its friends.

Don't forget that Windows and Mac computers can allegedly do more than one thing at a time. While those files are downloading you can read messages, look at the nice little thread map, or read some of the really interesting Forum Notices while the download continues. What you can't do is leave the forum, so the best way to use this feature is to start a download off and then use the time to search for more files. The Mac version of CIM does much the same thing, but the multitasking is better implemented in later versions of the software, say from version 1.4 up. Faster computers handle the multitasking with better grace, of course.

If you abort a download for any reason, like spilling curry into the keyboard, CompuServe can resume the download if you go back into the forum. You'll be offered an Overwrite or Resume option if this happens. The Resume option picks up the download from where it was abandoned.

Figure 6.13   *Your first Forum Message. Do it off-line. Use Mail/Create Forum Message, then navigate to the Forum you want. You must have joined it at some time previously for it to be listed here.*

Uploading files

You can upload a file to CompuServe for free, free that is of connect charges. You do it by selecting Contribute from the Library menu. All uploads are vetted by the Forum Sysops for viruses and content. The upload dialogue lets you fill in fields for type of file and so on, and is self-explanatory except for the 'binary' option. Use this if you're including a compressed text file, instead of the text option because compressed files turn into binary files by default. If you need help with any of this then mail the Sysop of the forum beforehand. They'll advise you fully on the process.

Conferencing

Conferencing, the art of talking remotely with someone you've never met about a topic of which you know just a little, is one of CompuServe's least used features, at least in the UK. It's used a lot in the USA, where owning a telephone doesn't equate to selling your soul to the phone provider, but in the UK and Europe telephone charges are much higher in comparison. This leaves UK conferencing as a minority sport, which is a pity because conferencing is actually quite entertaining.

Conferencing involves you typing on-screen responses to other users who are on-line at the same time. It takes several forms on CompuServe. Ad Hoc Conferences take place in forums if sufficient numbers of people are on-line; it takes place all the time in the CB services; and often there are scheduled live

Figure 6.14 *Retrieving messages. (1) Mark single messages or entire threads with a cross. When you Leave the Forum you'll reach this screen. Click disconnect when done, and the messages will be retrieved to your hard disk...*

'Celebrity' conferences in various forums, in which some poor unsuspecting CompuServe Book author is asked questions like 'What do you spend all your money, on then?'

There any numbers of apocryphal stories about CompuServe conferencing - it was used during the Gulf War to keep people updated - it gets used during Shuttle launches, was invaluable during the LA earthquakes and so on.

Conferences are either Scheduled, in which case they will be announced by the Forum operators in a Newsflash or a Conference Notice, or Ad Hoc in which case they just spring up. You get to them from the Conference/Enter Room menu, which will display a list of all conferences, and the number of people in each one. You can either Listen to what's going on or join in for a natter. If you're really bored you can Invite other people in the Forum for a chat.

Private Group discussions are often held, to which you can only join if Invited. Discussions held in Rooms are open to anyone, just use the Enter Room option to browse and choose.

Unfortunately Conferencing is not particularly busy during business hours and the UK Forums were devoid of all potential victims when this book was being prepared. But there are regular Friday night chats in the UK Forum (GO UKFORUM) so read the Notice and drop by.

Celebrity conferences are always paraded in the What's New notice which springs up when you log into CompuServe if you have this option set in your Preferences. Unfortunately, the time differences between Europe and the USA invariably mean you'll sit up until 3 AM to catch a glimpse of some USA conferences. But there are more Euro-conferences being planned, so keep an eye out in the forums, and in the What's New section.

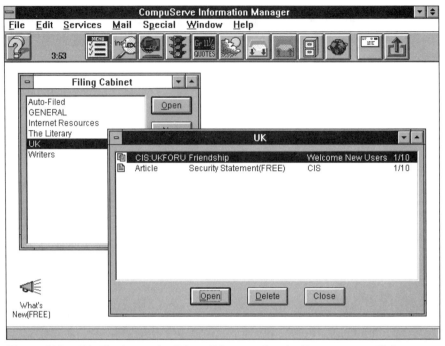

Figure 6.15   *(2) They're in the Filing Cabinet under the Forum name. Click open to read them.*

The Online Forum FAQ - Frequently Asked Questions from the HelpForum

What's the message area?

The "Message" area of a Forum is divided up into many sections, to better organize the conversations. Think of these areas as "cork boards." You can read the messages that others have posted, post your own, or staple a reply to someone else's, and then come back later at your convenience to see your replies. One of the nifty things about using the forum message areas is that you can do all of your message reading and reply composition OFF-LINE which gives you lots of participation at a very small cost. Use your time within the free support fora to become familiar with your messaging options, so that you'll soon be able to confidently select from the "real" fora which interest you, and start having fun!

I just posted a message, but I can't see it!

Although your messages post immediately, you can't see them right away because you are only able to see messages which were posted as of the beginning of your forum visit. It's as if CompuServe takes a "picture" of the

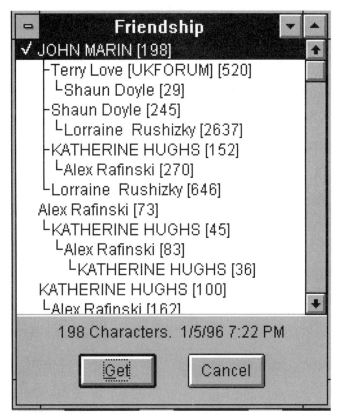

Figure 6.16 *(3) And you get a nice Map to help navigation. You post replies from the message screen. They're stored in your Outbasket until you next visits the Forum.*

messages available, when you enter. You can leave the forum and return, which will take an entirely NEW picture (tucking the ones that were here before, out of your way), or if you're using CIM you can use the "Freshen Messages" option in your "Messages" menu, which will include the messages posted since you entered the forum. ASCII-Terminal users can drop back to the Messages ! or Forum ! prompt and issue a new REA command, for the same effect. You'll then be able to see everything current, including the messages posted by you.

There were HUNDREDS of messages here a minute ago... where are they now?
When you leave a forum and return, you'll probably notice a marked decrease in the number of forum messages, visible. Don't let this worry or confuse you... they aren't "gone." Members don't want to have to wade through the SAME messages, over and over again... so the highest-numbered message you read during your last visit to the forum, along with any posted beforehand,

are all "tucked away", for your convenience. You can see these messages again (at least until the forum's scroll rate gets 'em), by backtracking with CIM's "Set Date" option, in the "Messages" menu, or by using one of the many specialized REA commands, in ASCII-Terminal mode.

How long do forum messages remain in the forum?

Each forum only has room for so many messages. When this limit is being met, new messages nudge the oldest ones from the board. The rate at which this happens (known as the "scroll rate") depends upon how many message slots that forum has, as well as how active the message board has been! Messages may scroll from a forum in as little time as a day, or a couple of months, for a forum which has a more relaxed activity level. A good, system-wide average is 3-7 days. It's a good idea to ask one of the Sysops of the fora in which you're especially interested, about the current "scroll rate," there, so that you can visit often enough not to miss anything good.

Won't replies to my forum messages just come to my Mail box?

The "Messages Waiting" notice which you get upon connecting to CompuServe, refers to MAIL area messages. Mail and Forum messages are two completely different things. Mail messages go privately and directly to the recipient, instead of posting for all to see, as forum messages usually do.

Mail is a great thing to use, to exchange "pen-pal" type messages with people, send and receive files, etc. When you send MAIL, the recipient will receive notice that it is waiting for them, immediately after connecting to CompuServe, before even entering a forum.

Some fora employ a "Scroll to Mail" option, which forwards any unread message to the recipient, as it's being pushed off of the forum by newer messages by the natural forum scroll. The desire not have to wait a week or more to see your replies, though, makes a pretty good case for just checking into the forum once a day or so, for replies to messages! Remember also, that not all fora use "Scroll to Mail"... and unread messages there, are simply lost.

Okay, you mentioned reading and composing replies OFF-LINE. How is this done?

You may read messages and compose replies off-line regardless of the communications software you're using... but the CompuServe Information Manager (CIM) programs such as DOSCIM, WinCIM, MacCIM and OS2CIM are geared to make the process simple and comfortable, especially for new members!

To work off-line with CIM software, you must first go into the forum and "mark" and retrieve the messages which interest you. You can get single messages one at time by selecting "File It," or you can retrieve entire conversations (threads, topics), at once. To do this with WinCIM or MacCIM, just mark [X] the boxes next to the topics. With DOSCIM, simply highlight the topic, and mark it... either with Ctrl+T or by going to the "Messages" menu and selecting "Mark Topic." When a topic is marked, DOSCIM will show a little triangle beside the name.

Choose the "Retrieve Marked" option from within your "Messages" menu, to double-check your selections, and hit "Get All" when you're ready! When retrieved, these messages are in your "Filing Cabinet" which can be easily accessed from off-line.

When you see these messages in your Filing Cabinet, you'll notice that they all have the same "REPLY" button, which will bring up the reply editor. You can also create original messages for any forum you've "Joined," with the "Create Message" option within your off-line "Mail" menu. When finished with an off-line message, simply put it into the "outbasket" for safe keeping. When you're ready, just hop into the forum, access the out basket, and there your messages will be, waiting to be sent. For additional help with using the CompuServe message areas, feel free to post a message addressed to SYSOP (no User ID# required), within the New Member Forum (GO CIS:NEWMEM), the Practice Forum (GO CIS:PRACTICE), or any of the CIM Support Fora (GO CIS:CIMSUP). This will catch the attention of the next SYStem OPerator to enter the forum, and get you a prompt response!

If you find yourself messaging heavily in several different fora, you may want to consider looking into one of the "Automated" software programs, which streamline the messaging process. They can be programmed to zoom from forum to forum, wherever you specify, and check for messages or do any of a number of other forum tasks. The file AUTOP.INF will familiarize you with what's available, and show you where to ask for more information. You'll find it within the Help Forum's (GO CIS:HELPFO) Library 1/Help Library, or within the New Member Forum's (GO CIS:NEWMEM) Library 15/Accessing CIS.

7 Places to go, things to do

Other services

CompuServe is dauntingly large for newcomers; new services and add-ons arrive almost daily, and the system never stands still. Consequently what follows is only a tiny list of the services available on CompuServe. The system is now so vast that you can almost guarantee that what ever you want is already on CompuServe somewhere, it's just a case of finding it.

There are a large numbers of gateways on CompuServe which lead you to other services such as the Ziff-Davies computer forums and private databases such as those run by Dun and Bradstreet. Use of these and other commercial services are marked with a $ (dollar) sign and are charged at a premium rate, extra to your membership fee. Readers should be aware that its possible to slip unnoticed into some very expensive research and public databases. However, you'll always get a final on-screen warning if you are about to trip unnoticed into an expensive commitment, including details of fees charged, and the service provided for that fee. For this reason alone you might want to supervise CompuServe sessions initiated by younger children, and not leave your password installed in CIM.

These services do add a lot of value to CompuServe if you're a researcher or business user. It's possible, for instance, to search the Dun & Bradstreet company index for details of UK companies, or to log into the news archives of UK newspapers. Automated news clipping services such as the Executive News service are also available, as are commercial, health and engineering databases. What's represented here are just a few of the many options available; readers are urged to browse - but watch those bills. You can find more details of these services either by going to the INDEX, by reading CompuServe magazine, or by asking in your regular forum. New services are announced in the What's New menu, updated for you automatically when you log in.

The UK explore menu

You can find many of the services on CompuServe simply by browsing from the Explore Menu. UK users now get their own Explore menu in 1996 making it easy to find places of interest. Set your computer to 256 colours to make the best of CompuServe's menu's and graphics features.

For instance, if you click on Education and Reference you'll be taken to a browser offering buttons to go to Hutchinson Encyclopedia, European Business Library, Magazine databases and the Uk Newspaper library. Additionally, you're offered a list of other reference sources, including British Books in Print, HealthNet and the Knowledge Index. Because the spread of reference material on CompuServe is so large, and readers needs so diverse it's impossible to fully documentthe reference services on CompuServe. The best advice is to use the Explore Menu (or Special/Find) to look around CompuServe, especially in your early days with the service. Browsing does not incur charges other than for connect time, so you can rummage at will.

The Browse menus currently offer direct access to: Internet, News, Magazines, Travel, Communications, Computers, Professional, Finance, Education & References, Sport, Shopping, Entertainment, Fun & Games, Home & Leisure, and Member Services. Each of those carries a sub menu of options, and browsing around these will give you a wonderful feel of what CompuServe has to offer.

If you're wondering whether to use CompuServe or the Internet as a starting point for research, you'll find it useful to remember that most of the services on CompuServe are provided by commercial service providers and that, while you'll pay a fee for access in many cases, the information you get should be reasonably accurate. Searching CompuServe is also faster than searching the Internet, and you may save money in phone charges by trying CompuServe first.

Finally, CompuServe is also full of useful professional and local advice. In 1995 I used CompuServe to track down medical information on drugs and

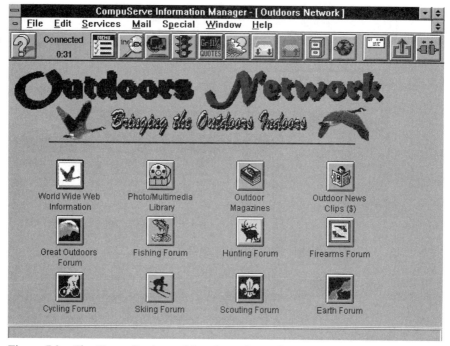

Figure 7.2 *The Great Outdoors. Meet lots of nice furry animals, then reach for the Firearms forum.*

medicine side effects in HealthNet; what was wrong with my cat's stomach in UKPROFF - Ask a Vet; checked the UK law on crash helmets in UKPROF - Ask a Policeman; and planned a trip to Edinburgh around the vegetarian restaurants mentioned in the UKFORUM Scotland section.

Terminal services

Many of the external databases hooked into CompuServe cannot be run under CIM. In these cases CIM will switch over to Terminal emulation. When this happens you'll need to use a command line interface, often presented to you as a single colon : . Many external databases use the CompuServe Focus gateway, which at least goes some way to formalizing commands. The two most important are /HELP and /OFF, for obvious reasons. What you're looking at when you come across these command line based systems is what people see when they access these databases directly as subscribers through the sort of desktop terminal you see in banks and offices. It does rather make you grateful for the huge amount of development behind CIM.

If you think you may need to access CompuServe through a terminal one day you can test your powers of perseverance by using the Terminal in CIM to

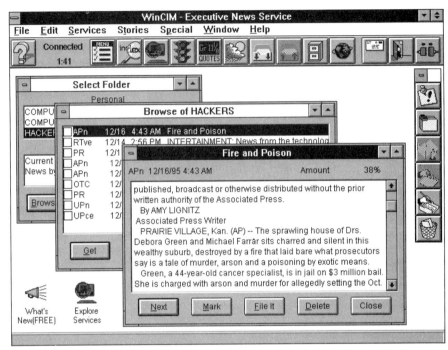

Figure 7.3 *The Executive News Service, here combing for articles on Hackers. It's highly useful for financial or corporate news too.*

access CompuServe. It's under Special/Terminal Emulator and will auto-dial into CompuServe for you.

The Executive News Service (GO ENS) or Special/ENS

ENS is a news 'clipping' service' You tell it what topics you are interested in and ENS then automatically compiles a personalized clipping folder for you to browse at your leisure. You're also allocated access to Public folders, in which CompuServe places items of general interest to everyone.

You can also create other personal folders by specifying a name, plus the news agencies you want searched. You then specify search keywords and ENS goes away and starts to fill your folders. Generally you'll start getting clippings placed into those folders within a couple of hours or less. You can specify boolean searches such as 'COMPUTERS+ WINDOWS' - 'COMPUTERS minus WINDOWS' or use the asterisk for a wildcard search. 'COMP*' will find not only 'computers', but 'component' and 'complications'.

Full instructions are in the Help file, or the Directory file on your hard

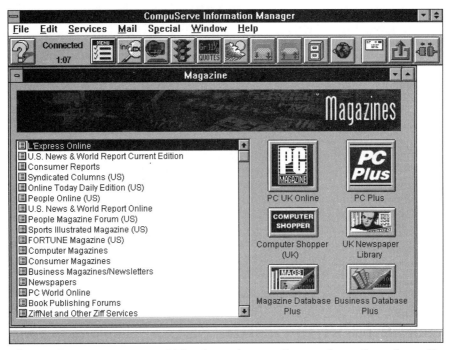

Figure 7.4 *Fancy a magazine? There's an almost endless supply on CompuServe. Not all of them are about computers.*

disk. Don't do as I did, and forget that the word 'windows' is in use outside of the computer industry. One of my first searches for 'Windows' information brought endless stories of German double-glazing innovations, and French smash and grab stories.

ENS is extremely useful - if you have a use for it. ENS is a surcharged service so doesn't come too cheap (GO RATES for pricing) but is great if you need access to news feeds, or just like browsing news from all over the world. Most of the world's top press agencies are listed, including French, German and other sources, and it's not uncommon to watch a news story break on ENS, then appear in the UK papers a day or two later, almost word-for-word. ENS provides copyright material which you're not allowed to reproduce without payment, but it is strange how many computer related stories appear first on ENS, and then in the UK computer magazines, few of whom have live news-feeds from press agencies.

There are some ingenious uses of ENS. One CompuServe magazine story relates to a busy American business man who downloads his ENS clippings every morning, feeds them into his Mac's voice synthesizer, and plays the resulting audio tapes back in the car on his drive to work. There's also a Windows Program called 'Journalist' which takes ENS clippings and formats them up into a newsletter.

There are other news wire services on CompuServe including the much loved PA NEWS, and the UKNEWS services listed below. Do a FIND NEWS to get a full listing.

Ziff/Net

CompuServe provides a gateway to ZiffNet, once part of the monolithic Ziff-Davies empire. ZiffNet deals almost entirely with computer related topics as an adjunct to the Ziff Davies computer publishing monolith. You pay a low membership fee to join, plus a small monthly subscription. Probably the best thing about ZiffNet is its provision of 'Shareware' programs you won't find in other CompuServe Forums. You only get them on ZiffNet because they are commissioned and copyrighted for and by Ziff-Davies, and often appear on CD ROMs bundled with Z-D mags. Other than that, you might regard ZiffNet as a useful extra set of forums to the computer forums on CompuServe. Ziff-Davies sold their computer publishing business in 1995 - perhaps the ZiffNet service will become a touch more human and varied as a result.

Some forums of interest

MEMBER HELP/ADMIN
GO BILLING View your charges or check current rates, allowing you to check your current bill; change your billing address; select the Executive Service Option or change your payment method.

GO OLI CompuServe's OnLine Inquiry service lets you enquire about, order or request further information on products advertised in CompuServe Magazine

GO PASSWORD Change your password. You should change it at least every 90 days. Use the full number of characters available and not choose something someone else might guess, like a child's name or make of car.

GO HELPFORUM CompuServe's customer service representatives answer your queries and help you with any CompuServe related problems you may have.

GO TERMINAL Change your terminal type and display settings, language preferences and logon action. You can also build your own personal menu to be displayed when you log on. Useful if you're not using using a CIM compatible computer.

GO WELCOME The Welcome Centre for new CompuServe members. If you need help getting started, CompuServe's Help Desk can assist...

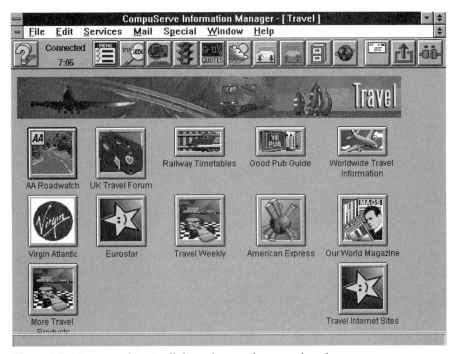

Figure 7.5   *Get away from it all, but take your laptop and modem.*

UK PLACES OF INTEREST

GO SEDOL The UK Stock Exchange Daily Official List. Locate SEDOL numbers which allow you to identify issues traded on UK exchanges. With the SEDOL number, historical quotes may be retrieved from the UK Historical Pricing Service.

GO UKLIB The UK Company Library offers financial and credit information on a large number of UK companies. Information is sourced from Dun & Bradstreet's European Dun's Marketing Identifiers, Extel Cards, Financial Times, ICC British Company Directory and Financial Datasheets, Infocheck UK, Jordans, Kompass UK and others. Searches by company name, industry or geographical location are supported.

GO UKNEWS UK News clips from Reuters World news wire. The content is broadly UK financial, political and economic, focusing on UK relations and business dealings with the US, Europe and Pacific Rim.

GO UKMARKETING The UK Marketing Library databases offer market research reports by top industry professionals, from sources including the ICC Key Note series, Marketing Surveys Index, Mintel Research reports, Mintel Special reports and others.

GO UKPAPERS The UK Newspaper Library holds The Daily Telegraph, Sunday Telegraph, The Financial Times, The Guardian, The Times, and the Sunday Times, among others. Extract the full text of articles from current issues, or going back several years, searching for a name, phrase or word.

GO UKPRICE UK Historical Stock Quotes offers daily updated information for over 5 thousand UK equity issues and over 350 market indices, with information dating from 1st July 1990 onwards.

GO UKTRADEMARK British Trade Marks. Check whether or not a Trade Mark has been registered.

GO UKWEATHER High and low resolution satellite images of weather patterns affecting the UK, Europe and beyond, plus detailed, short-term weather reports for major cities within the UK and Europe.

GO UKFORUM The UK Forum is a discussion platform covering politics, business, sport and culture. The forum features the popular "Rovers Return" pub, for more general discussion.

GO UKRECREATION All types of recreational activities based in the UK. Theatre venues and productions, film reviews, pub and beer guides, walking and hiking, motoring, voluntary work and much more.

GO UKSPORTS UK Sports Clips

GO UKIT A general computing forum for UK users

GO UKVENA (UK Vendor forum A) The first UK Vendors forum with support from companies such as Psion.

COMPUTING/TECHNICAL
GO AMIGATECH The Amiga technical forum has discussions on programming the Amiga using languages such as Forth, C, ASM, Mod-2, CanDo and Amiga Vision.

GO APLTIL Updated weekly, this is Apple's official technical support database offering articles on troubleshooting, compatibility, workarounds, peripherals and more.

GO UKSHOPPER The Computer Shopper forum. Each month the magazine prints a selection of the best threads from the many messages, usually about a computer related subject.

GO COMPDB Computer Database Plus provides access to abstracts or full texts drawn from over 230 magazines, journals and newspapers. Texts on hardware, software, engineering, electronics, communications and technology

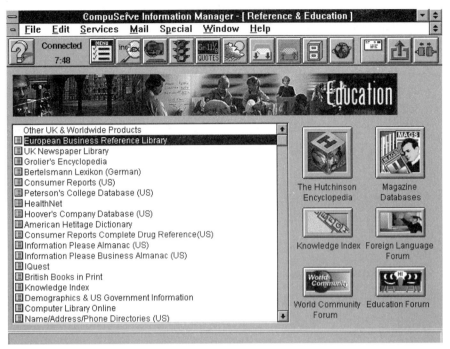

Figure 7.6 *The Education section contains large numbers of research and reference databases.*

applications are drawn from PC magazine, PC Week, MacUser and many more. Search the 400 thousand articles by subject, company, product, person, date and/or publication.

GO CONSULT The computer consultant's forum. The relative merits of different products, how they should be used and installed, and which software is most suitable for the job.

GO GRAPHDEV The Graphics Developers' Forum. Discover what techniques best suit your requirements, download software to create your own images or see the examples available on-line.

GO HAYFORUM Hayes modem users have access to product descriptions and upgrade information direct from Hayes.

GO IBMFF IBM File Finder is a database of applications and information culled from all the other IBM related forums. Keyword searches provide you with detials of PC files and where they may be found.

GO IBMHW IBM Hardware forum. Advice and information on every aspect of building, setting up, fault finding and repairing a PC. Software is available to test various aspects of your system's performance and assist with fault diagnosis.

GO MACAP The Macintosh Applications Forum. A collection of useful shareware, PD utilities and graphic images to help you get the best from your Mac.

GO MACHW Macintosh Hardware forum. Help files and information about upgrading your Mac. Compatibility, expansion and fault finding are among the subjects covered and software can be downloaded to assist fault finding and repairing your computer.

GO MODEMVENDOR Help files and upgrades from the most popular modem manufacturers including Multitech, Supra Corporation, US Robotics, Zoom and ZyXEL.

GO MSKB MicroSoft Knowledge Base offers thousands of product support documents normally used by the support staff, on just about every MicroSoft product ever released.

GO OS/2 Discussion area for users of the OS/2 operating system. Supplies user support, files, utilities, and technical assistance for IBM's operating system.

GO PCNET A group of forums covering everything PC related, from shareware and special offers to utilities and a useful 'file finder'.

GO DDJFORUM The on-line arm of Dr. Dobb's Journal provides a forum to discuss programming languages, techniques and tools. Sections cover object oriented languages, C, C++, UNIX and others, plus a help section for new programmers.

GO MACDEV The Mac Developers' Forum is home to discussion of BASIC, Pascal, C, C++ and object oriented programming languages. A number of experts and authors offer help and advice.

GO MSBASIC Visual BASIC and other MicroSoft BASIC products are supported, with advice from company representatives, and a large area of shareware files, extension code, samples and more.

GO CODEPORT With an emphasis on engineering applications that are portable between operating systems, notably Pascal, Modula 2, Modula 3 and Oberon, this forum supports programmers and users.

GO PBSPROF This ZiffNet forum contains on of the largest and highest quality collections of public domain software and shareware. The contents are given a rating on a five star scale, and their suitability for DOS or Windows is tested.

Figure 7.7   *Lost your dog on the way to the forum? Ask A Vet, Ask a Doctor, Ask a Policeman, all in UK Professionals.*

GO SDFORUM An on-line forum of the 'Software Development' magazine aimed mainly at professional programmers and developers offering support, advice and study groups. DOS and Windows dominate the discussion.

GO VBPJFORUM The Visual BASIC Programmer's Journal Forum carries VB user groups supporting OLE automation, applications, third party VBX support and VB programming books, plus a 'Beginners Corner'.

GO WINUSER The Windows Users Group Network Forum is for Windows professionals, with libraries carrying a variety of Windows applications and utilities, plus a number of lively discussion and support areas.

MISCELLANEOUS
GO ASTROFORUM A meeting place for professional and amateur astronomers to exchange ideas, theories and observations. The forum is often used to disseminate information about new discoveries. Graphic images and public domain astronomy software can be downloaded and there is a reference library of articles and facts.

GO CANCER The Cancer Forum provides information and support to people with cancer, their friends and relatives. Research, standard and supplemental treatments and cancer in children are among the topics covered.

GO CRISIS The Global Crisis Forum is a platform to express your views and discover the views of others on crisis points around the globe, including the monthly 'hot spot'. Files can be downloaded to provide more information about specific areas.

GO DIABETES The diabetes forum carries information and services for people with diabetes, hypoglycemia and related genetic autoimmune conditions. Libraries cover treatments, diet, medications, latest developments and more.

GO DISABILITIES The disabilities forum is an information exchange and support group for those living with disability. Disabled people, their carers and families share information, ideas and experiences to make day to day living easier.

GO EFFSIG The Electronic Frontier Foundation special interest group discusses how the new technologies will impact society in the near future, with informed comment and criticism on the way society responds to this change.

GO HOLISTIC A resource of information for those interested in holistic approaches to health. Vitamins, minerals, plants, herbs, exercise and massage are among the methods suggested to achieve a better balance and understanding of your body.

GO NEWAGE The new age forum is a platform to discuss topics such as psychic arts and sciences, Eastern religions, occult beliefs, yoga, meditation, natural healing and environmental issues.

GO ROOTS The genealogy forum provides advice on tracing relatives, with software and advice to simplify the job of building a family tree.

GO SUPPORT Access a comprehensive index of computer related products, then enter the support area for a product to obtain assistance.

GO TWCFORUM The Weather Channel forum. Download satellite images for your area, examine statistics, with the information presented as maps or graphs, or discuss meteorology with the experts.

GO WHITEHOUSE Access the latest political documents and proposals from America. There is a wealth of information for those interested in politics or researching for a project.

BUSINESS
GO APO Associated Press offers world news, political coverage, business news, reports from Wall Street, Dow Jones averages and more.

GO BUSDB Business Database Plus collates articles from over 500 business publications worldwide. Searches may be conducted to obtain articles on specific products, industry trends and analysis, sales and marketing ideas.

Figure 7.8 *Let's go to the movies. The UK What's On guide - the perfect antidote for couch potatoes.*

GO CLARIS This database carries articles about Claris products including answers to your technical questions, with ideas and suggestions to aid your creativity.

GO CNN The latest news and informed comment on the day's events, with pictures, plus reports from CNN's correspondents around the world.

GO DTP Access CompuServe's desktop publishing resources where you can access the Photos-To-Go database, and download fonts, graphics and clip art.

GO ECTF The European Community Telework Forum offers a platform for discussion of the innovative advances in communications and telecommuting. RACE (Research into Advanced Communications for Europe) is represented.

GO ENS CompuServe's Electronic News Service. Read the latest business news that's of interest to you by searching for a specific subject, or keep in touch with the world markets, with up to date figures.

GO ESO News articles by Associated Press, Reuters, Dow Jones, The Washington Post and many other international news wire services.

GO EUROLIB The European Company Library. A directory of information on more than 2 million companies, with information supplied by D&B, ABC Europe, Financial Times, Kompass Europe, Telefirm and others. Information can be keyword searched by name, industry or geographic location.

GO FLIGHTS An air information and reservation service which lets you plan your international journeys, find the lowest price and make a reservation. You'll be prompted for your departure city, destination and preferred date and time.

GO GERLIB The German Company Library. Forty-eight thousand companies are listed with information supplied by Creditreform, D&B German Dun's Market Identifiers, Kompass Germany and Hoppenstedt Directory. Information can be searched by name, industry or geographic location.

GO HOTELS An international hotel guide. Classify hotels by star rating, price, location, size and special facilities like conference halls.

GO INTL International Company Information combining the UK (GO COUK), US (GO COMPANY), Canada (GO COCAN), Germany (GOCOGERMAN), other European countries (GO COEURO) and Australasia (GO ANZCOLIB). Each section has a separate database to enable retrieval of company, product, employment and earnings information.

GO INVFORUM The Investors' Forum. Meet with those interested in investments and market trends, download investment software or discuss events with investors, managers and brokers.

GO LOTUS English and German support forums for Lotus products. Full access to the Lotus technical library, with online help and advice.

GO OAFORUM The office automation forum is a resource of information for IT managers and businesses grappling with new technology.

GO OAG The Official Airlines Guide. The OAG lets you plan your international journeys, find the lowest price, and check hotel availability. You'll be prompted for your departure city, destination and preferred date and time.

GO PRSIG The Public Relations and Marketing Forum. Discover the latest marketing techniques and PR methods, or discuss your ideas with an expert. Alternatively, peruse the library of PR and marketing ideas.

GO TBW The Business Wire is a US oriented news, press and information service for businesses. It combines news from hundreds of companies, continuously updated throughout the day.

GO WORK A forum covering everything associated with work. If you work

Figure 7.9   *Food, pubs, shopping and recreation and much more in the Home & Leisure section.*

from home, this is an invaluable resource of ideas and information to improve your efficiency and help you sell your services.

RESEARCH/REFERENCE

GO DPANEWS DPA-Kurznachrichtendienst carries articles from Deutsche Presse-Agentur, Germany's leading press agency. The headline, summary, business and politics sections are displayed in German.

GO DRUGS Discover the correct use, precautions and side effects of medicines listed in the US Pharmacopeia. Searches can be conducted using generic or brand names and provide basic information suitable for the lay person.

GO GROLIERS or GO ENCYCLOPEDIA Enter a keyword and Groliers Academic American Encyclopedia will give you the references you need.

GO HNT The Healthnet Forum. A reference library for consumers, giving concise information about health issues, medicines, sports injuries and allows searches by symptoms, disease, surgeries and drugs.

GO IISX The Human Sexuality Databank. Covers gynaecology, urology, phsychiatry and more. A number of support groups are based here, and searches can be conducted to help you find further information.

GO IQMEDICINE The IQuest Medical InfoCentre. AIDS Weekly, Cancer Research Weekly, Combined Health Information Database, MEDLINE, etc. are available. Searches can be conducted combining several databases, or individually.

GO KI Knowledge Index databases include Mental health Abstracts, Merck Index Online, PsycInfo, International Pharmaceutical Abstracts, CancerLit and more. Command and Menu searches are offered.

GO MAGELLAN Magellan Geographic can provide three types of cartographically exact maps. Varying details of level can be achieved and any area can be covered, from your local region to the whole world.

GO MAGILL Magill's Survey of Cinema carries information on film releases from 1902 onwards including film titles, release dates, countries of release, cast, credits, running time and production studio. A synopsis of the plots and significant influences are supplied.

GO MEDSIG The Medical forum. Search using a keyword to gain access to a library of information about any illness or disease. Locate support groups or be directed to where you can find further information.

GO MMS MMS International offer economic and financial research. Specialists in monetary theory and forecasting of banking policies and operations, they produce economic reports including a recommended MMS stock portfolio.

GO NORD The National Organization for Rare Disorders. The causes, symptoms and therapies of rare diseases are explained in detail, with a search facility to assist you.

GO PAPERCHASE The National Library of Medicine's MEDLINE is the world's largest biomedical database. The eight million references to articles in four thousand articles are searched using a system of menus.

GO PATENT The Patent Research Center offers access to summaries from the World Patents Index (1963 onwards) and US chemical, mechanical, design and electrical patents (1950 onwards).

GO PDQ Physicians Data Query. Four databases: Cancer information files (professional and consumer), Directory and Protocol. Information on stage expectations, general prognoses and alternative treatments is available.

GO PSYCIN PsycINFO Psychological Abstracts contains article abstracts on the behavioural sciences. General, developmental, applied and experimental psychology are among the specialties covered.

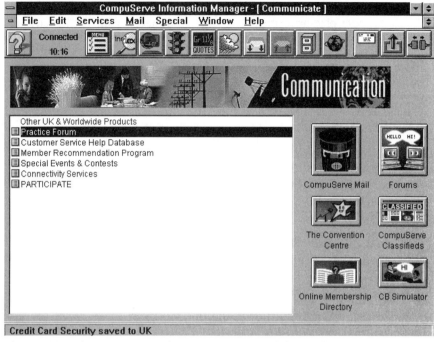

Figure 7.10   *The starting point for communicating with four million other CompuServe members.*

RECREATION

GO ACTION The Action Games Forum. Participate in multi-player games, including the near-classic Doom, or choose one of the many other action games available in this forum.

GO AIT Adventures In Travel. Professional travel writers offer their opinions on thousands of travel destinations with advice and information on local customs, foods, languages, travel arrangements, hotels and more.

GO AMIGAARTS A large collection of graphic images, produced on Amigas, which you can download in different formats.

GO APSPORTS The Associated Press Sports Wire will keep you informed of the latest scores and news on soccer, basketball, baseball, hockey, golf, tennis and other sports.

GO ARTS From classical music and classic literature to chart music and TV greats. The arts, music and literature forum is the place to discuss the finer points of Strauss or Superman.

GO AWAY Create and control your own animated alter ego or 'avatar' in this role playing game. Meet other characters, with the added dimension of graphics.

GO BEER The Beer forum carries all the information you need to make any type of brew; lager, stout or ale, with ideas on minimizing costs and getting the best results.

GO BIORHYTHM Discover your physical, emotional and mental state now and at any time in the future, with a monthly analysis. Information is presented in an easy to understand graphical form.

GO BRIDGE Bridge players looking for a match can find partners around the world. You can play a game with others, or sit in on one of the many matches already in progress.

GO CHESSFORUM Play against opponents around the world in games of electronic chess in an effort to climb the ratings. Also carries the latest news and chess tournament results from around the world.

GO COOKS The cook's on-line forum. Exchange recipes from around the world, try new dishes and find out why your bread won't rise properly, or read reviews of newly released cookery books, retrieve nutrition and dietary information or get involved in a food fight!

GO DINOFORUM The world's leading paleontologists and scientists offer their knowledge and answer your questions in the dinosaur forum. Competitions, dinosaur facts, drawings and chat forums, are available for younger fossil hunters in a section moderated by teenagers.

GO ETRADE E*Trade's stock market game allows you to trade on-line. Win or lose millions buying and selling imaginary shares with cash prizes for the monthly winners.

GO FSFORUM Fly solo, or join one of the regular "virtual fly-ins" where you arrive at an airfield waiting for permission to land, then you can compare notes on civilian, space, combat and air traffic control simulations with other simulator pilots.

GO GARDENING Find out what conditions plants need, or the best way to re-design your garden. Grow flowers or vegetables, then find out how you can best store and prepare what you've grown.

GO GLF The Golf Guide On-line carries details of 14,000 golf courses around the world. Many courses are listed with par, total yardage, a course rating and a list of challenging features.

GO GOODHEALTH The health and fitness forum provides information and support including discussion of exercise, fitness, diet and nutrition, mental health, alcohol and drug abuse, alternative healthcare and more.

GO HOLLYWOOD The Hollywood Hotline is a source of information detailing events from the movie capital of the world. An online encyclopedia details previous Oscar winners and other movie facts, and the Hollywood Hotline reviews all the latest film releases.

GO HOTGAMES The forum for the most popular games. There is a download area where you can get public domain versions of your favourite games.

GO ITALFOR The Italian forum is conducted in Italian and English, with sections covering tourism, language and culture, food, politics and debate, business news and computing.

GO LEGENDS A multi-player game where the objective is to collect treasures, score points and survive long enough to become a Wizard, at which point you'll be endowed with the magical powers of invisibility and more...

GO LITFORUM Discuss all aspects of literature, including writing techniques, preparing manuscripts and getting them published. If that fails there's a self publishing section covering how to print and distribute your own book.

GO MENSA A place for intelligent people to exchange ideas on the application and development of human intellect. Message and library sections cover topics including puzzles, gifted children and scholarships etc.

GO MODEMGAMES A games forum offering you the chance to match wits with human opponents rather than mere machines. Golf, logic games, flight simulators and beat 'em ups are among the gaming fare on offer.

GO MUSICARTS The music and performing arts forum. Join fellow enthusiasts in discussions about music, including jazz, blues, big band, classical, ethnic, country, folk, new age, rock and pop music. Ballet, dance and drama are covered too. A diary section lists and previews major music and arts events, and a careers section hosts discussions and advice sessions for aspiring hopefuls.

GO OUTDOORS People seeking fresh air can discuss camping, backpacking, climbing, cycling, sailing and winter sports, with detailed equipment reviews. Additionally, there is a section devoted to nature and wildlife.

GO PEOFRM The People Magazine forum. Discuss current events as covered in the paper version. There are several sections covering the day's events so you can chat about people in the news.

GO PETS A forum for owners of cats, dogs, birds, horses, reptiles and snakes. Discover the best ways to keep your pet healthy and happy. Vets give advice on training, feeding and medical matters, and pet loss bereavement group.

GO PHOTOFORUM A photography forum offering advice, information and latest product news. Sections include latest product news, techniques, dealing with people and selecting the correct film.

GO RACING The Motor Sport forum offers trackside reports, schedules, driver biographies and live reports direct from major events worldwide. Contact information is provided for all the official motorsport organizations.

GO RIDE Focusing on motorcycles, pro racing, touring and other motorcycling topics. An indispensable guide to the motorcycling scene.

GO ROCKNET The Rock music forum. Information on where classic groups are playing, discographies, bibliographies, and discussion of artists' careers. Insiders release information here, often before it hits the press.

GO SAILING The sailing forum has conferences with celebrities and experts. Members of this electronic yacht club exchange ideas, techniques and product information in an informal club setting.

GO SCIFI Everything Sci-Fi, including information and reviews of the latest TV series, books, comics and films. Read excerpts and short stories or contribute your own thoughts about the future.

GO SCUBA Scuba diving is one of the most safety conscious activities. Safety, equipment, equipment maintenance and diving medicine forums are among those available. Discuss diving with fellow divers, instructors, underwater photographers and diving physicians.

GO SHOWBIZ Films, celebrities, television and personalities fall under the spotlight of your attention in this forum. Find out what's a box office hit, chat with fans or gossip on the message board.

GO SPACEFORUM Latest news and discoveries, theories and discussion. NASA's latest exploits in space or UFO reports, with many graphic images available to download. A message section allows you to discuss the news of the day, or put forward your own theories.

GO TBONLINE Travel Britain Online is a guide featuring theatres and shows, a London pub guide, details of all the major festivals and more.

GO VEGETARIAN Find recipes, tips on getting started as a vegetarian, and talk with others who share your views.

GO WCN The Worldwide Car Network is the world's largest provider of information about rare and collectible cars. The forum hosts discussion on everything from driving performance cars to locating rare parts for cars, motorbikes or trucks.

GO WCOMMUNITY Speak with people in a foreign language. CompuServe's machine translation software converts between English and French, Spanish or German. The people in these countries reply and their comments are translated back into English.

GO WINE Discuss the merits of fine wines with people who share your interest. Find out which good wines are available, and how much you should pay.

GO YDRIVE An entertainment forum for and by under sixteens where you can chat, find out about the latest movie releases, find penpals and read other kids' fanzines.

Section 3

Internet made easy™

8 CompuServe and the Internet

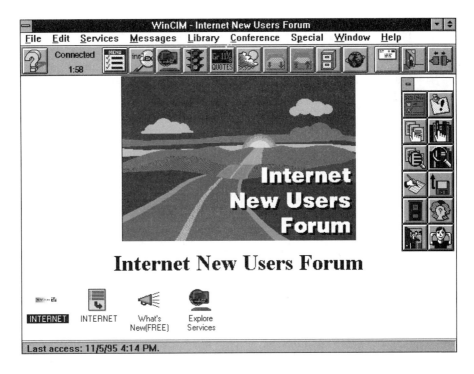

The merging of CompuServe with the Internet was inevitable. Internet-savvy Email has been available from within CIM for a number of years, the next logical steps of providing FTP, Usenet News and Telnet from within CompuServe occurred in 1995 and today's CompuServe gives users full interaction with the World Wide Web from the safety of the CIM range of software. In some ways this is an ideal position for both CompuServe and its customers. Being able to access the Internet from within a well tried and tested single application is exceptionally useful for customers.

However, there are many users who either don't want or don't need the inner offerings of CompuServe such as forums and commercial databases, but just want to lurk around the Internet itself. CompuServe has done the decent thing and made it possible for users to select for themselves the degree of interaction with either CompuServe or the Internet.

But, before we delve into CompuServe and the Internet let's go through the obligatory history lesson, better for you to understand where the Internet came from, and where, if anywhere, it might be going to.

Internet origins

Charles Herzfeld winces at the sound of a Rolling Stones tune drifting through the open window. It's been a busy year but he's finally signed off all the approvals for the joint scientific research network that's going to link three American university computers together. The project, kicked off by the Pentagon's Advanced Research Projects Agency will eventually become ARPA-Net, and will run on DEC computers. ARPAnet can never grow larger than 256 computers, but some joker remarks that there aren't more than ten reliable computers in the whole of America. The first sites to be linked are the University of California at Los Angeles and Santa Barbara, the Stanford Research Institute, and the University of Utah.

Thirty years on and an email arrives in the mailbox of a writer in Sussex. It has come from the USA, routed through several different mail handling computers to arrive two hours later. This is the Internet in action, the all-singing all-dancing global communications system descended from ARPAnet. There are no limitations on its use, no costs incurred for sending traffic over it, and no censorship.

The Internet is now so large and so varied that you can write your own facts and figures, and no one will challenge them. So let's start with say, forty million users, 2 million on-line computers, and more data files than you could count in a lifetime.

You need a computer to access the Internet which lessens its usefulness as an all purpose info-tool. Much of the information on it isn't indexed, so while you can pull information down quickly you'll have trouble collating knowledge. And unless you've got a free connection through a University or business network using the Internet over the phone in Europe can be expensive.

But 1996 will be the Year Of the Internet. In the last three years there's been a massive burst of consumer interest, and new Internet-ready software is now built into the latest software from Apple, Microsoft, and IBM. Graphical browsers such as Netscape and WinWeb let users navigate thorough remote servers quicker than you can turn a page. Easy to install software turns any laptop computer with a modem into a virtual window onto the Internet, with access to terabytes of information.

ARPAnet

The Internet as we now know it was created by the Pentagon's Advanced Research Projects Agency (ARPA) in the Kennedy era. The aim of ARPA was to bring together scientific minds to research and develop technology that would enable America to stay ahead in the Cold War. The guiding light in ARPA was Bob Taylor, a computer visionary who started trying to find better ways of working with computers while he was at NASA. Taylor eventually moved to the Defense Department and was one of the first founders of ARPA.

Taylor launched ARPA by setting up a number of research projects at American universities, and then came up with the idea of ARPAnet, the very

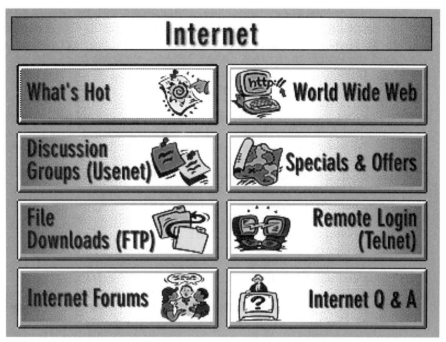

Figure 8.2 *Internet services and help available from within CIM. CompuServe also supports direct PPP access and TCP/IP software.*

first trans-national computer network. Its purpose was to link the scientists and researchers together. The technology used to transfer data between computers had been developed in the early sixties by Paul Baran, who was working on ways of preventing telephone systems from being destroyed by the electromagnetic pulse (EMP) effect during thermonuclear bomb blasts. Baran developed the first packet switching techniques, which were then incorporated into wide area network (WAN) technology. The first tests of NCP – Network Control Protocol – were carried out at Britain's National Physical Laboratory in 1968, and were successful enough to convince the Pentagon's Advanced Research Projects Agency to install the first nodes in 1969, creating ARPAnet. NCP was later superseded by TCP/IP the dual pair of protocols still in use today.

Despite the military connections, ARPAnet was primarily designed to link scientists and academics together to share research - it wasn't designed as the military nuclear-proof command network some writers are fond of inventing, although Baran's packet switch technology may contribute to this idea. ARPAnet operated using DEC PDP-10 computers and the message and data handling were carried out using separate minicomputers known as TIPs (terminal interface processors). The TIPs were linked to other TIPs over leased phone connections, and by 1973 the ARPAnet had turned into a national network, but access to the system was limited to universities, research establishments, and defence contractors.

The network operated with a great sense of wonder and there was no security anywhere on the system. Virtually any student (or friend of a student) who had access to a terminal connected to a TIP could log into any other computer, and spend hours or days cruising round its insides. Many of the academics who used the system found that using electronic mail was much more interesting than transferring research papers around, and so the beginnings of the social structure of the Internet emerged.

In 1975 the ARPAnet was turned over to the Defense Communications Agency, an organization dedicated mainly to overseeing military and government radio and data traffic. Security on the net was tightened somewhat, but to no great degree. The ARPAnet was at that time limited to 8-bit addressing techniques, which meant that no more than 256 sites could be connected directly at any one time. A new network addressing scheme was introduced in 1982, which meant that thousands of networks could be connected to each other, and the true Internet was born. ARPAnet split from the Internet in 1983 and became Milnet. About the same time America's National Science Federation commissioned NFSNET to hook together five supercomputer centres. This move was to open up supercomputer access to academic users, and NFSNET was spliced into the existing ARPAnet infrastructure. This created traffic and administration problems so NFSNET eventually decided to build its national network to connect academic sited together. Computing centres were linked together over relatively fast 56 Kbps phone lines, creating regional centres. These were eventually inter-networked together with many speed and capacity upgrades along the way, to form the basis of today's Internet.

The growth of the Internet was rapid, and spread not only to research establishments, but also to the corporate sector. In the early days the ARPAnet was used mainly for communications and data generated or sustained by research projects, but by the mid-1980s the Internet was becoming saturated with electronic mail from all corners of the world, including private individuals. This was an anathema to those involved at the start, mainly because the costs of connecting to the Internet had dropped to the sort of levels where small corporations could afford connections. By the start of the 1990s it was estimated that the Internet carried over 2 million regular users, much to the chagrin of the universities and government departments who were directly funding the backbone of the service. As time passed many commercial networks became part of the Internet and the American telephone company packet switch nets gained access, becoming just a small part of an ever larger whole. Today the Internet has spread into the home and your PC in the back bedroom is as much a part of the Internet as the early Cray supercomputers crunching military trajectory figures, way back in the late seventies.

Hey, let's invent UNIX

In 1969 Ken Thompson, a worker at the Bell Laboratories Science Research Murray Hill labs, decided to invent UNIX. Thompson's idea was to write an operating system for his own use, one that would multitask, and eventually become processor-independent. Thompson's project quickly caught the enthusiasm of co-workers and UNIX blossomed. Various universities also caught

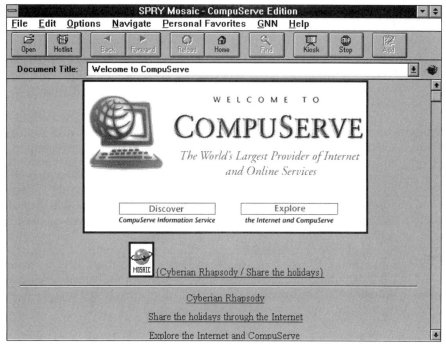

Figure 8.3 *The CompuServe Mosaic Browser operating over a PPP link to the Internet.*

the bug, and many of the larger American faculties eventually developed their own implementations of Thompson's work.

UNIX was tailor-made for use on computer networks. Utilities such as ftp, finger and sendmail became standards for accessing and using the computers connected to the Internet. The early UNIX implementations were often bug-ridden, because anyone and everyone had a hand in its development and there was no central coordination of development amongst the academics who used and 'improved' UNIX. In fact there were so many implementations of UNIX that it was possible to find different versions sitting on adjacent terminals in most of America's universities.

The combination of flaws in UNIX, the curious minds of students, the utter lack of security on the Internet, and the 'hacker mentality' led to huge problems for the Internet on many occasions, especially when the arrival of cheap personal computers in 1982 started an explosion in Internet use. Almost any sort of computer can now be hooked up, as long as the TCP/IP software is available for it.

TCP/IP is now truly multi-platform and it's often very difficult to tell just what type of computer is providing the service at the remote end of the link. Conversely UNIX has become a backwater operating system outside of Academia but is still used on tens of thousands of Internet-connected host computers.

The present

The current Internet works well for sending and receiving electronic texts. It's not quite so good as CompuServe for research because much of the information on the Internet's computers isn't indexed. If you want a quote from Shakespeare you may well find it with a Gopher search, if you seek details on Hebrew literature you may have to look in a library.

The World Wide Web may change all of this. It has good search facilities and many of the sites connected to it offer information in a well structured and accessible manner. Web sites are becoming increasingly complex, and it's now possible to grab full motion videos, or make live telephone calls from many of them if your personal computer is fast enough. The downside is that popular sites are often inaccessible because of user overload.

New fibre networks are already being installed which will provide a true Information Superhighway. This will carry entertainment, messaging and almost everything else that the Internet currently carries, but it will be larger, run wholly by commercial companies, and paid for either by advertising or by subscription. Expect it in around five years time or less as experiments by the BBC, BT and other communications companies are already well established. Whether you need it or not, the Internet is already snaking its way to your door along fibre optic cables and fast digital links.

Internet today

The Internet started to distend with new users in the mid-nineties. The huge sales of personal computers in the West is one reason; the availability of cheap telephone modems is another. It's estimated that there are 50 million personal computers in the USA, and about the same number in Western Europe, although less than a quarter of these are fitted with modems or network access of any kind. That gives a population of about 25 million modem users – about the same as some estimates for the number of Internet users in 1994 – although not all modem users have Internet access. 1995 UK surveys indicate that 30% of all homes have a computer of some sort. However modem sales seem to give a best indication of Internet use, with nearly half a million units being sold in 1994.

The real reasons for the explosion in European Internet availability are probably more to do with a haphazard 'chaotic' process, rather than the planned expansion of commercial interests. The end of the Cold War brought many upheavals in both the USA and Europe, including a relaxation of formalities about the supremacy of International Standards over the earlier IP protocols.

On the down side

Hyperbole about the Internet is rife. It's dubbed the Information Superhighway, the InfoBahn, or the Digital Revolution, depending on the thickness of glossy

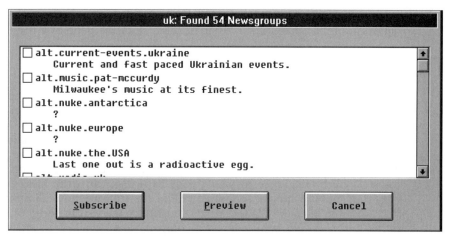

Figure 8.4   *Searching for UK newsgroups in CIM. 'Milwaukee' and 'nuke' both include UK.*

paper your favourite computer magazine is printed on. Some of this might actually be true if you had an Ethernet connection to the Internet, but modems present the Digital Superhighway to the user as an information traffic jam, and few UK journalists writing about the Internet emphasize the tedium or expense of modem use. Services like Internet Talk Radio demand transfers of files up to 30 megabytes in length, and are not realistically available to many users of current modem technology, because of the phone charges.

The Internet traffic snarl-up is unlikely to improve even with the recent arrival of V.34 modems, as there's always more data waiting to be downloaded than there is bandwidth available to get it. At the moment the theoretical bandwidth of modems over European networks is believed to be about 32 kilobits per second. This roughly equates to 2000 words of ASCII text per second, but it's likely that new transport techniques such as ATM will eventually erode the supremacy of the analogue telephone modem. In the meantime new modems planned for 1996 include V34 bis voice data modems. These will operate over existing lines to give a carrier speed of 32 K/Bits per second, faster still than the recent V34 modems.

Unfortunately, alternatives to dial-up access are expensive. A leased line with 64 K/Bits per second, enough for a couple of heavyweight users, costs around £8,000 per year to install and maintain, and the much-vaunted ISDN is still too expensive to install for the average UK punter to contemplate, although UK running costs for ISDN are lower than in most of Europe.

But enter the Information Superhighway. The phrase itself comes from a visionary speech by Vice President of America Al Gore and points towards a system of unlimited bandwidth connections direct to businesses and homes in the USA. It's envisaged that the network will be more or less complete in the first decade of the next millennium, bringing unlimited amounts of data and information to businesses, schools and homes.

Restrictive telecoms policies prevail in much of Europe, and despite Europe being the home of the much-vaunted ITU/U (ex CCITT), European telecomms are a mishmash of systems, technology and policy. The Information Super-highway will be a long time coming to this side of the pond as a result.

The future

Systems which offer video on demand have been demonstrated and there's currently a pan-European test to run ATM (asynchronous transfer mode.) ATM is a technology which allows virtually unlimited bandwidth to be made available over dial-up lines or Ethernet, and looks set to get here in about five years' time. The implications for Internet users are enormous and the promise of unlimited transmission bandwidth means that the only limitation to data transfer will be the speed at which your hard disk can write files. Data will consist of moving images, sound, and all of the stuff we now call multimedia, instead of the plain ASCII text which constitutes the vast majority of Internet traffic today. As we went to press a company has launched an international software product which allows voice calls over the Internet.

Services like World Wide Web will become more sophisticated, and multi-media, Internet based voice-mail in real time, and elementary on-line video conferences are already here. The future, it would seem, holds unlimited promise for both CompuServe and Internet users, and the writing is certainly on the wall for providers who continue to lope along with character based terminal interfaces. The days of typing arcane UNIX commands into a distant computer are now past, and many Internet providers are beginning to realize this. Some never will, and will slowly fade into the past, just as MS-DOS 2.1 did.

Beware the hype

The Internet is what the computer market needs to lift it into the next generation of bolt-on computer accessories. It follows from this that ninety percent of what you read about the Internet will be either hype, or 'news' stories lifted from the Internet itself. What you should also know is that you, dear reader, will not be able to form an objective vision of what you'll get from the Internet until you sign up, because everybody's Internet is different.

To confound matters further, the Internet itself puts out chaff to ensure a continuous stream of hyperbole. Take the Cookie Recipe story. This 'true' story concerns a lady who was so taken with a cookie in a New York restaurant that she asked for the recipe. The waitress said that there would be a charge of 'two-fifty' for the recipe, added to the customers credit card. When said lady got her credit card bill she found that she'd been charged two hundred and fifty dollars for the recipe, and so posted it on the Internet in revenge. Half a dozen UK newspapers printed this story verbatim, until one John Diamond, writer on The Times, phoned up the restaurant concerned. Naturally the story was a hoax, and goes back over twenty years. The end to this story is that John Diamond was interviewed for 'The Spin' TV programme, thus ensuring that the myth got onto National Television. Its success, and its life was complete and the Internet had triumphed once more over the international news media.

Other urban myths abound, many of them generated by a group of Internet users in the alt.memetics newsgroup. Their theory is that any fiction can be placed on the Internet, where it will grow and spread like a virus. Success is measured by how far the story will travel. You, the unknowing punter are at the receiving end of these stories, re-packed as The Truth and pre-digested for you in the daily papers.

CompuServe and the Internet - reprise

Faced with massive interest in the Internet, CompuServe could do one of two things; they could have ignored it, and lost considerable market share; or they could have decided that the Internet is a valuable resource and needs to be amalgamated into CompuServe's 'brand identity'. Many of the UK companies who have tried to do this have failed, mainly because of a lack of understanding of how the Internet is perceived by customers, or how best to integrate it into their own service provision. CompuServe have to date got this vital integration almost 100% correct, and it's possible to take as much or as little from the Internet as you need, with a just single subscription to CompuServe. As we'll see in the next few chapters you're offered a variety of methods to hook into the Internet, and that's where we're going next.

Hardware & software

To access those computers and the services they offer you need to setup 'client' software on your personal computer. This then talks with the remote 'server' over the link provided by the Internet and you've got a working system. The various servers store information; client software goes and retrieves it. Two years ago you'd need separate programs on your computer to get your mail, run gopher searches and pickup your news. Today, many of the graphical Web browsers for Windows, Apple and other computers can access everything from News, through to Gopher searches without extra software, and this trend is set to continue. Soon you'll only need a single program to access all of the Internet services.

CompuServe is constantly adding to its Internet toolkit, and many of the following utilities and tools are available from within CIM or CompuServe. GO INTERNET for a full list of Internet utilities. If the utility you need isn't available from within CompuServe you'll need to use the CompuServe PPP service with third party client software to access it. The following chapters explain how.

ARCHIE (available through CIM & CompuServe Telnet)

What it means:
Nothing. Named after an American cartoon series. Culturally inept Internet writers think it means 'Archive Server'

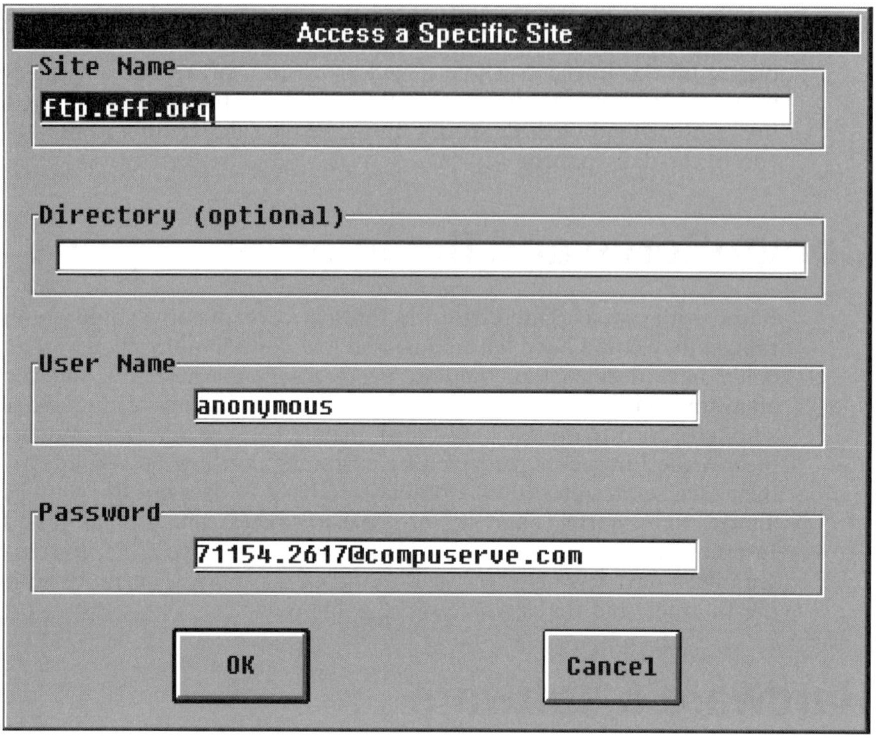

Figure 8.5 *Anonymous FTP in CIM . . .*

What it does:
Lets users search for particular files, a bit like a card index.

Useful for tracking down computer files on the Internet. You'd use ARCHIE to search for a file called BIBLE.TXT, or files for a particular computer type, such as the Amiga. ARCHIE is slow, but can be accessed by email, and has a lot of obscure search commands. Good for academics, and anyone not paying for the phone bill.

EMAIL (CompuServe and Internet Electronic Mail is built in to CIM)

What it means:
electronic mail
What it does:
Sends and receives text files, computer files, pictures, sounds.

The most popular pursuit in the known universe, but only if you've got a computer. Highly useful for keeping in touch, cheaper than fax or other point-to-point links. You send mail from your computer to a mail server. From there it gets transmitted around the Internet until it reaches the mailbox of

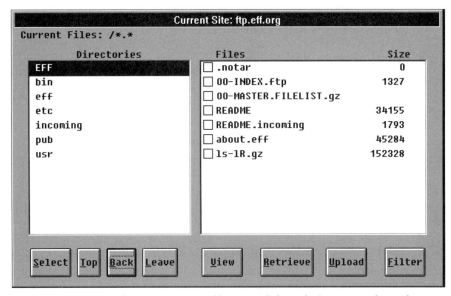

Figure 8.6   . . . and the remote site itself, accessed through CIM. No other software is needed.

the recipient, who either receives it on his screen or dials in to pick it up if he's using a modem. The best thing next to your computer, other than a winning lottery ticket. And it's free with your CompuServe membership.

GOPHER

What it means:
An in-joke from the University of Minnesota whose mascot is a Gopher. As in Go fer it (Fetch it)

What it does:
Searches by filename or keyword. Thus if you wanted a text file on how to deal with estate agents when buying a house you'd search the Gopher servers with keywords 'crook' and 'rip-off'. Gopher is fast and highly useful. Those keyword searches will pickup everything from Monty Python scripts to medical treatises on ingrown toenails; as long as they're stored in indexed directories on Gopher Servers. Gopher has a friend called Veronica (again from the 'Archies' cartoons). Veronica can search either Gopher directory titles, or for specific files using AND/OR /NOT constructs. Veronica lets you look for Monty AND Python NOT snakes.

WAIS (available through CompuServe Telnet)

What it means :
Wide Area Information Server

What it does:
Finds files by searching indexes at multiple servers.

WAIS sounds good in principle but often only comes up with a pointer to other documents. If you run a search on 'woodlands' you might well get three hits listing a paper published by an Australian University, together with the postal address to send your money to. Much loved by academics, but not as immediate as the World Wide Web.

FTP (available through CIM & CompuServe - GO INTERNET)

What it stands for:
File Transfer Protocol

What it does:
Transfers files over the Internet

FTP is used in many ways. Gopher and the WWW software uses FTP to get files from afar and transfer them to your computer. You can also use an FTP program by itself to log into and rummage around on live servers on the other side of the planet. Your rummaging happens in real time so searches and transfers can be slow and expensive. Many sites now support FTP by mail - as long as you know what the file is called, and where it's buried on the server you can request it to be emailed. You then collect at your leisure.

TELNET (available through CIM & CompuServe Telnet)

What it means:
Networking from afar. But it looks like teleporting.

What it does:
Lets you use remote computers anywhere in the world.

Telnet gives you access to any computer on the Internet which supports it. You use TELNET to login to say, a NASA database to run searches, or to CompuServe instead of dialling out on a phone line, or to a library to search their indexes. TELNET lets you access live applications running on the remote computer, so you could in theory run the next Shuttle launch from your back bedroom. TELNET is the method hackers use to enter one computer, than 'hop' into another computer which may be in a different country. Also used to access IRC, ARCHIE and other services.

USENET (available through CompuServe)

What it means: Network News service

What it does:
Provides a bulletin board type service. Often called Network News. Users post mail to a news group, which makes them available to other readers. Newsgroups

cater for all interests, and have lurid names like ALT.SEX.ALIENS and so forth. News groups also carry computer images in coded form, giving the Internet most of its reputation as a haven for pornographers; conversely the Newsgroups carry huge amounts of worthwhile and relevant information from lost children searches to computer help texts. Newsgroups are broadly similar in concept to CompuServe forums, except CompuServe forums are managed, and rather safer for timorous users who don't want the hassle of fighting with Usenet fascists over every trivial point. Usenet can be useful, but anarchy often rules, whereas on CompuServe forums are managed and therefore usually more rewarding. CompuServe now limits access to some contentious Usenet groups after a tightening up of European pornography legislation, especially in Germany.

LISTSERV (available through CompuServe Mail)

What it means: List Servers

What it does:
Sends information by email.

LISTSERVS are automated systems which send you the contents of magazines, newsgroups, and special interest topics by email. You subscribe to a list server by sending your email address, and a Subscribe message. The list server then puts you on its mailing list and the text arrives in your mailbox. It's a great way of filtering and receiving information about your own special topic. List servers cover evening from knitting bed quilts to computer security and many interesting electronic magazines (ezines or just zines) are available.

IRC (available through CIM & CompuServe Telnet)

What it means
Internet Relay chat

What it does:
CB radio for computer geeks

IRC lets anyone with nothing to say get up and shout it to the world. Other IRC users logged into the same channel see the text messages and respond by typing text into their remote computer. Messages scroll up the screen. Most IRC channels are clogged with people saying either 'Hi' or Good-bye' or swapping verbal abuse, although there are exceptions. Great for letting off steam, or just seeing what a complete waste of time some human beings are. IRC 'BOTS are automated systems which engage unwary newbies in futile conversations. You might think you're exchanging climactic tips with Sexy Sadie, but in reality you're chatting up a knackered old computer while other people on the channel fall over themselves at your expense. IRC was used at the 1995 Labour Party Conference to transmit live transcripts over the Internet.

CompuServe has its own CB system which is somewhat better managed than IRC, which isn't managed at all. Parents and those of a nervous disposition take note..

WWW (available through CompuServe WinCIM 2 and Mosaic)

What it means: World Wide Web

What it does:
Everything

A system of presenting textual and visual information in a navigable fashion. The best method yet of navigating the Internet and getting useful information from it. WWW systems can access Gopher and Archie Servers, grab your Newsgroups, log you into IRC channels. They also let you flip from computer to computer or document to document by means of links. You click on a link and you're immediately connected to the site which has the document you want. WWW systems are becoming increasingly sophisticated, and a fast computer armed with a WWW Browser such as Spry Mosaic can display movies, pictures, play sounds, and even offer instant voice mail over the Internet. The Downside? It's so addictive you might lose your social life and become a cyber-geek.

PING

What it means:
Packet INternet Groper

What it does: Tests remote connections over the Internet.

PING is used like sonar to 'ping' a remote computer over the Internet to see if it's dead or alive. To PING something you need a PING utility on your computer. The Internet Resources forum has lots of them, but PINGing over a modem link can get expensive, as you can wait some time for not much response.

FINGER

What it means:
Foraging INformation Gets Erratic Results
What it does:
Brings back information about users. FINGER-ing jmajor@commons.gov.uk might bring back the news that jmajor is out to lunch, on holiday, or in bed with Mad Prime Minister Disease. UNIX FINGER users can put information about themselves into a PLAN file which gets sent to you if you FINGER them. A second PROJECT file is sometimes used to send out more information.

WHOIS

What it means: Who Is Who at your site?/ On the Internet?

What it does:
Lets users search for other users, or Internet computers.

WHOIS is often used by academic sites to construct personnel directories of staff and students. In that case each University will have its own WHOIS directory. (You need a WHOIS client to search them). There are a few International WHOIS databases, such as the European RIPE database, but WHOIS is generally used to forage for the name of that guy at Leeds University who borrowed a tenner off you, fourteen years ago. WHOIS was widely used by the German Chaos computer group to obtain Internet addresses of military computers from the central NIC registration computers.

9 Starting out, setting up on the Internet

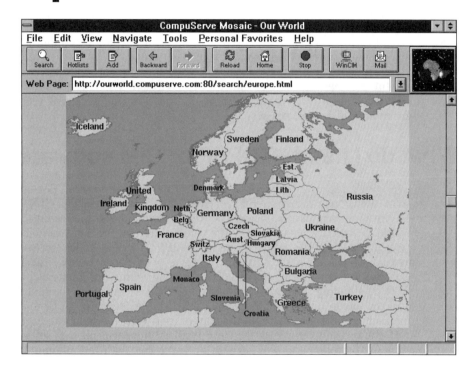

The first thing you need for access to the Internet is an Internet access account. It takes the form of provision of an access point to the 'Net, and generally speaking, you'll pick up that node – or permission to use it – from an Internet Service Provider (ISP in the jargon).

CompuServe is an ISP, and you access the Internet through CompuServe, either via CIM which hooks indirectly into Internet services such as Telnet, FTP, and Usenet news, or directly, by using CompuServe's telephone nodes to set up a temporary TCP/IP connection with CompuServe PPP (point-to-point) software. This lets you use Internet client software over the Internet itself. However, you'll still be using CIM and CompuServe Mail for your all email, unless you have another email account with another provider.

If that provider has given you a POP3 mailbox, you can go into it over CompuServe's PPP connection and retrieve mail from there. You'll need a secondary (non-CIM) email program to do this, but it's a handy way of connecting up to say, your University or Company's email, using CompuServe PPP as the link.

The first method using CIM means you don't need any special software to get into the Internet, the second means that you need special dialler and login software (known as a 'TCP/IP stack' and implemented by CompuServe as 'CompuServe PPP') and special TCP/IP compliant communications software to do things like send mail, browse the World Wide Web and so on.

If all of this sounds baffling, that's because it is baffling, and no amount of waffle on the part of this writer should disguise the fact that setting up a TCP/IP connection to the Internet is not particularly easy. However CompuServe do make things as simple as possible, and they have a range of install and go options for users. They also have a wonderful telephone support team who will soothe your troubled brow, if things go wrong.

Before you get as far as setting up your Internet software, have a look in the Internet New Users Forum. (GO INETFORUM). This contains message sections dealing with the problems you will face and will give you a good grounding on Internet basics.

What do I need - TCP/IP or CIM software?

Everyone's use of CompuServe and the Internet is different. You may only want occasional access to FTP, Telnet and News for which CIM and the CompuServe service is sufficient. On the other hand you may want to use the World Wide Web, which is now the whole 'Internet' for many people. In that case you'll need to use CompuServe PPP Internet dialer software, and in-built Mosaic browser software to drive your connection to the Internet. CompuServe gives you the choice of staying within the managed world of CIM or stepping outside of it to use TCP/IP software, but the first thing to do is to set up CIM, which will then give you access through CompuServe's Internet support forums to all the support software and help you need.

If you're using Windows then the Dialler utility will take its settings from your CIM profile, and will get you onto the Net with the minimum of fuss. You then use the Mosaic Web browser directly from within CIM from the Special menu option.

Mac users

Things aren't (yet) so simple for Mac users. You need the MacTCP Control Panel, found in System 7.5, plus a 68030 or better Mac to run Web Browser software such as Mosaic. You'll also have to use a utility called ConfigPPP to get onto the Net, and ConfigPPP is not a particular secure application. (It stores your password as visible text.) Users of older 68000 based Macs have a couple of options, the first is to use CompuServe's excellent FTP and Usenet features from within CIM, the other is to upgrade. However, many users of those early 68000 Macs such as SE's and Classics will not want to upgrade from these excellent machines to larger and more expensive kit and for them the only, and easiest option is to use the managed Internet options from within CIM. Unfortunately this will preclude access to the World Wide Web, at the present time.

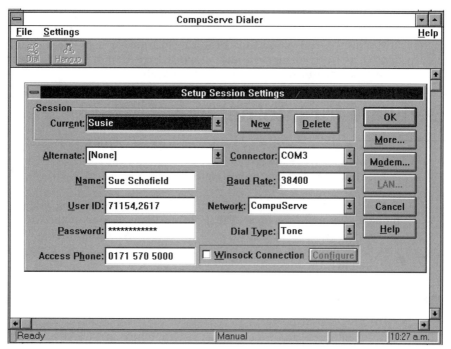

Figure 9.2   *CID - CompuServe Internet dialler. This is all you need to make a Windows TCP/IP connection to the Internet. It takes its settings from CIM and was formerly part of NetLauncher.*

Connecting up via TCP/IP

To access the Internet you simply connect your computer, through its Internet software (the 'stack') to the host computers of your ISP. Remember that when this happens the user is actually logged into a distant host computer, not directly to something called the 'Internet'. It's CompuServe's remote computer which has the direct connection to the Internet, not your modem.

Connecting via TCP/IP allows multitasking. You can use as much of the available modem or Ethernet bandwidth as you can grab and that means with a fast modem you can send and receive mail while grabbing files from a remote site. Each task you run is called a 'session' and it's common to have multiple sessions open in various windows. Multitasking saves money, or at least it does if you have a personal computer and software capable of doing it.

Early versions of CIM used a combined TCP/IP stack and dialler for use with Windows machines, and ConfigPPP for Mac users. From Version 2.0 of WinCIM you don't need anything else to get going other than WinCIM 2.0 itself. These utilities get your machine logged into to CompuServe's Internet services over a TCP/IP connection - and that's it. You have to provide your own Internet 'client software' to drive your non-CompuServe mail, fetch files, or browse the Web. The latter operation is made easier by a special version of

the Mosaic Web Browser software accessed from the Special menu in
WinCim 2.0 You can either use this to rummage around the Internet, or use
any other TCP/IP compliant browser software such as Netscape. However
Mosaic is licensed already and supported by CompuServe, so try that for
your first stroll through the World Wide Web.

Software for Internet use

For an indirect connection to the Internet via CIM and CompuServe, use
CIM and GO INTERNET.

For a full connection to the Internet you need:

* SLIP or PPP dialer software to access the Internet if you're using a
modem. CompuServe uses PPP (Point-to-Point Protocol) the 'driver' which
allows TCP/IP to work over serial lines. For Windows, that's WinCIM 2.0
and its CompuServe Internet Dialler (CID) which is a combined dialler and
PPP handler, for Macs it is MacPPP.

Client software supplies

The difficult problem for newcomers is getting hold of TCP/IP client software, a
problem which will ease as more commercial programs come onto the market.
In the meantime all the software you need is in the CompuServe Internet
Resources forum (GO INETRESOURCE). However you'll be able to do
most Internet things from within Mosaic, as it handles FTP, gopher and so
on, automatically for you.

If you want to got the whole hog you'll need discrete client applications.
For FTP you'll need FTP software, for email you'll need email software and
so on. These let you hook into the various application servers you'll find on
the Internet. These programs communicate through the TCP/IP link, which is
operating through your modem, which is being managed by PPP. You choose
client software just as you would choose a word processor or other computer
application, that is, you listen to what all the experts tell you, and then go
and buy the same program as the guy next door has.

In practice you will probably end up using the Shareware software found
on CompuServe, unless you're a business that can afford the services of a
consultant or dealer. Early generations of Shareware programs for the Internet
were slightly lacking in many respects, but have improved drastically over the
last year. There's also been a flood of updated software for WAIS, Gopher and
the World Wide Web and it's now possible to get going for very little outlay.

It's important to remember that whatever software you end up using will
be out of date in months rather than years, because the Internet is growing
and changing at a phenomenal rate. The basics will remain the same, but
WWW services are evolving rapidly. This may influence your decision as to
whether you'll use Shareware or commercial software to get going with the
Internet.

Figure 9.3   *The Mosaic Web Browser using CID. Getting onto the Web is as simple as clicking the Mosaic icon.*

Start-up Q & A

What is the difference between PPP and SLIP?

SLIP (Serial Line Internet protocol) also allows computers direct dial up access to the Internet. However, PPP is newer, faster and considered more flexible and feature-laden than SLIP. CompuServe's PPP access uses, Point-to-Point Protocol.

I am having problems with my non CompuServe Internet software. Who do I call for support?

Obviously, CompuServe cannot be expected to support all of the Internet software packages available on the market. For problems with your Internet access software, contact the vendor of the particular software package. If you have problems with CompuServe Dialler software you can call CompuServe's Customer Support desk or leave a message by using GO FEEDBACK.

Can I use the CompuServe PPP gateway to access USENET Newsgroups and electronic mail?

CompuServe is providing access to a news server for use with the dial up PPP access. This means that you have the freedom of using the USENET

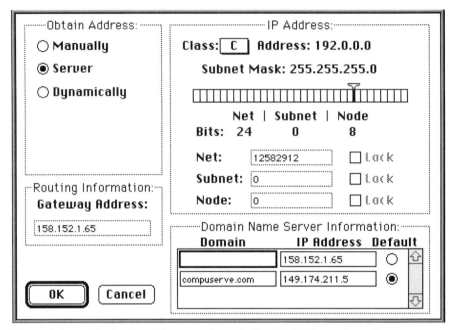

Figure 9.4   *Inside the MacTCP control panel. No MacTCP, no direct Internet access for Mac users although you can use CIM Internet services.*

newsreader software of your choice; simply configure it to read from the news.compuserve.com server. Or you can use the News support built into Mosaic, or from within the CompuServe Services via CIM. There are currently no plans to support CompuServe mail through PPP. CompuServe members will continue to be able to access their e-mail by logging onto the Information Service.

What do I need to use to browse the World Wide Web?
FOR WINDOWS:
   1. CompuServe Internet Dialler (CID) built-in to the WinCIM 2.0 software which gives you a temporary TCP/IP connection direct to the Internet.

FOR MACS:
   1. Internet Access Software (NCSA Mosaic is available on-line).
   2. MacTCP - included in Macintosh System 7.5 (see notes above)
   3. MacPPP to handle the dialling and modem.

FOR OS/2
   1. IBM's WebExplorer

It is recommended that when using the World Wide Web that you disable he loading of images, unless you are accessing at 14400 baud or more. When

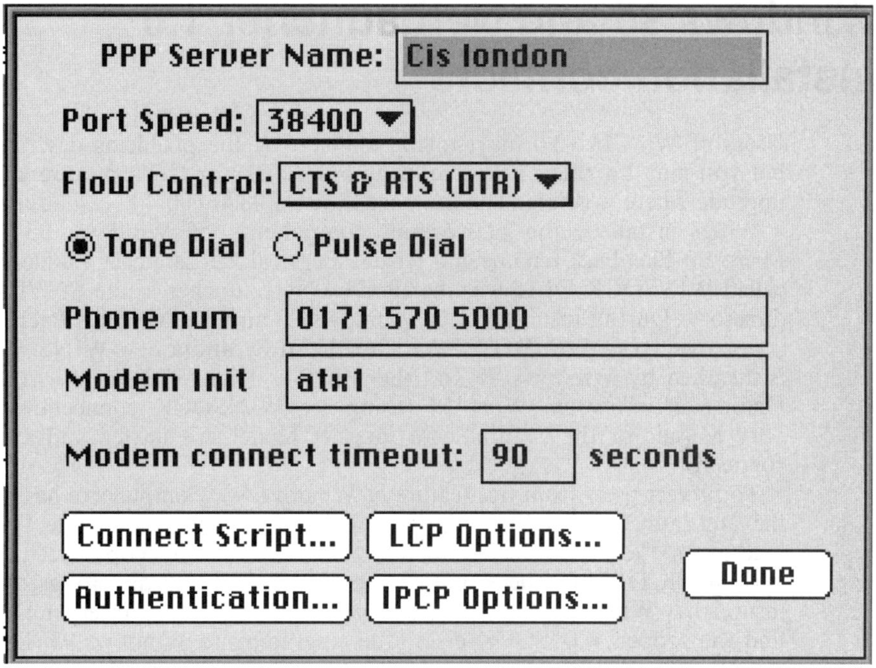

Figure 9.5 *Inside the MacPPP dialler. Your set up should look similar.*

using the CompuServe Mosaic Web browser you can choose the OPTIONS
pull-down menu, and de-select AUTOLOAD INLINE IMAGES. You can
still access individual graphics items by double-clicking them.

Are there any security concerns with using PPP?

There is no security risk in using CompuServe's dial PPP service. Your
computer is not accessible to people on the Internet. As always, we suggest
that you follow standard security measures with this, as well as any other
service, and do not send your credit card or any other sensitive information
over the Internet.

* Mac Users should note that ConfigPPP discloses the User password in the
Script Section if they use an automatic script to log into the PPP service.

Can I use the PPP connection to provide information on the Internet?

No, not directly. With CompuServe's PPP service, you are assigned a
dynamic IP address from a bank of IP addresses available to CompuServe
members. This means your IP address will change each time you establish a
new PPP connection. In order to provide information on the Internet (i.e. run
your own World Wide Web page), you need a static (permanent) IP address.
CompuServe now offer subscribers their own Web page area.

Windows 95 and NetLauncher 1.0 installation conflicts

Users of WinCIM 2.0 may not be afflicted by the problems described here, but you may hit snags if you're using older disks or CD's. You're advised to upgrade where possible. The Support Line on 0800 000 400 can advise.

When installed, the networking components of Windows 95 and the Microsoft Plus Pack rename and replace a critical NetLauncher 1.0 file. This file, called WINSOCK.DLL, was installed by NetLauncher in the C:\WINDOWS directory. During installation of Windows 95 and the MS Plus Pack, this file is renamed to C:\WINDOWS\WINSOCK.OLD, and a new WINSOCK.DLL is installed by Windows 95 and the MS Plus Pack. This results in a "Fatal Dialing Error" when WinCIM (using the WINSOCK connection option), Spry Mosaic or the CompuServe Internet Dialer are started and attempt to connect.

To protect users from this feature of Windows 95, CompuServe has produced the NetLauncher 1.0 Move Utility. This small utility, available for download from the NetLauncher menu, will automatically copy NetLauncher's WINSOCK.DLL to the CompuServe application sub-directories. This will insure that WinCIM, Spry Mosaic and the CompuServe Internet Dialer can find the proper WINSOCK even after upgrading to Windows 95. Download the NLMOVE.EXE file from the NetLauncher menu, and run it before or after upgrading to Windows 95.

If you do not wish to use the NetLauncher 1.0 Move Utility, and prefer to manually reconfigure your PC, follow the steps listed below.

If you have NOT already installed Windows 95 and the Plus Pack

If you are using NetLauncher and have not upgraded to Windows 95 and the Plus Pack, you can easily avoid the WINSOCK renaming problem. From the DOS prompt, simply copy C:\WINDOWS\WINSOCK.DLL to the each of the following directories:

```
C:\CSERVE\WINCIM
C:\CSERVE\CID
C:\CSERVE\MOSAIC
```

—prior to upgrading to Windows 95 and the Plus Pack. This will insure that WinCIM, Spry Mosaic and the CompuServe Internet Dialer can find their NetLauncher WINSOCK.DLL, even after the MS Plus Pack has been installed.

If you HAVE already installed Windows 95 and the Plus Pack:

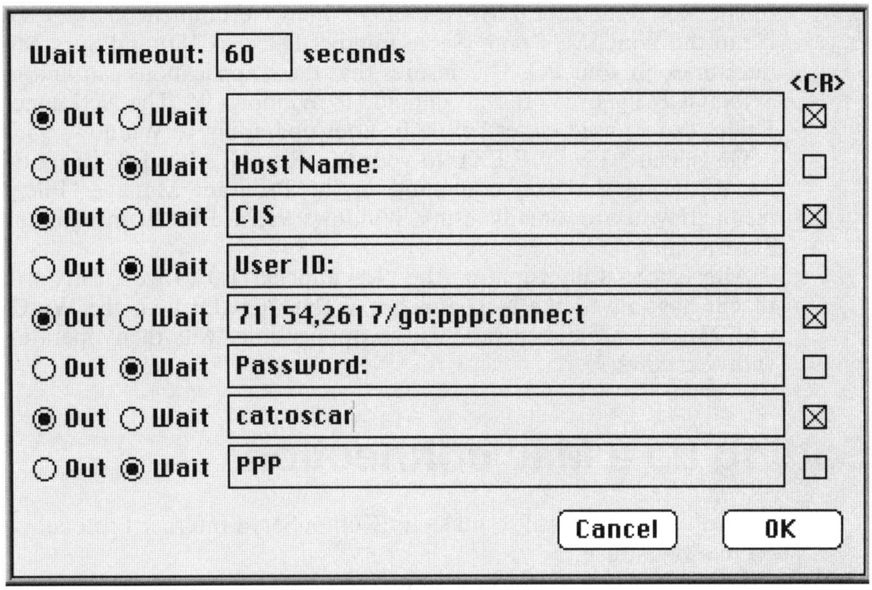

Figure 9.6   *The MacPPP script. Your set up should look similar, but remember that Mac PPP discloses passwords on dialling.*

If you have already installed Windows 95 and are now experiencing dialing problems with NetLauncher, simply re-install NetLauncher. This will allow NetLauncher to reload its WINSOCK.DLL in the C:\WINDOWS directory. After re-installation, copy C:\WINDOWS\WINSOCK.DLL to each of the following directories:

    C:\CSERVE\WINCIM
    C:\CSERVE\CID
    C:\CSERVE\MOSAIC

The next time you start up your PC, Windows 95 will again rename the Net-Launcher WINSOCK.DLL to C:\WINDOWS\WINSOCK.OLD. But because you copied the NetLauncher WINSOCK.DLL to the WinCIM, CompuServe Internet Dialer and Spry Mosaic directories right after re-installing Net-Launcher, these applications will now be able to find the correct version of the WINSOCK.DLL that will allow them to connect.

WinCIM 2.0 offers flexible installation options that will eliminate the need for the steps listed above

NetLauncher 1.0 MOVE utility

Upon installation of certain networking components, Windows 95 renames and replaces NetLauncher 1.0's WINSOCK.DLL file.

The NetLauncher 1.0 Move Utility copies NetLauncher's WINSOCK.DLL file to the WinCIM, CompuServe Internet Dialer (CID) and Spry Mosaic sub-directories on your PC. This insures that these applications can find the correct WINSOCK file even after an upgrade to Windows 95. The NetLauncher Move Utility can be used either before or after upgrading to Windows 95.

Download NLMOVE.EXE to your PC. Run NLMOVE.EXE on a Windows 3.1 PC using the Run command in the Program Manager File pulldown menu. If you are already using Windows 95, use the Run command in the Start menu.

After successfully running, the NetLauncher 1.0 Move Utility will confirm that it has moved the NetLauncher WINSOCK.DLL to the WinCIM, CID and Mosaic sub-directories. These applications will then operate correctly with Windows 95.

Setting up a Mac connection

The software you need to make an CompuServe Internet Protocol connection on the Macintosh:

1. MacTCP - Control Panel that handles TCP.
2. MacPPP - Extension and Control Panel that allows a Dialup PPP connection with a modem.
3. CompuServe Information Manager (MacCIM) 2.4.2 or greater - Its settings can be used to easily configure MacTCP and MacPPP.
4. CompuServe PPP Utility - This product quickly configures MacTCP and MacPPP using your existing MacCIM Settings.
5. Internet Access Software (eg. a web browser such as Netscape).

Details

1. OBTAIN MACTCP. MacTCP is a software product sold by Apple and is included in System 7.5. If you do not have System 7.5 or MacTCP, you should obtain either System 7.5 or the stand-alone MacTCP software from your authorized Apple dealer.

2. OBTAIN MACPPP. If you do not have MacPPP, download Version 2.01 from the menu. Select to decompress the Stuffit (.SIT) file when you leave MacCIM.

3. CONFIGURE MACPPP and MACTCP. To do this, download the CompuServe PPP Utility (CompuServe PPP Utility.sea) GO PPP and run it. It will extract a file called "CompuServe PPP Utility". Run this file to auto-matically configure MacTCP and MacPPP for a Dial PPP connection into CompuServe.

Several notes for Mac users

a) MacPPP Version 2.01 must include your password to run correctly. The CompuServe PPP utility will place your unencrypted password in the "Con-

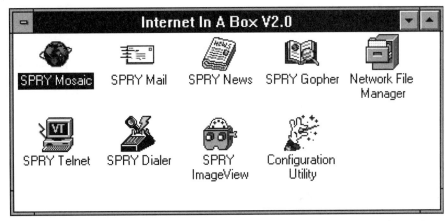

Figure 9.7   *The CompuServe PPP connection lets you use any TCP/IP software. This is Internet in A Box, a full suite of commercial software. Mac users can try similar software, such as VersaTerm.*

nect Script" settings in the "Config PPP" Control Panel. The upcoming version 2.20 of MacPPP will allow you to enter $password$ as your password if you want to be prompted for it, but in the meantime be careful if others will be using your machine!

b) The CompuServe PPP Utility uses settings from the CompuServe Information Manager (MacCIM) to set up your Internet connection. You must have MacCIM Version 2.4.2 or 2.4.3 installed BEFORE using the CompuServe PPP Utility. The latest MacCIM product can be downloaded on-line (GO MACCIM). Note: If your machine does not meet the necessary hardware/software requirements to run MacCIM 2.4.2 or higher, or if you would prefer to manually configure your PPP setup, GO PPP and select "Macintosh Setup" for more details.

c) MacTCP can only have one configuration file. If you have an existing Internet setup, it will be renamed, but you may undo any changes by running the CompuServe PPP utility again. You can download the MacTCP switcher (TCPSWTCH.SIT) from the Mac Communications Forum (GO MACCOM) to easily manage multiple configurations.

4. OBTAIN INTERNET ACCESS SOFTWARE. Netscape and CompuServe Mosaic are examples of Web browser software that will work on the Mac. You may obtain these browsers from CIS by doing the following:

Netscape Navigator

Make an FTP connection to ftp.mcom.com and access the /netscape/mac directory. To do this in MacCIM, GO FTP and select to access a specific site. Type in ftp.mcom.com and press Enter.

Mosaic

Ftp to ftp.ncsa.uiuc.edu and access the /Web/Mosaic/Mac directory OR visit the Internet Resources Forum (GO INETRESOUR) and access Library 5 to download either NCSAMO.68K (for 68000 microprocessors) or NCSAMO.PPC (for PowerPC chips). Both NCSAMO.68K and NCSAMO.PPC are currently v2.0 beta. If you would like to download v1.0.3 which is a release version, you can download the file MACMOS.SIT in the same library.

Your questions about Macintosh Internet connectivity can be answered in the MacCIM Support Forum (GO MCIMSUP).

Setting up OS/2

To establish a PPP connection through CompuServe, you must have Warp's Internet Access Kit (IAK) installed on your machine. You must also have the PPP update installed which you can ftp from ftp.ibm.net as /pub/PPP/PPP.ZIP or you can download the file from the OS/2 USERS forum (GO OS2USER) in library 20 with the filename PPP.ZIP.

Once you have the PPP update installed, you need to open the Dial Other Internet Providers object in the Internet Utilities folder. Then choose the Add Entry object, or select Add Entry from the Configure pull-down menu, then configure dialer as follows:

Login Info page of the settings notebook:

—In the Name: field, type CIS or PPP or some other "name" for this connection.
—In the Description: field, enter a description for this connection.
—For the Login ID: field enter your CompuServe User ID number.
—Enter your password in the Password: field.
—In the Phone Number: field, you need to enter the dial up number that you use to connect to CompuServe.

Then enter the following information into the Login Sequence:

field
\r
ame:
CIS
ID:
[LOGINID]/GO:PPPCONNECT
ord:
[PASSWORD]
PPP

—Set the Connection Type to PPP.
—Set the Inactivity Time Out to the desired minutes for the dialer to wait before automatic hangup.

Connect Info page of the settings notebook

—Set the MRU (Maximum Receive Unit) to 1500.
—Place a check in the VJ Compression checkbox.
—Enter 149.174.211.5 in the Domain Nameserver: field.
—Enter compuserve.com in the Your Domain Name: field.

Server Info page of the settings notebook

—If you would like to use a news reader through your PPP connection, you may enter news.compuserve.com in the News Server: field.
—Leave the other fields blank.

Modem Info page of the settings notebook

—Select your modem type, COM port, desired baud rate, data bits 8, and parity NONE.

After adding the above information you need to close the settings notebook and choose SAVE. Then to establish your PPP connection, select the NAME of the connection and choose DIAL. You will then see the initialization of the modem, the dialing, the logging in, and you should see messages in the Status Window reporting the remote IP address, VJ compression enabled, and that the default route address has been assigned.

When you see the above messages, then the connection is complete. You must leave the dialer running while you have the PPP connection active. You may want to minimize the dialer after the connection is established.

10 The World Wide Web

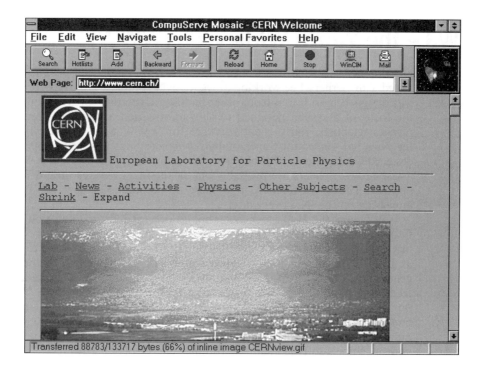

If you go back through some of the early hobbyist computer magazines you'll find that a lot of journalists were getting very hot under the collar about something called Hypertext, as long ago as the early 1980s. Hypertext was going to revolutionize the way that computer users were presented with information – because a single document could provide links to other documents and services. If this chapter were a Hypertext document you would be able to click on 'Doom', either to pick up a brief description of what Doom is, or to go on to shoot up aliens (or whatever they are) with a shotgun. If it were a good implementation of the Hypertext concept, you'd be able to leave Doom running in a window and go on to knock up a few sales figures in Visicalc, or spread abuse on IRC, all at the same time. Your Hypertext browser would leave the links to the original document in place so you could pop back at a moment's notice without having to reload the images or the text.

The technology to make Hypertext hum along didn't really start to become available until the end of the 1980s, by which time Visicalc was just a fond memory. (Many of today's Internetters and personal computers users won't know what part Visicalc played in the history of personal computer-ing.) But Hypertext has found its place as a navigation and search tool for the Internet, and the World Wide Web is flavour of the month, mainly because it uses a decidedly handsome piece of client software to let users wander around the Internet.

W3 – the World Wide Web (WWW)

Development on what was to become the WWW was started in 1980 by a guy called Tim Berners-Lee working at the CERN complex. His Hypertext system was designed in isolation from other budding Hypertext software, but became the focus of a system designed to ship information around between particle physics scientists. Early client software for WWW was character based but the National Center for Supercomputing Applications (NCSA) stepped in and designed GUI based WWW browser clients for Mac, Windows and X-Windows. These browser clients are probably one of the main reasons that WWW is so popular. Today it's reported that there are hundreds of new WWW servers appearing on the 'Net every day.

WWW uses the Hypertext metaphor to present information. You access it through a GUI client such as CompuServe Mosaic, Netscape, WinWeb, MacWeb or Cello, or you can get at it via telnet and one of the character based clients such as Lynx. The character based clients aren't of much interest to the current generation of Amiga, Mac or Windows users, because WWW provides a rich feed of graphics and sounds in addition to text based information. You click on an icon and a picture appears, or a sound erupts. The graphics and sound handling is provided by the graphics and sound handling programs you have on your computer; the WWW client serves only to hook information into your machine's software support routines and display hardware.

Information about information

The trouble with the Internet is that it's so big. Gigabytes of information are poured into it every day, making rapid collation and indexing of millions of new files impossible. Add the complexity of a jargon ridden computer-centric system, and the average punter doesn't stand a chance. Enter the World Wide Web a relatively simple method of publishing and presenting information to users. WWW lets users navigate by means of Hypertext links. These links point to graphics, music, text or any other computer-readable data. All the user has to do to hop from one link to the next is to click on a picture or an underlined piece of text. The link takes you to the URL (Uniform Resource Locator) - geek-speak for address of the site or document you want to go to. Interesting URL's are frequently compiled into lists of Bookmarks which can then be loaded into your Web browser software, or traded for other lists of even more interesting bookmarks. Used in this way WWW becomes a useful on-line personalized knowledge base.

WWW has revolutionized the Internet, and is the main vehicle for the rapid

Figure 10.2   *The National Lottery home page, featuring balls.gif. Lucky old you.*

colonization of the 'Net by commercial companies. It's both the most exciting thing to happen to networked computers - anyone can devise and program their own WWW 'page' via a word-processor and the Hypertext Markup Language (HTML) - and the most prosaic, for the same reason.

The World Wide Web lets users flick effortlessly around the Internet. It also handles email, FTP, Gopher and Usenet News, usurping the geek-appeal of those once vital utilities. Consequently a browser like CompuServe Mosaic could be all the Internet software you'll need.

Searching the Internet

WWW brings the Internet alive, not just with sound and vision but also with sophisticated search engines. These can be used to track down sites containing keywords or listings of related sites. The Yahoo search engine lists sites by subject so that you can navigate by point and click around your topic. The Lycos system crawls around Web sites and logs them to its database. When a new site is found the crawler visits the sites in the links too, and adds those, automatically building and maintaining an ever-growing database. A third system called Savvy-Search rummages around other search engine sites, gathering information by a variety of methods, including using other search mechanisms where needed.

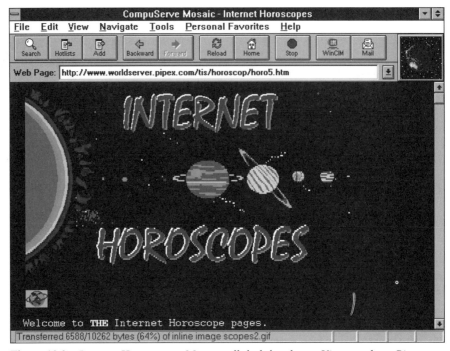

Figure 10.3   *Internet Horoscopes. Meet a tall dark handsome Virgo, and get Pisces.*

These systems make the World Wide Web the best research tool on the Internet so far, and with a thousand new Web sites a day being added, enable users to keep their heads above a tide of unrelated information. You get to the Search mechanisms in CompuServe Mosaic by clicking on the Search Button in the Toolbar, or Edit/Search Internet from the menu.

Internet, the Web, and business

Scarcely a day goes by without a UK business setting up a new Web page. New additions to browser software means that users can make credit card payments, phone calls, retrieve music and video on a Pay As You Go basis, and much more. In fact the Web is becoming the victim of its own success, as more users and more providers cram into the limited server and transmission capacity available. Most of the businesses on the Internet report high levels of interest from their small investment in setting up a Web page, and the search engines on the Web make it very easy for users to browse their way to the suppliers they need. For businesses the hardest parts of getting on the Web are finding an information provider, a graphic artist and a page compiler. Direct leads to all of these people can be found in the Internet Forums on CompuServe, including the newly set up Internet Commerce Forum. A year ago the Internet was not really the place for business due to the adolescent

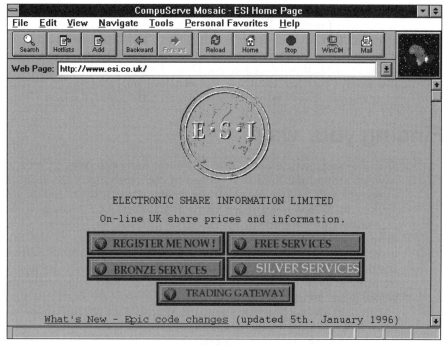

Figure 10.4   *On-line UK Share Information from ESI Ltd.*

nature of much of it. But the World Wide Web has forced the Internet to re-assess its future, and the privatization of many of the Net's technical resources mean that businesses are here to stay.

The CompuServe Mosaic browser

Mosaic is one of the most widely used WWW browsers. You use it to navigate around Internet resources by point-and-clicking on links or pointers to other services. These have HTTP addresses (HyperText Transport Protocol) which are resolved by the TCP/IP connection to take you straight to the site containing the relevant data. This method of navigation supersedes all other methods of rummaging around the Internet – it provides a seamless way of getting from server to server, and country to country, without the technology of navigation or the complexities of UNIX getting in the way. You'll see the HTTP addresses appear in the status bar of Mosaic, if you have this option turned on in the Options.

Mosaic lets you select a 'home page' to which you'll always be taken when you start the software up, although you can change this to any other page you wish. You start to navigate by clicking on text links, which appear in blue, or underlined, or both. Once you've been to that link, the text for the link turns red and may be cached in your computer's disk memory to speed up access if you return. You can click on picture icons to see graphics files displayed on screen – like a colour magazine page. You can also grab pages and save them to disk, either as text files or as HTML native files. The latest versions of Mosaic and other browsers are commonly available on CompuServe in the Internet Resources Forum. Don't forget that the HTTP prefix means you need a browser to access the site. Full instructions for setting up and using the versions of Mosaic supplied with CIM are in the next Chapter.

Finding your way

As we've seen with Gopher and Veronica, and with WAIS, your ability to navigate around the Internet is limited by the capability of the client programs or server based utilities that you use to find data. Just as Gopher supersedes Archie, so WWW supersedes Gopher and Veronica because it will hook seamlessly into Gopher or WAIS servers, if the link appears to take you there. You don't have to know about the technicalities of the Internet to make use of it, which is why WWW is so important to non-technical users. It's the first real tool (or maybe the second after the GUI Gopher clients) for traipsing around the Internet which doesn't demand a grounding in UNIX before it can be used.

The best way to find out about the World Wide Web is to jump straight onto it by clicking on the CompuServe Mosaic icon. Mosaic needs no pre-configuration although you can extensively tailor it to your needs (See Chapter 11). You'll be able to navigate around the menus with ease. If you are running a slow modem then go to View/Auto-Load Images. Deselect this before you start and the graphic images will not be sent to you unless you click on the icons.

Setting up your own Web Home Page

CompuServe makes it easy for users to set up their own WWW Home Page on the Internet via an automated Home Page Wizard. This is an authoring tool which lets for members to create a home page on the World Wide Web (WWW) through CompuServe's Personal Home Page Service. It offers drag-n-drop editing, templates, tips and context-sensitive help to assist members in the creation of their home page. The Wizard also has a "TEST" button that will display the page in a browser before placing it out on the Web. The Appendices give detailed instructions for using the Wizard. All CompuServe members are allocated up to a megabyte of free Web Page space on signing up.

Do it the hard way - Writing in HTML

HTML is the page mark up language of the World Wide Web. It lets users 'write' a Web page using either a basic text editor and a lot of brain power, or a lot of word processing power, and not much brain. The hard way to create a Web page of your own is to sit and learn the HTML text tags needed to produce a page.

Figure 10.5 *You've bought the records, now try the movie. Virgin Interactive Entertainment on the 'Net.*

Tags look like this:

```
<HTML>
<HEAD>
<TITLE>Buy this book or Die!</TITLE>
</HEAD>
<BODY>
<H1>All About East German MZ Two Stroke Motorbikes</H1>
</BODY>
</HTML>
```

and so on.

The key to successful Web page design is innovation and good graphic design. Unfortunately not many of us have both in equal quantities, so many of the amateur pages on the Web look, feel, and sound ghastly. Web Pages should be innovative too, the worst ones contain pictures of virtual celebrities like the guy next door, or Mom's favourite recipe for Instant Whip. The best Web pages provide unique information about a specific topic, with relevant links to a few carefully researched alternative sites. Bad Web pages are just a waste of time.

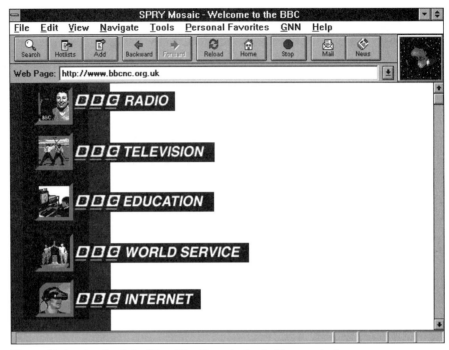

Figure 10.6   *Auntie of the 'Net. Blue Peter badge holders get in free.*

Accordingly, if you're tempted to lay out a Web page, do it on paper first and get a few second opinions. If you're a Company venturing out on to the Web go see a professional outfit such as any of the many graphic designers currently working with Web sites. Remember folks, a naff Web site can seriously damage your wealth.

The easy way to create HTML documents is to use an add-on for your word processor to do the hard work. Learning HTML basics takes about a day, at the end of which you'll have created a page which looks just like all the others. With an editor you can create really awful pages in minutes, without the disadvantage of having to learn to programme to do so.

For general information about HTML including plans for new versions, see :

http://www.w3.org/hypertext/WWW/MarkUp/MarkUp.html.

and for a comprehensive list of HTML elements see

http://www.sandia.gov/sci_compute/html_ref.html.

Look out for the HTML 3.0 specification on the Internet which will give you a good idea of the way HTML is going. The spec. is currently up to nearly 400k in length..

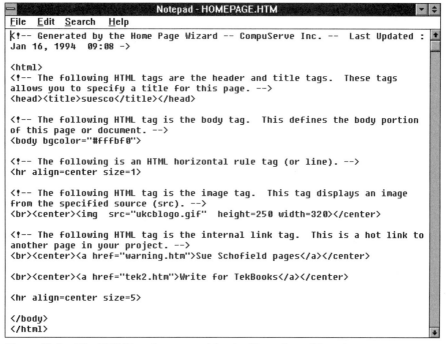

```
Notepad - HOMEPAGE.HTM
File   Edit   Search   Help
<!-- Generated by the Home Page Wizard -- CompuServe Inc. --   Last Updated :
Jan 16, 1994   09:08 ->

<html>
<!-- The following HTML tags are the header and title tags.  These tags
allows you to specify a title for this page. -->
<head><title>suesco</title></head>

<!-- The following HTML tag is the body tag.  This defines the body portion
of this page or document. -->
<body bgcolor="#fffbf0">

<!-- The following is an HTML horizontal rule tag (or line). -->
<hr align=center size=1>

<!-- The following HTML tag is the image tag.  This tag displays an image
from the specified source (src). -->
<br><center><img  src="ukcblogo.gif"  height=250 width=320></center>

<!-- The following HTML tag is the internal link tag.  This is a hot link to
another page in your project. -->
<br><center><a href="warning.htm">Sue Schofield pages</a></center>

<br><center><a href="tek2.htm">Write for TekBooks</a></center>

<hr align=center size=5>

</body>
</html>
```

Figure 10.7   *The HTML code generated by the Home Page Wizard.*

The Web and the future

Much of the development of the Internet lies within the framework provided by the multitude of servers which form the World Wide Web. At the moment the Web provides mainly static images and text, but it will become the vehicle for moving pictures, and much more. Further enhancements comes from the abilities of new Internet programming/scripting environments such as JavaScript, a combination of Netscape's LiveScript and Sun MicroSytems Hot Java. These will pave the way for the Web to become a feature rich source of information.

JavaScript can link directly to other servers running remote applications. These will make the Web blossom with home banking, home movie selection, shopping and may of the applications wondered about in the Epilogue of this book. Readers shouldn't under estimate the expansion of the Web, when my first Internet book was published in 1994 the Web was a minority access mechanism to the Internet. Today, just a over year later, the World Wide Web and the applications which run over it form the backbone of the Internet for many people. While academics and youthful users will still grope myopically through the dubious pleasures of command line interfaces, Web users wander through a dazzling world of interactive real-time applications.

More information

The best way to find out more about the Web is to start rummaging. The CompuServe Internet forums already have a WebMasters forum and a Commerce forum and both are interesting places to visit.

One useful Web index to UK sites is the Internet Magazine's 'What's On' guide. You'll find it at HTTP://WWW.EMAP.CO.UK/.

Almost all the other information you need is on the Web itself, and can be found with the Yahoo or Lycos search engines from within Mosaic. These mechanisms do move sites occasionally, so use the Mosaic Search feature to find search engines and new sites and then add them to your own Hotlists.

The On-line WWW Bibliography

Courtesy Sally Justice, South Bank University (sally@sbu.ac.uk)

Use CompuServe Mosaic to obtain these documents by typing the URL into the Web Page Window, or by using File/Open. Remember that sites come and go frequently, but these addresses did work at print time.

HTML Documentation

http://www.utirc.utoronto.ca/HTMLdocs/NewHTML/htmlindex.html
Dr. Ian Graham, University of Toronto

World Wide Web Frequently Asked Questions
http://sunsite.unc.edu/boutell/faq/www_faq.html
Thomas Boutell

A Beginner's Guide to HTML
http://www.ncsa.uiuc.edu/General/Internet/WWW/HTMLPrimer.html
National Center for Supercomputing Applications
(pubs@ncsa.uiuc.edu)

HTML Quick Reference
http://kuhttp.cc.ukans.edu/lynx_help/HTML_quick.html
Michael Grobe, the University of Kansas

Composing Good HTML
http://www.willamette.edu/html-composition/strict-html.html
James "Eric" Tilton (jtilton@willamette.edu)

HyperText Markup Language (HTML)
http://www.w3.org/hypertext/WWW/MarkUp/MarkUp.html
Daniel W.Connolly, World Wide Web Consortium (W3C) in the
Laboratory for Computer Science, MIT

HyperText Markup Language Specification
http://www.hpl.hp.co.uk/people/dsr/html/CoverPage.html
Dave Raggett, W3C

A Beginner's Guide to URLs
http://www.ncsa.uiuc.edu/demoweb/url-primer.html
Marc Andreessen (mosaic@ncsa.uiuc.edu)

Crash Course on Writing Documents for the Web
http://www.pcweek.ziff.com/~eamonn/crash_course.html
Eamonn Sullivan, PC Week

Elements of HTML Style
http://bookweb.cwis.uci.edu:8042/Staff/StyleGuide.html
JK Cohen, UC Irvine (jkcohen@uci.edu)

Hypertext Terms
http://www.w3.org/hypertext/WWW/Terms.html

The Common Gateway Interface
http://hoohoo.ncsa.uiuc.edu/cgi/
Rob McCool, NCSA (robm@ncsa.uiuc.edu)

Style Guide for Online Hypertext
http://www.w3.org/hypertext/WWW/Provider/Style/Overview.html
Tim Berners Lee, W3C (timbl@w3.org)

Entering the World Wide Web:A Guide to Cyberspace
http://www.eit.com/web/www.guide/
Kevin Hughes, Enterprise Integration Technologies

A Basic HTML Style Guide
http://guinan.gsfc.nasa.gov/Style.html
Alan Richmond, NASA GSFC

IETF HyperText Markup Language (HTML) Working Group
fftp://www.ics.uci.edu/pub/ietf/html/index.html

The HTML 3.0 Hypertext Document Format
http://www.w3.org/hypertext/WWW/Arena/tour/start.html

Daniel W. Connolly's Welcome Page
http://www.w3org/hypertext/WWW/People/Connolly/
Daniel W Connolly

The WWW Virtual Library
http://www.w3.org/hypertext/DataSources/bySubject/Overview2.html
vlib@mail.w3.org

SGML (Standard Generalized MArkup Language)
http://nearnet.gnn.com/wic/comput.39.html

The World Wide Web
http://www.w3.org/hypertext/WWW/TheProject.html
Tim Berners Lee, W3C (timbl@w3.org)

Authoring WWW Documents - Overview
http://rsd.gsfc.nasa.gov/users/delabeau/talk/
Jeff de La Beaujardiere (delabeau@camille.gsfc.nasa.gov)

HTML - Writers-Guild
http://ezinfo.ucs.indiana.edu/~awooldri/www-writers.html
awooldri@indiana.edu

The Web Developer's Journal
http://www.awa.com/nct/software/eleclead.html
NCT Web Magazine - Markland Communities Inc.

WAIS, A Sketch of an Overview
Jeff Kellem, Beyond Dreams (composer@Beyond.Dreams.ORG)

World Wide Web Primer
http|://www.vuw.ac.nz/~gnat/ideas/www-primer.html
Nathan Torkington

The Internet Index
http://www.openmarket.com/info/internet-index/current.html
Win treese (treese@OpenMarket.com)

HTML Documents: A Mosaic Tutorial
http://fire.clarkson.edu/doc/html/htut.html
Wm. Dennis Horn, Clarkson University

How To Create High Impact Documents
http://home.mcom.com/home/services_docs/impact_docs/creating-high-impact-docs.html
Netscape Communications Corporation

Bad Style Page
http://www.earth.com/bad-style/
Tony Sanders (sanders@bsdi.com)

The Web Communications Comprehensive Guide to Publishing on the Web
http://www.webcom.com/html/
Web COmmunications (support@webcom.com)

WebTechs and HTML
http://www.hal.com/~markg/WebTechs/
Mark Gaither, HaL Computer Systems (markg@hal.com)

SGML
http://www.w3.org/hypertext/WWW/MarkUp/SGML.html
Tim Berners Lee, W3C (timbl@w3org)

Perl FAQ
http://www.cis.ohio-state.edu/hypertext/faq/usenet/perl-faq/top.html
Stephen P. Potter and Tom Christiansen (perlfaq@perl.com)

PERL - Practical Extraction and Report Language
http://www-cgi.cs.cmu.edu/cgi-bin/perl-man
Larry Wall (lwall@netlabs.com)

University of Florida's Perl Archive
http://www.cis.ufl.edu/perl/
Steve Potter, Varimetrix Corporation (spp@vx.com)

* Any discrepancies in the URIs please notify Sally Justice

Some good (and bad) WWW sites

Readers please note that CompuServe does not control access to the Internet but users are reminded that anything they access on the Internet is entirely out of CompuServe's control....

Banks
Bank Of Scotland
http://www.foremost.co.uk/bos/bos.html

Lloyds Bank
http://www.lloydsbank.co.uk

Royal Bank of Scotland
http://www.royalbankscot.co.uk

World Bank
http://www.worldbank.org

Books
Banned Books
http://www.cs.cmu.edu:8001/Web/People/spok/banned-books.html

Blackwell's Bookshops
http://www.blackwell.co.uk/bookshops/

Cambridge University Press
http://www.cup.cam.ac.uk

 Future Fantasy Bookstore
http://futfan.com/home.html

Natural History Book Service
http://www.nhbs.co.uk

The Computer Bookshop
http://www.easynet.co.uk/compbook.htm

The Internet Bookshop
http://www.bookshop.co.uk/

Education
Animal Information Database
http://www.bev.net/education/SeaWorld/homepage.html

Channel 4 Schools
http://www.schools.channel4.co.uk/c4schools

Further Education Colleges in England
http://www.wwt.co.uk/colleges.html

Grolier Encyclopedia
http://www.grolier.com

Theology
Anglicans Online!
http://infomatch.com/~haibeck/anglican.html

Catholic Resources
http://www.cs.cmu.edu:8001/Web/People/spok/catholic.html

Cults
http://www.observer.co.uk

Global Jewish Networking
http://www.mofet.macam98.ac.il/~dovw/t01.html

Hell - The Online Guide
http://www.marshall.edu/~allen12/organ.html

Homosexuals and the Church
http://vector.casti.com/QRD/religion/

Islamic Resources
http://latif.com/

The Bible Gateway
http://www.calvin.edu/cgi-bin/bible

Screwball

Body Piercing
http://indyunix.iupui.edu/~dlbewley/body-p/body-p.html

Codpiece International
http://www.teleport.com/~codpiece/

Crop Circles
http://www.hub.co.uk/intercafe/cropcircle/connector.html

Disaster of the Day
http://www.ora.com:8080/cgi-bin/crash-cal

House of Lost Socks
http://www.caprica.com/~jmares/house-of-socks.html

News of the Weird
http://www.nine.org/notw/latest

Online Toilet
http://wps.com/toilet/index.html

Phantasmagoria Graveyard
http://libstaff.lib.lehigh.edu/

Squashed Bug Zoo
http://albert.ccae.virginia.edu/~dcm3c/zoo.html

Strawberry Poptart Flame Thrower (busy site)
http://cbi.tamucc.edu/~pmichaud/toast/

Wall Of Shame
http://www.milk.com/wall-o-shame/

Work

CareerMosaic
http://www.careermosaic.com/

Computer Contractor
http://www.vnu.co.uk/vnu/cc/

Employment Opportunities on the Internet -Riley's Guide
http://www.wpi.edu/~mfriley/jobguide.html

IBM UK C&TS Recruitment
http://www.europe.ibm.com/go/ukjobs/index.html

IT Jobs
http://www.britain.eu.net/vendor/jobs/main.html

JobServe
http://www.jobserve.com/

Jobs at Microsoft
http://www.microsoft.com/Jobs/

Net Contractor
http://www.demon.co.uk/syntaxis/contract/agency.html

Reed Personnel
http://www.reed.co.uk/reed/

Scribblers
This author
http://ourworld.compuserve.com/homepages/suesco/

11 The compleat Mosaic

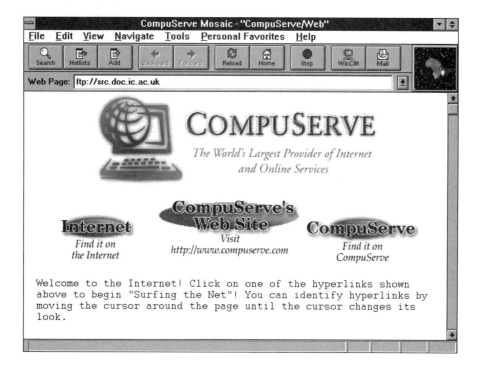

Mosaic is one of the most widely used WWW browsers and one of the first. It offers Internet users a fast and powerful way to navigate the World Wide Web. If you have a previous version you are strongly urged to update it, as the newer versions are faster and easier to use. Click 'Install' on the CD to upgrade, or use the floppy disks. Your original CIM settings will remain in place.

There are other browsers around, but Mosaic has the great advantage that it's supported by CompuServe UK Staff. You do not need to pay an extra license fee to use Mosaic as issued on the CompuServe CIM CDs and floppy disks. We've used the Windows version of Mosaic for this book. The Mac version is in the Internet Resources forum on CompuServe. Once you've got Mosaic running you can use the Search Button to search on the keyword 'mosaic' for updates and product news.

Users of WinCIM version 2.0 will find a link to Mosaic under the Special menu Option or next to the Filing Cabinet on the ToolBar and a return link to WinCIM in the Mosaic Toolbar.

Using Mosaic

You use Mosaic to navigate around Internet resources by point-and-clicking on links or pointers to other services. These have HTTP addresses (HyperText Transport Protocol) which are resolved by the TCP/IP connection to take you straight to the site containing the relevant data. This method of navigation supersedes all other methods of rummaging around the Internet – it provides a seamless way of getting from server to server, and country to country, without the technology of navigation or the complexities of UNIX getting in the way. You'll see the HTTP addresses appear in the Document title bar of Mosaic and in the Configuration options, where you select an address as your Home Page.

   The 'home page' is where you'll always be taken when you start the software up, although you can change this to any other page you wish. You start to navigate by clicking on text links, which appear in blue, or underlined, or both. Once you've been to that link, the text for the link turns red and may be cached in your computer's memory to speed up access if you return.

   You can click on picture icons to see graphics files displayed on screen – like a colour magazine page. Pages already received are cached into memory or to disk, which means that Mosaic can run adequately over a fast modem link. ('Fast' in this case means a modem to V32 bis standards, or preferably V34.) You can also grab pages and save them to disk, either as text files or as HTML native files.

Finding your way

As you'll see with Gopher and Veronica, and with WAIS, your ability to navigate around the Internet is limited by the capability of the client programs or server based utilities that you use to find data. Just as Gopher supersedes Archie, so WWW supersedes Gopher and Veronica because it will hook seamlessly into Gopher or WAIS servers if the link appears to take you there. You don't have to know about the technicalities of the Internet to make use of it, which is why WWW is so important to non-technical users. It's the first real tool for traipsing around the Internet which doesn't demand a grounding in UNIX before it can be used.

HTML

HTML is the Hypertext markup language used to construct pages for the World Wide Web. It's simple to master, and full details can be found on the Web itself. There are a number of utilities which let users construct pages in Microsoft Word, and other word processors. HTML is proving to be a great way of providing information, via the Web. This means that the Web has suddenly become the de facto standard for electronic mass picture and text publishing, and there are many interesting publications available as a result.

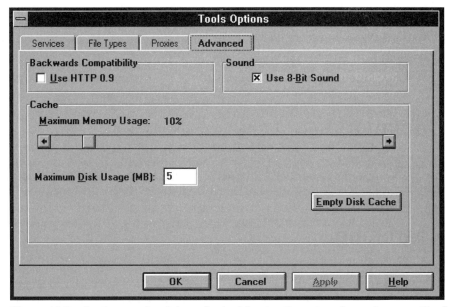

Figure 11.2 *Setting up the disk cache in Mosaic. Emptying the cache gets rid of corrupt pages.*

WWW is currently recognized as the 'killer application' that Internet providers have been waiting for. Access to the Web is being touted as the easiest way to get to most of the Internet services, and providers are distributing WWW client software on the basis that it's all you need to start working with the 'Net. In many cases they may be right, although not all Internet services are currently available via WWW. But it may well be the case that WWW provides all the information and research tools you need, in one simple-to-use package.

Proxies

Proxy servers are primarily there to let users protected with firewall security to get out onto the Net. 'Caching proxies' cache the most popular items, or take the load off main servers by receiving diverted requests from others. Mosaic can use proxy servers for FTP, Gopher, and News and those addresses should be entered into the Preferences. Proxy servers change almost daily and the best way to get an up to date list is to do a Net search for proxy. In the meantime you can use Mosaic by leaving these areas blank.

Surf City

Click on an underlined link to be transported to the site or server carrying the Web page. Links you've been to are cached, up the maximum you set in the

Cache & Network Screen. Cached links change colour to show that you've been to there and that they are stored. You can navigate backwards and forwards through your cached links with the back/forward buttons. The home button takes you to the site designated in the Preferences. If a site is taking forever to appear click the Stop button to abort the access and save your phone bill.

Bookmarks

If you find a site you can't live without then add it to your bookmark file. Bookmarks retain the Universal Resource Locator (URL) in a look-up table for fast navigation. They're called from under the Hotlists menu in Mosaic.

Searching

Use the Yahoo Search dialogue to rummage around the Internet for items of interest. The search mechanism will accept boolean searches and is probably the easiest way to use the Internet for research. You can search for files, documents, noises, movies and pictures. If you've installed the correct Helper Applications Mosaic will un-stuff your files or play back your film clips for you. Use the search mechanism to pick up your first few gigabytes of Bookmark files.

Other search engines can be used to track down sites containing keywords or listings of related sites. The Yahoo search engine lists sites by subject so that you can navigate by point and click around your topic. The Lycos system crawls around Web sites and logs them to its database. When a new site is found the crawler visits the sites in the links too, and adds those, automatically building and maintaining an ever-growing database. A third system called Savvy-Search rummages around other search engine sites, gathering information by a variety of methods, including using other search mechanisms where needed. All of them can be accessed indirectly, from the Search button in Mosaic.

These systems make the World Wide Web the best research tool on the Internet so far, and enable users to keep their heads above a tide of unrelated information.

Helper applications

Mosaic is only half a Killer Application. You'll need file unstuffers, GIF viewers, WAV file gizmos and a heap of other applications to provide the other half. Mosaic will automatically call the other applications when it needs them. The effect is clever, but only when you've completed your collection. Again you can get all the file viewers and noisemakers you want from the Internet. Search for them from within Mosaic or the Internet Resources Forum. You set them up in the options/configuration dialogue.

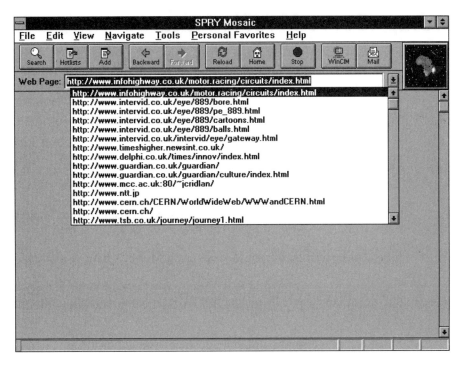

Figure 11.3 *Mosaic keeps a track of each session under Personal Favourites. This is a track of the session used to capture the screenshots for this book.*

Working with CompuServe Mosaic

CompuServe Mosaic is a graphical, sophisticated Internet Browser application, allowing you to access the Internet World Wide Web also referred to as WWW, W3, or the Web

Mosaic features Hotlists and advanced menu support, allowing you to easily incorporate your own Internet "finds" into Mosaic and quickly jump to the information you want to access. Fonts, colors, viewers, and performance are easily configured using integrated configuration screens.

NB. These instructions are for version 04.00 shipped with WinCIM 2, but should work with earlier versions. Users who haven't upgraded will find most of the configuration options in the Configuration Menu. Later versions split configuration into two parts under View/Options and Tools/Options. Mosaic is constantly being updated so the version you have may differ slightly from that illustrated here.

If you don't understand terms such as Gopher, Telnet etc. then browse the following Chapters, and then return here to see how Mosaic works with these services.

CompuServe Mosaic features

* Support for in-line GIF and JPEG graphics.

* Use the Hotlists feature to group World Wide Web pages into folders and subfolders, so that you can easily revisit them. You can also have favorite Hotlists appear in the Mosaic menu bar for quick access.

* Configure Mosaic preferences (colors, fonts, viewers, default home page) via a straightforward Configuration dialog.

* Control how and how often screen images are loaded.

* Read and post news to USENET newsgroups using Mosaic's built-in news support. Built-in News support can display threaded messages.

* Send electronic mail from Mosaic, using Mosaic's built-in send mail feature.

* Connect to the last World Web pages you accessed, via the History list or the pull down Document Title/Document URL menus. Caching keeps documents in memory.

* Search for information in any document you are browsing.

* Save, edit, or copy HTML document source code.

* Drag and drop Mosaic documents to other Windows applications.

* Use GIF graphics you find on the World Wide Web as your Windows desktop wallpaper.

* Use Kiosk mode to hide the Toolbar and other information. Ideal for presentations, it also allows you to set up Mosaic for "unattended" use.

* Quickly load and save documents and graphics, and view Mosaic hyperlink information, with the Mosaic Quick Menu feature.

* Print Mosaic documents, including in-line images.

What is the World Wide Web made of?

When people talk about the World Wide Web, they are often referring to HTML documents located on the Internet. HTML (HyperText Markup Language) documents, also referred to as home pages, attractively display information (text and graphics) and allow you to easily access other documents across the Internet.

The World Wide Web is made up of the (constantly growing) collection of

Figure 11.4   *You can add favourite sites to the Hotlist, then edit them at a later date.*

WWW home pages available on the Internet, as well as other Internet resources such as ftp, gopher and news. The World Wide Web environment was designed to incorporate a great many resources, so information is inter-linked (hence, a Web). Therefore, you can click on an item on a home page to access an ftp server or gopher server, or another home page.

Many of the home pages you can find on the World Wide Web lead in turn to other interesting home pages; the amount and scope of the information you can find using Mosaic is quite impressive.

Starting Mosaic

Start Mosaic by clicking on the Mosaic icon or by selecting it from the Services menu in CIM. Mosaic will immediately start connecting you to a home page, so that you have somewhere to start finding other World Wide Web resources. (If you start Mosaic from CIM you must have the Winsock option selected in the Special menu). You can also start Mosaic by selecting Special/Go from CIM and typing in the URL of the site you want to visit. CIM will start up Mosaic and GO directly to the site or page you want'

You can change the home page that Mosaic automatically connects to by choosing Configuration in the View/Options menu and changing the Home Page option.

The Mosaic console contains a lot of information. The Toolbar at the top of the Console contains buttons that serve as shortcuts for Mosaic menu items. The Status Bar at the bottom of the Console displays the locations of resources you connect to, as well as indicating when a transfer is in progress or a graphic is being loaded.

Below the Toolbar is the Document Title Bar, containing the Document Title and Document URL drop down lists. The two lists contain a listing of the last several documents you've accessed. The lists are identical, but one shows the Title of the document (such as "The Internet Movie Database") and the other shows that document's URL (http://www.msstate.edu:80/Movies). You can go back to any of the displayed documents by choosing its title or URL from the lists. You can change the number of documents that are displayed in these lists using the Configuration option in the Options menu.

The Document Title Bar also contains a status icon, which moves when a document is being loaded or a graphic is being transferred (roughly, it indicates that Mosaic is busy.)

Exiting Mosaic

You can exit Mosaic by choosing Exit from the File menu. You can also double-check on the Windows System Menu to exit Mosaic. If you are currently retrieving a new Mosaic document, it is recommended that you wait to exit until that document is retrieved, or stop retrieving the document by clicking the Stop button or choosing Cancel Current Task from the History menu.

Browsing with Mosaic

World Wide Web uses hyperlinks (also referred to as anchors or hot spots) to allow you to jump to other resources. Hyperlinks are indicated by blue, underlined text, or by graphics surrounded by a blue border (you can change the color that is used). Another way to tell that you are on a hyperlink is to highlight the text or graphic with your mouse. The mouse will turn into a pointing hand, and information about the hyperlink URL (Uniform Resource Locator) will appear in the Status Bar. This URL information tells you where the resource you are highlighting is located and provides additional information about the resource.

You can then click on a hyperlink to connect to another Mosaic document. The new document will be opened (you will see the radar indicator in the upper right hand corner of your Mosaic Console begin to spin). If at any time you need to stop loading in a document, you can click the Stop button or choose Cancel Current Task from the Navigate menu. You can continue to browse through WWW documents by simply clicking on the hyperlinks you find in the document. You can also travel through documents you encounter as described below.

Jumping back and forward

You can click on the Back button (the third button on the Toolbar) to move back to the last document you viewed. The Forward button (the fourth button on the Toolbar) can move you forward after you have moved back. You can also type B for Back or F for Forward, or choose Back and Forward from the Navigate menu.

Opening previous documents

The Document Title: and Document URL: drop-down lists, found under the Toolbar, contain a listing of the last several documents you've accessed in this session. The lists are identical, but one shows the title of the document (such as "GNN Home") and the other shows that document's URL

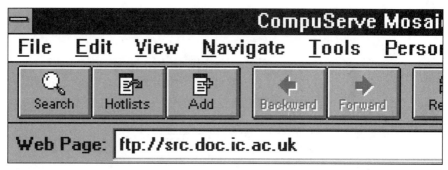

Figure 11.5   *Using Mosaic for FTP. Put the URL in the box and press enter . . .*

(http://nearnet.gnn.com/gnn.html). You can go back to any of the displayed documents by choosing its title or URL from the lists.

You can also click History to access the History dialog. The History dialog allows you to view and easily access documents you've already accessed in this session. You will see a hierarchical view of the documents you have accessed. If you want to move to a previous document, select the document you want to go back to, and click on the Load button.

At any time, you can click the Home button on the Toolbar, or choose Home from the Navigate menu to return to the document defined as your Home Page. When you start using Mosaic, a home page is defined as your default home page; you can set up a new home page (or set Mosaic to start without opening a home page) using Configuration in the View/Options menu.

You can reload the current WWW document at any time by clicking the Reload button or choosing Reload from the Navigate menu. You might want to do this if the document did not load properly.

Using Mosaic's quick menu

Mosaic features an easy to use menu that can help you easily access load, save, and get information about a document.

Mosaic's Quick Menu is accessed using the right mouse button. With your mouse pointer over a hyperlink, click the Right mouse button. The Quick Menu appears. The Quick Menu will be different depending on whether you have selected on a regular hyperlink, an image, or an image that also leads to a hyperlink. If you selected a regular hyperlink, the Document options below will display; if you selected an image, the Image Options below will display, If you selected an image that also leads to a hyperlink, you will see all the listed options, since the object is treated as both an image and a hyperlink.

The quick menu options

Load Document Loads the document that is pointed to by the hyperlink. Choosing this option in exactly the same as clicking on the URL with your left mouse button.

Figure 11.6   *Ths means try using FTP:/ /yourname@compuserve.com/FTP://sitename. Lets try nic.switch.ch as a site . . .*

Save Document to Disk Saves the document that is pointed to by the hyperlink (without loading the document). The document is saved with the extension .htm and can later be opened using the Open URL command.

Get Document Information Displays the document header information; i.e. the resource type, size, full pathname, etc. This is a good way to decide whether you will want to load in a document (and whether you have the appropriate viewers for it), before actually loading it.

Copy Document URL Copies the Document URL (i.e. http://www.compuserve. com/) to the Windows Clipboard, so that it can be pasted into other Windows applications (or other Mosaic dialogs).

Load Image Same as the Load Document option, above, but loads the currently selected image. This is a useful option to use in conjunction if you have turned off the Autoload In-line Image option; see the next section for information.

Save Image to Disk Saves the displayed image to disk.

Get Image Information Displays the image header information; i.e. image type, size, full pathname, etc. As with Document Information, above, this will help you decide whether you want to load in an image.

Copy Image URL Same as the Copy Document URL option, but copies the images URL to the Windows Clipboard.

Viewing in-line images

Mosaic home pages frequently display graphical in-line images. By default, Mosaic will load in text, then load in in-line images; you can control whether

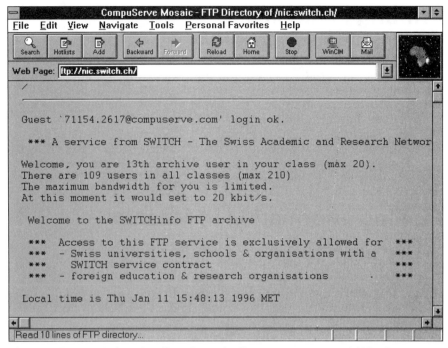

Figure 11.7 ... *And you're allowed into the Swiss site, just you and 109 other users.*

or not the in-line images are loaded, and how often they are loaded, using View/Options in Mosaic. If you are using Mosaic over a slow connection, you may want to change these settings. You may also want to change these settings if you are not interested in viewing the images.

The Autoload In-line Images option found in the View/Options menu and in the <Configuration> dialog will allow you to specify whether or not images are loaded. If you choose not to use this option (due to a slow connection, or other reason), you can load in images that you need selectively using Mosaic's Quick Menu feature. See the previous section for information on using this feature. Some images in Mosaic are used as hyperlinks; if you turn off Autoload In-line Images, most home pages will display an alternate method for accessing the hyperlinks. However, some images, called image maps, have multiple hyperlinks included in them; in these cases, you will often have no other way of accessing hyperlinks.

When you connect to a Mosaic document, Mosaic loads in the entire document, using image "placeholders" for any images in the document. Mosaic will then load in the images one by one, and redraw the screen (replacing the place-holders with images) as images are loaded in.

You can change how often the screen is redrawn by changing the When loading images, redraw every minutes option found in Mosaic's <Configuration> dialog. See "Configuring Mosaic Options" for more information on using this option.

Printing in Mosaic

You can print the information in a document to your printer using the Print command in the File menu. Click the Setup button in the <Print> dialog to specify the printer you want to print to, and to set up different options for that printer.

If you want to see how the output will look, you can choose Print Preview in the File menu to see a preview of how the document will print.

The Print Margins command in the File menu allows you to specify the margins to use when printing Mosaic documents to a printer; by default, no margins are used. Set the Top, Bottom, Left and Right margins to the settings you prefer.

Finding information in Mosaic

You can search a WWW document for particular text using the Find command. Click the Find option in the Edit menu, and type the text you want to search for in the dialog that appears. The search will occur from the top of the document to the bottom. If you want to search for additional occurrences of the text, you should choose Find Next in the <Find> dialog.

Using hotlists

One of Mosaic's strongest features is its ability to organize the information that you find on the World Wide Web. There are so many documents out there with useful jumps to resources you might be interested in, that it is common to want to access these documents again and again. You can save these documents and open them again later (see "Saving Documents in Mosaic" later in this chapter), but Mosaic provides an easier way to re-access documents.

Mosaic's Hotlists can be used to remember WWW document locations, so that you can easily locate and access them. You can group Hotlists by subject (Games, Sports, Weather, Fun Stuff) or by any other criteria (if several people use one computer, they might each have their own hotlist).

Hotlists you create can then be accessed two ways: they can be accessed with a couple of mouse clicks from the convenient Hotlists dialog, or you can make Hotlists into drop-down menus, so that you can choose them directly from the Mosaic menu bar.

The Hotlists dialog

You work with Hotlists in the <Hotlists> dialog, (accessed by pressing the Hotlists button or by choosing Hotlists in the File menu). The <Hotlists> dialog initially will show all the different Hotlists you have. Mosaic comes with several Hotlists pre-loaded. You can remove any of the provided Hotlists, or add additional Hotlists of your own.

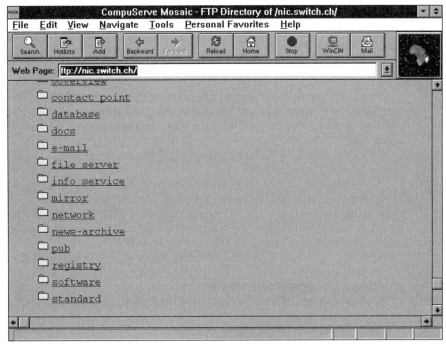

Figure 11.8   *Remote Directories are presented as yellow folders. Try PUB first, as it means Public.*

The Hotlist itself is shown as a flaming document in the <Hotlist> dialog. Initially, Hotlists may be shown closed; you can open up (expand) the Hotlist by double clicking on the Hotlist icon. Each Hotlist can contain many WWW documents, or it can contain folders that contain additional documents (you can use folders and subfolders to organize your documents any way you want).

In the <Hotlists> dialog, you can create new Hotlists, add new Hotlist items, edit your existing items, or delete them.

At any time, you can check Use Hotlist as menu item to have a Hotlist added as a menu item. You can add as many menu items as can fit in your Mosaic menu bar. When you choose this option, the Hotlist icon in the <Hotlists> dialog will change to a dialog containing the letter H. If you add a Hotlist as a menu item, any folders within that Hotlist will appear as menu items that have sub-menu items beneath them.

Creating a new hotlist

Choose Hotlists from the File menu, or click the Hotlist button on the Toolbar. The <Hotlists> dialog, described earlier, will appear.

Click the Open/New button. You will see a Windows file open dialog. (You could specify the name of an existing Hotlist at this point, to open and load it into the <Hotlists> dialog.)

Choose a filename for your Hotlist, and click OK. This must be a legal DOS filename (using up to 8 characters, with the extension .hot).

The next dialog asks you to specify a name for this Hotlist. This can be any name you want (keep in mind that you may want to use this Hotlist as a Mosaic menu, so you might want to keep the name short.) Type a name, and click OK.

The Hotlist will be created, and you will see it appear in the Hotlists dialog (as a "flaming" document).

As mentioned earlier, you may want to create folders and subfolders to help organize your information. To do this, click Add and specify Folder in the dialog that appears. (To create a subfolder, first highlight the folder you want to add a subfolder to). You will be asked to name the folder. Give a name for the folder and click OK; the folder will be created.

Now that you have a Hotlist, you can begin to add documents to it.

Adding a Document to a Hotlist

There are several different ways to add documents to a Hotlist:

* Add the current document to a Hotlist.

* Drag and drop a document URL (address) into a Hotlist

* Copy a document URL (address) and paste it into a Hotlist.

* Add a document to a Hotlist manually.

The first three options allow you to add a document to your Hotlist without having to know or remember the document's URL (the document's "address", described in the next section). These options are described below.

Adding the Current Document to a Hotlist In Mosaic, display the document that you want to add to a Hotlist. You can then add it to the current Hotlist, or add it to any of your Hotlists, as described below.

Add using the Add Document option Click Add Document to Hotlist in the Navigate menu to add the document to the Hotlist you are currently using. The document will be added to the end of the last Hotlist or folder you selected. You can open the <Hotlists> dialog if you are not sure which Hotlist is currently selected.

Add using the Hotlists Dialog:
1) Click the Hotlist button, or choose Hotlists from the File menu.

2) Select the Hotlist (or Hotlist folder) to which you want to add the current document.

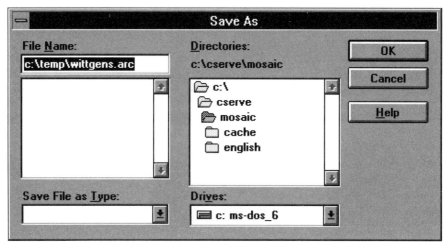

Figure 11.9   *When you find the file you need Mosaic will save it to disk.*

3) Click Add (or click Insert to insert the document under the currently selected document). You will be asked whether you want to add a document or folder; select Document. You will see a dialog containing the Name and URL of the document you are currently viewing. If you wish, you can change the name of the document. Do not change the URL!

4) Click OK. The document will be added to the Hotlist you selected.

Drag and Drop a Document URL into a Hotlist.
You can drag and drop a document into a Hotlist, if you wish. The hyperlink ("jump") to the document should be displayed on the screen in order to do this.

1) Click the Hotlist button, or choose Hotlists from the File menu. Open the Hotlist and folder you want to move the document into. Move the <Hotlists> dialog on your screen so that you can also see the hyperlink for the document you want to add to the Hotlist.

2) Select a document hyperlink by holding down your mouse until the cursor changes to a document icon, and drag it to the Hotlist or Hotlist folder you want. You will be prompted to give the Hotlist a name.

Copy and Paste a Document URL to the <Add Hotlist> Dialog

If you wish, you can copy a document's URL information to the Windows Clipboard and then easily paste it in the <Add Hotlist> dialog, so that you do not have to type a long URL in the <Add Hotlist> dialog.
You can copy a document URL from any Windows application by using the Copy command in that application. You can also copy a document URL

that you see on your Mosaic screen by clicking on the document URL with your right mouse button and holding it down, then selecting the Copy Document URL option in the Quick Menu that appears.

You can then open the <Hotlists> dialog, select the Hotlist and/or folder that you want to add the document to, and click the Add button. Choose Document to add a new document. In the <Add Document> dialog, put your cursor in the URL field, and click Ctrl-V (the Paste shortcut key) to paste the document URL into the URL field.

Adding a Document to a Hotlist Manually

You might do this if you want to add a document to a Hotlist, but do not currently have the document open. To do this, you need to know the URL (address) for each document; URLs are described in more detail in the next section. For instance, someone may give you a list of WWW documents containing travel information. You might create a Travel folder in one of your Hotlists, and add all the documents to it. This process is described below.

1) Click the Hotlist button, or choose Hotlists from the File menu.

2) Select the Hotlist to which you want to add a document by highlighting it using your mouse.

3) Click Add. You will be asked whether you want to add a document or folder; select Document. You will see the <Add Document> dialog. If you currently have a document open, the information about that document will appear in this dialog.

For the Document name:, type any name you want for this document. It should be a name that will help you recognize this file.

For the Document URL: field, type the Document's URL. See the "Understanding URLs" section for more information on using URLs.

4) Click OK. The document will be added to the Hotlist you selected.

Exporting Hotlists

You can, if you choose, export any of your Hotlists as an HTML file (i.e. a Mosaic-format document). This feature might be useful if, for instance, you have compiled a Hotlist with an interesting collection of Mosaic home pages, and want to put it up on a World Wide Web server for others to access. Or you may find it handy to use the Hotlist as your default home page, so that you immediately have a list of your favorite resources available when you start Mosaic.

You export a Hotlist by clicking the Export button in the <Hotlists> dialog. This dialog prompts you for a name and location for the HTML file. Select the directory you want for the file, and assign a name to the file. The file will be saved with the extension .htm by default.

After you export the file, you can open the file by using the File Open

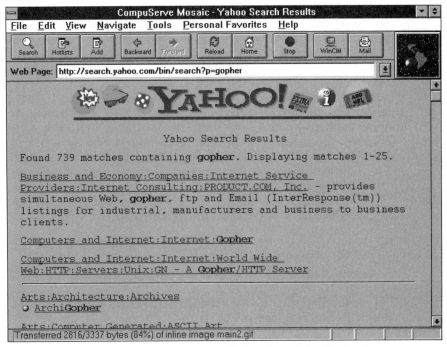

Figure 11.10   *Searching with Mosaic and Gopher, first find a Gopher Site, then add it to your Hotlist . . .*

command. Your Hotlist will be displayed as a Mosaic document which resembles your Hotlist and contains hyperlink jumps for documents in your Hotlist.

Opening Local HTML Documents

You may need to open a local HTML file at some point. A local HTML file is a file on your PC containing HTML code. This could be a Mosaic document that you saved using the Document Source command, or a Mosaic document that someone wrote and gave to you. A Local File usually has extension .htm.

You can open a Local File by choosing Open Local File in the File menu or clicking the Open button on the Toolbar. A file open dialog will appear, displaying any files in the current directory with extension .htm. Specify the name and path for the local file, and click OK. Mosaic will try to open the file you specified.

Mosaic also supports drag and drop for HTML documents. Just drag an HTML document from your Windows File Manager to the Mosaic Console; the document will automatically be opened.

Opening Documents using URLs

Mosaic locates documents by using URLs, Uniform Resource Locators. URLs are a standard notation for WWW resources, designed to be able to identify information stored on a variety of machines, in a variety of different ways. A URL can point to resources such as an HTML document (a WWW home page), an ftp server, a gopher server, or a local document. When you access a document in Mosaic, you will see the URL for that document shown in the Document URL: field displayed below the Mosaic Toolbar.

If you know a document's URL (Uniform Resource Locator; a standard "address" for WWW documents), you can access a document directly by typing the document's URL. If someone tells you the URL of a popular WWW site on the Internet, you can go to it directly using that URL. You will also need to know a document's URL to set it up in a Hotlist or as a default home page. Opening documents using their URLs is described below.

If you know the URL of a resource, you can access it using the <Open URL> dialog, as described below.

1) Click Open URL in the File menu You will see the <Open URL> dialog.

The most common URL you will specify in the <Open URL> dialog is the URL for an HTML home page. This is always preceded by http:// followed by the address of the HTML document (e.g. http://www.bakerstreet.com/221B.html)

2) Type the URL you want to connect to and click OK. If the URL is valid, Mosaic should begin connecting to it.

You can paste a document URL into this dialog. Use the Copy command in the application from which you wish to copy the URL, and click Ctrl-V to paste the URL.

Alternately, you can type (or paste) a URL directly into the Document URL: field located underneath the Status Bar. Click [Enter] to load the URL.

Understanding URLs

URLs typically provide information about a resource type, location, and path.

You might find a document called "Unsolved Cases" with a URL of

http://www.bakerstreet.com/sholmes/cases/unsolved.html

This URL can be broken into three components

http: //www.bakerstreet.com /sholmes/cases/unsolved.html

or

Resource Type //Resource Location /Resource Pathname

These three portions are described below.

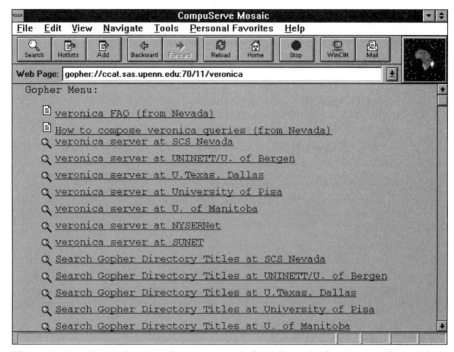

Figure 11.11   *Use a Veronica Server to search for 'Monty Python' or your keywords.*

Resource Type

The Resource Type tells you the type of server on which the resource resides. The resource type is actually the kind of protocol will be used when retrieving the document.

WWW resource types and formats include:

http://HTTP (HyperText Transfer Protocol) Server. This is a site containing hypertext WWW documents.

ftp://FTP (File Transfer Protocol) Server.

file://Local HTML File (also sometimes used to denote FTP Servers).

telnet://Telnet Server.

gopher://Gopher Server.

wais://WAIS Server (not directly supported in Mosaic)

news:USENET news site

The news: URL uses a slightly different format; it takes the format news:newsgroup.name, since you already have a news server defined in Mosaic (using the <Configuration> option).

Resource Location

This is the Internet address of the machine where the resource resides.

In the example above, www.bakerstreet.com is the name of the World Wide Web server that contains the home page. In some cases, you will be able to tell where a machine is located based on the address; for instance, www.websites.de would be a home page in Germany; .de is an extension for home pages in Germany.

Resource Pathname {filename}

In many cases, the URL for a document or other resource contains a full pathname for a file. If you're familiar with DOS or UNIX pathnames, the path in a URL is very similar. (Note that URL paths always use the forward slash /).

In the example above, the path is /sholmes/cases/unsolved.htm. Note that the path for a home page can contain a filename, but does not have to; /sholmes/cases/ is also a valid pathname. Certain URLs, such as a URL for an FTP site, may not contain a pathname at all; i.e. ftp://ftp.bakerstreet.com.

Sample URLs

Some sample URLs are shown below:

http://www.federation.gov/Enterprise/Missions

ftp://ftp.circe.com

ftp://jwatson@ftp.bakerstreet.com

file://localhost/c:\mosdocs\myhome.htm

telnet://odysseus.circe.com:70

gopher://gopher.deathstar.com:70/11/fun/Movies

news:alt.tv.seinfeld

For advanced information on URLs, a URL primer is available from NCSA on the NCSA home page, at http://www.ncsa.uiuc.edu/demoweb/url-primer.html.

Accessing FTP, Gopher, news, and mail

Although you may navigate principally between HTML documents ("home pages") when using Mosaic, you can also use it to access other Internet resources such as ftp and gopher sites and USENET news. It can also be used to send out but not to receive electronic mail.

Mosaic has built-in support for FTP, gopher, Internet mail, and news. The sections that follow describe when and how Mosaic's ftp, gopher, news, and mail functions work.

FTP using Mosaic

You will frequently find FTP (File Transfer Protocol) sites when using the Internet. FTP sites are remote computers that store files which you can download. Mosaic can be used to browse and retrieve files from FTP sites. When you access an FTP site using Mosaic, the files on that site will be displayed in a hierarchical folder format in the Mosaic Console.

You will only see two types of items, folders (directories) and files. You can navigate through folders by double clicking on them to move deeper into the folders; if you want to move back, click on the up arrow shown at the top of the folder list.

When you double click on the name of a file, Mosaic will automatically download (copy) the file to your \...\DATA directory, using the displayed filename.

Getting to an ftp site:

You may find hyperlinks that take you to ftp (file transfer protocol) sites when you're using Mosaic. You can also, if you wish, connect to an FTP site directly if you know its URL (address). The format for an ftp URL is:

ftp://ftp.narnia.com

where ftp.narnia.com is the site you want to reach using ftp.

Alternately, if a username is required to ftp to the site, you would type

ftp://edmund@ftp.narnia.com

where edmund is your username on the remote site. You will be prompted for a password. Alternately, you can provide the password using the following format: ftp://edmund:cslewis@ftp.narnia.com, where cslewis is edmund's password on ftp.narnia.com.

Gopher Using Mosaic

Gopher sites are also found on the Internet; these are lists of files, similar to FTP sites. However, in addition to files that you can download, Gopher contains hierarchical lists of resources like searchable databases, graphics files, and telnet sites, that you can immediately connect to and use. Mosaic can be used to browse and retrieve files from Gopher sites, as well as access information that Gopher resources point to.

The gopher site will be displayed in a hierarchical file format in the Mosaic Console. You will see folders (directories), and several different types of items: files such as image files, sound files, and applications; database search tools; links to telnet and 3270 sites. Double clicking on a file in gopher will either download it to your \...\DATA directory or will open it, depending on whether you have a Viewer for that file configured in Mosaic (Mosaic examines the gopher file extensions to decide which viewer to use). If you click on a telnet or tn3270 link, Mosaic will use the telnet or tn3270 application defined in the <Viewers> dialog.

Getting to a gopher site:

You may find hyperlinks to gopher sites when you're using Mosaic, or you can connect to a site directly if you know its URL (address).

Gopher URLs take the form:

gopher://gopher.narnia.com

where gopher.narnia.com is the gopher site you want to reach.

News using Mosaic

USENET news is a forum for discussion (similar to a bulletin board system, but on a greater scale) that is found on the Internet. Some World Wide Web home pages contain links to newsgroups that you may wish to access. You may also want to directly connect to news using Mosaic; see the end of this section for information on directly connecting to news.

Mosaic allows you to access news Mosaic's built-in news function. If you use CompuServe Mosaic's built-in news function, you should select the Use Built-in Mail/News option in the Mosaic configuration dialogs in order to have Mosaic use the built-in news function.

Whichever method you use to read and post news, you will have to have access to a News Server to read News. For CompuServe users this will normally be news.compuserve.com

Reading news using Mosaic's built-in news function:

When you list newsgroups, descriptions of all the newsgroups will be displayed; to disable this feature, uncheck Extended News Listing in the <Configuration> dialog. Note that unchecking this option will disable threading in news.

Once you have connected to News using Mosaic, and display a newsgroup Mosaic displays news articles as bulleted items on the screen. Articles are

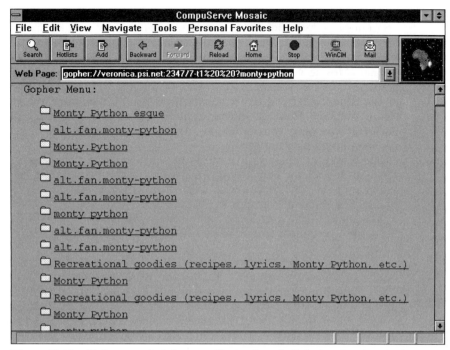

Figure 11.12   *If the server isn't busy you'll get a list of all the hits found in GopherSpace.*
Click one to go the site holding the file . . .

usually grouped together by threads, articles posted in response to an original
article will be shown indented below that article and will be identified using
the poster's name, rather than an article subject.

Mosaic displays hyperlinks at the top of the screen that you can click on to
navigate through threads. When you are viewing an article that is part of a
thread, you will see either Next thread or Next article in thread and Previous
article in thread, depending on where you are in the thread.

To view an article, simply click on its title in the article list. You can use the
Back button on the Toolbar to move back to the original article.

Posting news articles using Mosaic's built-in news function:

You can add an article to a newsgroup (post an article) in Mosaic. Note that
you must have rights to post on the current news server in order to post a
news article.

When you are viewing a list of news articles in Mosaic, you will see a Post
to newsgroup hyperlink at the top of the screen. Clicking on this hyperlink
will produce a News posting dialog allowing you to post a news article.

When you are viewing an individual article in Mosaic, you will see a Follow-up to message hyperlink. This also produces the News posting dialog, but will automatically include the text of the currently displayed article in that dialog (using standard follow-up format).

The <Mosaic News> dialog will be displayed, allowing you to post news messages to a News Server.

The Sender field will be filled out automatically with your e-mail address; this is obtained from the Email Address option in the CIM Configuration dialog. If this value is incorrect, you should change it; otherwise, no one will be able to reply to your posting.

The Newsgroup field will be filled out with the name of the newsgroup you were viewing, or the newsgroup you specified using the newspost: URL. You can change this field, if you wish to post the article to a different newsgroup, or add additional newsgroups to post the message to.

The Subject field is optional (but strongly recommended); fill this out with the subject of your message. (This will be filled out automatically if this is a follow up posting).

The Keywords field allows you to specify keywords that will appear in the header of the news posting; these keywords are used by some news readers when searching for messages. Some sample keywords are: politics, simpsons, jobs.

Type the message body in the space provided. All standard Windows editing keys (arrow keys, Home, End, Delete, etc.) are supported.

You can drag and drop text files from Windows File Manager into your news article, if you wish. To do this, drag the file and drop it into the text window of the Mosaic News dialog. The text in the file you dragged and dropped will display in that window; you can then edit the text or add new text, as desired.

You can also indicate the MIME type of the item you dragged and dropped. Currently, only text files are supported; text/plain will be selected by default. You can change the MIME type to another text type, if desired.

Click Send to post your news article.

Directly posting a News article:
You can post or follow-up a news article directly using a URL, with the following syntax:

newspost:newsgroupname{,newsgroupname,newsgroupname} {/followup}

where

newsgroupname is the name of the newsgroup you want to post to (you can specify multiple newsgroups by separating them by commas)

/followup indicates that you want the posting to be a follow-up posting and include the currently displayed article text (if no article is displayed when you do this, no text will be included)

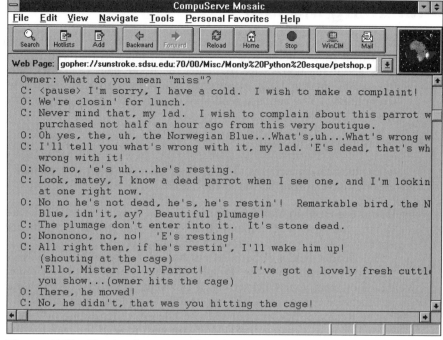

Figure 11.13 *Here's the script for the Parrot sketch, from the gopher at sunstroke.sdsu.edu. How we laughed . . .*

Examples:

newspost:alt.tv.seinfeld

newspost:rec.bicycles,rec.sports.cycling

newspost:alt.suburbia/followup

Connecting to a newsgroup directly:

You can directly connect to a newsgroup using Mosaic by specifying the news URL in Mosaic dialogs (such as the Open URL dialog) in the format

news:alt.smurfs

where alt.smurfs is the name of the newsgroup you want to access.

If you use Mosaic's built-in news function, wildcards are also supported. This means that you can list multiple newsgroups by typing news:* to list all the newsgroups on a news server, or news:alt.tv.* to show all the newsgroups with names starting with alt.tv, etc.

Mail using Mosaic

Mosaic can be used to send out electronic mail. You may find hyperlinks that send mail (many home pages provide such links so that you can send feedback about the home page, or reach the home page's creator). Mosaic also has a link in the Help menu that allows you to send feedback mail to CompuServe. You can also send mail directly from Mosaic by choosing Open URL in the File menu, and typing

mailto:lucy@narnia.com

where lucy@narnia.com is the e-mail address you want to send mail to. Later versions have a Mail button in the Toolbar.

Using the Built-in Mail function:

When you use a command that sends out mail, a mail dialog will appear allowing you to compose a mail message.

The Sender field will be filled out automatically with your e-mail address; this is obtained from the Email Address option in the <Configuration> dialog or from your CIM setting. If this value is incorrect, you should change it; otherwise the recipient will not be able to reply to your mail.

The Recipient field may already be filled out, depending on how Mail was started. You can change this field, if you wish to send the mail to other people. This field only accepts standard e-mail addresses (such as lucy@narnia.com). A CC field is also provided; you can type e-mail addresses of other people to whom you want to send a copy of the mail.

The Subject field is optional; fill this out with the subject of your message.

Type the message body in the space provided. All standard Windows editing keys (arrow keys, Home, End, Delete, etc.) are supported.

You can drag and drop text files from Windows File Manager into your mail message, if you wish. To do this, drag the file and drop it into the text window of the Mosaic mail dialog. The text in the file you dragged and dropped will display in that window; you can then edit the text or add new text, as desired.

You can also indicate the MIME type of the item you dragged and dropped. Currently, only text files are supported; text/plain will be selected by default. You can change the MIME type to another text type, if desired.

Saving documents, files, and images

You may sometimes want to save documents, files, and images you find using Mosaic. There are several different ways to save items in Mosaic:

* Use the Mosaic Quick Menu to save an item to disk.

* Drag and drop the item to another application (such as the File Manager), or your Windows desktop.

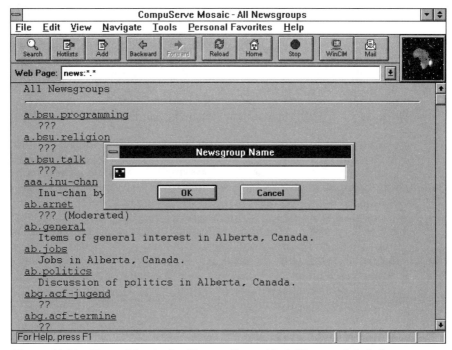

Figure 11.14 *Using Mosaic for Usenet. Go to Tools/News and find the newsgroup you're interested in from the full list . . .*

* Use the Load to Disk Mode command to save the item to disk.

These methods of saving documents are described below.

Saving Items using Mosaic's Quick Menu You can use Mosaic's Quick Menu feature (described earlier in this chapter) to save a document, file, or image to your PC. Click on the item's hyperlink with your right mouse button and hold it down, then select the Save Document to Disk or Save Image to Disk option (whichever is appropriate) in the Quick Menu that appears.

Dragging and Dropping Mosaic Items You can drag and drop Mosaic items to the Windows File Manager, or to other applications that support drag and drop, such as Microsoft Word. When you drag items to the File Manager, they will be saved as files on your system. When you drag items to a Windows application, they will be treated in the same way as other items dropped in that application. You can also drag images to your desktop, and use them as your Windows wallpaper.

When you drag and drop images from Mosaic, they will be saved as bitmap images, regardless of their original format. If you want to save an image in its original format, save the image by using the Quick Menu option, as described above.

To drag and drop a Mosaic item:
1) With your mouse cursor over a hyperlink, click and hold down the mouse button until the cursor changes from a pointing finger to a document icon.

2) Continue holding down the cursor, and drag the item to its destination. If the image cannot be dropped on that location, the cursor will change to a symbol, and you will not be able to drop the item. You may be prompted for a name (and path) for the item, depending on the type of the dropped item.

If you drag it to the File Manager, the item will be copied into the directory where it was dropped. Note that images will always be saved as .BMP files.

If you drag it to another Windows application, the item will be treated the way dropped items are typically treated in that application. You can only drop items on applications that support drag and drop.

If you drag an image to the Windows desktop (not an open application), you will be asked to confirm that you want to use the image as wallpaper. You will then be prompted to save the image. You can change the name that is suggested, but do not store the image in a directory other than the \WINDOWS directory. When you save the image, it will immediately be used as wallpaper; see the Windows Control Panel, Desktop option to change the Wallpaper or how it is displayed.

Load to disk mode

You can also save all of the Mosaic documents you encounter by using Load to Disk mode. Load to Disk mode is a mode you can turn on, that will prompt you to save each item that you click on to your system, without loading it. It is a good method to use to save all the information pointed to by a home page quickly and easily, without having to load in each image.

Select Load to Disk Mode in the View/Options menu (a check mark will indicate that the mode is enabled). When Load to Disk Mode is enabled, each time you try to access a document you will be prompted for a name and location to save the item to. Note that the items you access will not be loaded; they will only be saved. Mosaic will continue to try to save documents until you disable Load to Disk Mode by again selecting the Load to Disk Mode option from the menu.

If you wish to use Load to Disk Mode selectively, you can turn it on for one download by holding down the [Shift] key while you click the item.

Configuring Mosaic options

You can easily configure Mosaic using the Tools/Options dialog. This dialog allows you to specify options for displaying elements in the Mosaic Console, such as the Toolbar, Status Bar, images, hyperlinks, sounds, the default servers for Mosaic, fonts, colors, and viewers.

You can access the dialog by choosing Options from the Tools menu. The options are described in the sections that follow.

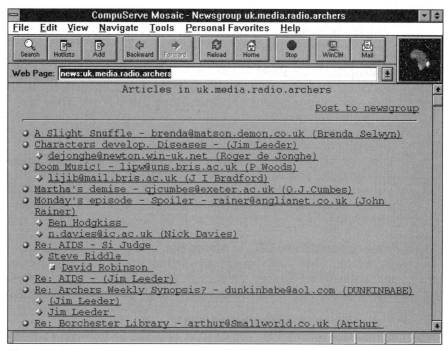

Figure 11.15 *Mosaic presents messages as 'threads'. Click a link to go to the thread. You can read, or reply to messages from Mosaic.*

General options

View/Show Toolbar/Show Web page Bar

These options control whether or not the Toolbar and Status Bar are displayed. You may not wish to hide the Status Bar (Web page bar) as it displays the locations of resources you connect to, as well as indicating when a transfer is in progress or a graphic is being loaded. By default, these options are displayed; check them again to hide them.

Show Document Title/Show URL

These options control whether or not the Document Title: drop down list with the Mosaic radar indicator and the Document URL: drop down list are displayed. You can show both options, hide both options, or show only the Document Title Bar. You cannot display only the Document URL: list. By default, these options are displayed; check them again to hide them. (These options are not found in later versions of CompuServe Mosaic.)

Use Built-In Mail/News

(These options vary in some versions of CompuServe Mosaic.)
    This option allows you to use Mosaic's built-in Mail and News browsers

instead of the external Mail and News applications. If you do not have external Mail or News, check this option. See "Accessing FTP, Gopher, News, and Mail" for more information.

View options/Autoload in-line images
By default, images (such as logos, fancy titles, small photos) are automatically displayed on your system when you connect to a World Wide Web site. This is done by automatically downloading the image to Mosaic, where it is kept in your system memory. This downloading process can be very time-consuming, depending on the speed of your Internet connection.

Mosaic allows you to disable this feature, so that the images are not automatically downloaded/displayed. Uncheck this option to stop viewing graphics. In the place of the graphics, you will see graphic placeholders. See the section on "Viewing In-line Images" earlier in this chapter for more information.

View options/Show URL in Status Bar
By default, when you highlight a hyperlink (by moving your mouse over it), the destination URL for that hyperlink will be displayed in the Status Bar. You can uncheck this option to disable the URL display, if you choose.

View options/Underline hyperlinks
Typically, hyperlinks are displayed in blue and underlined. You may want to turn off the underlining. This is a personal preference; it will not affect the speed that the document is retrieved in any significant way.

Animate logo (varies in some versions)
This refers to the radar/globe indicator on the Document Title Bar. By default, this is turned on, as it offers you some useful information about whether or not a document or image is being retrieved (and gives your mind something to do while you wait-although you can always work in other Windows applications if a document is loading too slowly). The time you'll save by turning off the logo animation is not substantial; you will probably only want to turn off that option if your connection is very slow.

This option is primarily provided in case you are using a remote access program such as Symantec's PC-Anywhere to use your PC remotely. In these cases, the animated logo may cause problems, and you should uncheck this option.

Tools Options/Use 8-bit sound
Mosaic features internal sound support for .AU and .AIFF files, using your sound card (if you have one). This option assumes you have a high quality sound card. If these file types do not play properly, or you have a lower quality (or 8-bit) sound card, choose this option.

Tools Options/ Extended News Listing
This option, when checked, will display all the newsgroup descriptions when you are listing newsgroups in Mosaic. Note that unchecking this option will

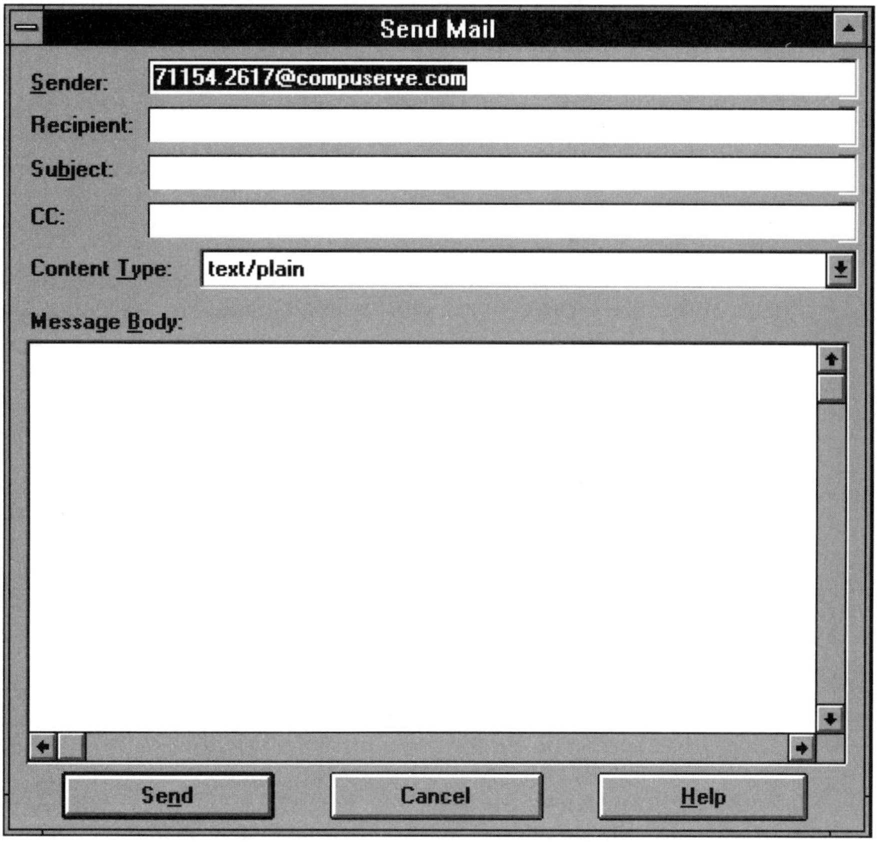

```
┌─────────────────────────────────────────────────────────────┐
│ ▭                        Send Mail                      ▲    │
├─────────────────────────────────────────────────────────────┤
│  Sender:    ┌─────────────────────────────────────────────┐ │
│             │71154.2617@compuserve.com                    │ │
│  Recipient: ┌─────────────────────────────────────────────┐ │
│             │                                             │ │
│  Subject:   ┌─────────────────────────────────────────────┐ │
│             │                                             │ │
│  CC:        ┌─────────────────────────────────────────────┐ │
│             │                                             │ │
│  Content Type:  ┌─────────────────────────────────────┬──┐ │
│                 │text/plain                           │ ± │ │
│  Message Body:                                              │
│  ┌───────────────────────────────────────────────────┬──┐ │
│  │                                                   │ ▲ │ │
│  │                                                   │   │ │
│  │                                                   │   │ │
│  │                                                   │   │ │
│  │                                                   │   │ │
│  │                                                   │   │ │
│  │                                                   │ ▼ │ │
│  ┌──┬───────────────────────────────────────────────┬──┐ │
│  │← │                                               │ →│ │
│  ┌───────────────┐  ┌───────────────┐  ┌───────────────┐   │
│  │     Send      │  │    Cancel     │  │     Help      │   │
│  └───────────────┘  └───────────────┘  └───────────────┘   │
└─────────────────────────────────────────────────────────────┘
```

Figure 11.16   *You can send mail in Mosaic, but not receive it.*

also turn off news threading. See "Accessing FTP, Gopher, News, and Mail" for more information.

When loading images, redraw every __ seconds

You can change how often the screen is redrawn by changing this option. When you connect to a Mosaic document, Mosaic loads in the entire document, using image "placeholders" for any images in the document. Mosaic will then load in the images one by one, and redraw the screen (replacing the placeholders with images) as images are loaded in. Changing the redraw value will affect how the Mosaic document appears as it is loaded in. For instance, if you want Mosaic to load in most/all of the document's images before redrawing the screen, you would set this value to a high number (i.e. 5 seconds), to give Mosaic time to load in all the images. If you want Mosaic to redraw the screen each time a new image is loaded in, set this value to a lower number (2 seconds, for instance). The value you will want to use is also dependent on the speed of your connection. If you are operating over a slow modem connection, images may not load in very quickly, and you may want to increase the screen redraw value to a higher number (so that the screen only redraws when new images are loaded in). Another reason for changing this value: if your Mosaic screen is redrawing the screen very often, you may find the flicker of your screen as the screen is redrawn to be annoying. If so, increase the value of the redraw option until you are happy with the screen performance.

View options/ Home Page

Mosaic lets you set up a default Home Page that you can quickly access using the Home button on the Toolbar. Type the URL for the home page in the URL: field to set up this home page. See "Opening Documents Using URLs" for more information on understanding URLs.

You can also set up Mosaic to automatically load this Home Page on startup; if you want to see this home page whenever you start Mosaic, check the Load automatically at startup option.

Tools/Options Email Address

You can specify which address will be used as your return address when mail is sent out using Mosaic. Note that Mosaic will only send mail, not receive it. In order to receive mail, you must have a valid mail account and you will have to use a separate mail application. Fill out this field with your correct e-mail address, if you have one; if not, leave this field as it is.

Tools Options/SMTP Server

You must specify this value in order to send out mail. A default mail server address has been supplied for you with WinCIM 2.0

Tools Options/ News Server

In order to read news, you must have a news server address defined here. A news server is the machine that you connect to in order to read news.

A default News server is supplied. If you have a news server you prefer to use to read news, type its address here.

Cached Documents (varies in some versions)

This item represents how many documents are cached, or kept active, in your PC's memory. If this number is 10, for instance, 10 documents will remain "available" to you; if you go back to them, they will appear immediately, and will not have to be loaded.

If you have a lot of available system memory, you may want to increase this number. Keep in mind that a high number for cache may affect other applications' performance, although Mosaic performance will probably improve quite a bit.

Documents in Drop Down (varies in some versions)

This value indicates how many of your last-accessed documents will appear in the Document Title: and Document URL: drop down lists (displayed beneath the Toolbar). A value of 5 would mean that the last five documents you accessed would display in these lists.

The three buttons at the bottom of the dialog allow you to configure viewers, choose fonts, choose the hyperlink color and define proxy servers. These features are described in the sections that follow.

Viewers

The World Wide Web includes many different types of items: text, pictures, sound, movies, and almost every conceivable type of computer file. Although Mosaic has the ability to display text and graphics (GIF and JPEG format) and play .AU and .AIFF sound files, certain items you will find on the Web require applications ('helper' applications) other than Mosaic in order to work. For instance, MPEG multimedia movies will require you to run an MPEG movie player application in order to view the movie. Applications like the MPEG movie player application are referred to as external viewers.

Mosaic is already set up to use two external viewers: ImageView, a viewer for JPEG and GIF files that comes with Mosaic, and Media Player, a sound player that comes with Microsoft Windows. When you try to access JPEG or GIF files, ImageView will be started; accessing WAV or MIDI files will cause Media Player to open.

Although Mosaic has built-in support for GIF and JPEG files, ImageView is included with Mosaic so that you can open these files in a high resolution format, save them, and convert them to other formats, if desired.

You may find other items on Mosaic home pages (or FTP or Gopher sites you are viewing using Mosaic) that require external viewers. You can set up external viewers for those applications as described below.

Click the Viewers button in the <Configuration> dialog; the <Viewers> dialog will appear. This dialog allows you to change the viewers and tools that are used to access Mosaic resources. The tasks you can perform in this dialog are described in the sections that follow.

Setting up viewers

Mosaic uses MIME types to decide how to treat items you try to access on a World Wide Web home page. MIME (Multipurpose Internet Mail Extensions) is a general purpose encoding method for exchanging multimedia data over the Internet; files that you find on World Wide Web home pages will have predefined MIME types associated with them. For instance, MPEG movie files have type video/mpeg, and TIFF graphics have type application/tiff. You can find out the MIME type of an item by clicking on it with the right mouse button and choosing Get Document Information (or Get Image Information). (Note that this information is only available for items on HTTP servers).

When you find an item for which you want to set up a viewer, you will need to know the MIME type of the item in order to set up a viewer for that item. Most standard MIME types are included with Mosaic. If you do not see the MIME type for the item you want to define, you will have to add that MIME type to the MIME type list; see the next section, "Creating a new MIME Type" for information.

Setting up a Viewer:
1) In the Tools/options Type drop down list, select the MIME type for the item for which you want to set up a viewer.

When Mosaic accesses files from an HTTP site, it uses only the MIME type to decide what type of file it is accessing and how to treat the file; therefore, you must be sure that the MIME type you specify is accurate.

2) The Extensions field allows you to define file extensions (i.e. .GIF, WAV, .DOC) that are used to recognize a file. Note that file extensions are only used when accessing files on an FTP or Gopher site; therefore, you only need to provide extensions if you think you will be downloading this type of item from FTP or Gopher sites. If you are providing several extensions, you should separate the extensions with commas. Note that UNIX servers sometimes have case-sensitive filenames; you will probably want to add both upper and lower cases for the extension (e.g. .txt, .TXT).

3) In the Viewer field, type the full path and filename of the viewer you want to use for items with the MIME type you selected, or click Browse if you are not sure of the path for the viewer and want to search for it on your system.

4) You can set up as many viewers as you like. Click Close when you are done configuring viewers. The changes will take place immediately.

You can change any of the viewer or extension information for a MIME type at any time by selecting that MIME type from the drop down list and changing the information that appears; clicking Close to exit the dialog will save your changes.

Setting up applications for Telnet, rlogin, and TN3270 (see Chapter 13)
The Telnet, RLogin, and TN3270 fields in the <Viewers> dialog allow you to define which applications are used by Mosaic to access telnet, rlogin, and tn3270 URLs. Type the full path and filename for the applications you want to use in the appropriate field, or click Browse if you are not sure of the path for the application and want to search for it on your system.

When you Close the dialog, the changes you made will be saved.

Adding a new MIME type:
Many standard MIME types are included with Mosaic; see the table at the end of this section for a list. However, you may at some point need to define an entirely new MIME type.

You might want to do this because you find an item on an FTP or Gopher server for which you have a viewer, and want to set up that viewer for that item. Note that when Mosaic accesses an item on an FTP or Gopher server, it uses the item's file extensions, not the MIME type, to recognize the item. Therefore, you can create a new MIME type just for that item. For instance, you might find an FTP site which contains diagrams created in Shapeware's Visio program. If you have a copy of Visio, you might want to create a new MIME type for Visio, called application/x-visio, so that you can directly open Visio files from Mosaic using Visio as a viewer.

Also, you might be accessing an HTTP (World Wide Web) server which contains a new or non-standard MIME type, and you want to define that type so that you can specify viewers for it. If you are doing this, be sure to use the exact same syntax for the MIME type that the server is using.

MIME types are composed of two parts, a type and a subtype. The type should be one of the following: application, audio, image, text, or video; the subtype defines the actual file type. See the MIME Type table in the next section for a list of types to use in Mosaic. You specify MIME types by specifying first the type, a forward slash and then the subtype, e.g. application/x-visio, where application is the type and x-visio is the subtype. New, undefined MIME types should be pre-fixed with an x; i.e. application/x-visio.

You can add a MIME type as follows:
1) Click the Add New Type button in the <Viewers> dialog. A <New Document Type> dialog will appear, allowing you to add new MIME types to the Mosaic MIME type list.

2) Type the MIME type name for the new MIME type. See the previous section for information on how MIME types are specified.

3) Click OK to add the new MIME type. The new MIME type will be added to the Type drop down list, and you can add viewer information to that MIME type as described earlier.

MIME Types Included in CompuServe Mosaic
The table below lists the MIME types that are included in CompuServe Mosaic. The MIME types are broken down into type and subtype, and include a brief description of the type of file they apply to.

Type Subtype	Description
application/commonground	Common Ground files
application/iges IGES files	
application/mathematica	Mathematica files
application/msword	Microsoft Word files
application/pdf	Adobe Acrobat files
application/postscript	Adobe Postscript files
application/rtf	Rich Text Format files
application/wordperfect5.1	Word Perfect 5.1 files
application/zip	ZIP (compressed) files
audio/aiff	Audio Image File Format audio files
audio/basic	Sun/DEC/NeXT audio (*.AU) files
audio/wav	Microsoft Windows WAVE (RIFF) audio files
audio/x-midi	MIDI audio files
image/gif	CompuServe GIF images
image/jpeg	JPEG compressed images
image/targa	AT&T Targa images
image/tiff	Tagged Image File images
image/x-win-bmp	Microsoft Windows Bitmap images
text/html	HTML formatted text files

Type	Subtype	Description
text/plain		Plain ASCII text files
text/richtext		Richtext text files
video/mpeg		MPEG movie files
video/msvideo		Microsoft Video (.AVI) files
video/quicktime		Apple Quicktime movie files

Further information about MIME

Technical information about MIME can be found in the Internet Request For Comments document RFC 1521 and 1522. A complete list of RFCs can be found at:

ftp://DS.INTERNIC.NET/rfc

The frequently asked questions documents for MIME can be found at

http://www.cis.ohio-state.edu:80/hypertext/faq/usenet/mail/mime-faq/top.html

A list of currently registered MIME types can be found at:

ftp://ftp.isi.edu/in-notes/iana/assignments/media-types/media-types

View options/color

The Hyperlink color is the color that is used to highlight Mosaic hyperlinks (jumps to other documents or document areas, or jumps to resources). Text hyperlinks are entirely highlighted, and graphics hyperlinks are surrounded by a highlight. The standard Hyperlink color is blue.

To change the Hyperlink color, click Color. The <Color> dialog will appear. Select the color you would like to use for Hyperlinks, or click Define Custom Colors to select a color. Click OK; the Hyperlink color will be changed immediately.

View options/fonts

You can change the fonts that Mosaic uses to display documents. You can change the font that is used for a particular item, or the font size. You might want to do this to make documents easier to read, or to fit more information onto your screen.

Different items in documents use different font styles (similar to styles in word processors). Most regular text is displayed in Normal style, and headers are displayed in a Header style, such as Header 1, Header 2, Header 3, etc.

You can change these font styles clicking the Fonts button. You will see the <Fonts> dialog.

If you want to change just one style, you can choose the style that you want to change from the drop down menu, and define a Font for that style by clicking the Change Font button.

Specify the font type and style you want, and click OK. The style will be changed until you change it again.

If you are not sure what style it is you want to change, you will have to do some experimenting. Mosaic cannot tell you what styles are being used in a particular WWW document.

If you want to change all the styles in a document, you can choose Enlarge All or Reduce All to enlarge or reduce the styles. You can choose this option as many times as you like.

Click OK when you are finished changing styles.

Viewing document source

A Document Source command is provided in the File menu to enable you to view, and save HTML document source code. Click Document Source or Web Page Source in newer versions to view the current document's source code.

You can now choose Save from the File menu to save the source code to a file. Remember that all the HTML codes will also be saved. You will be prompted for a name for this file.

You can also choose Copy from the Edit menu to copy some or all of the HTML text to the Windows Clipboard, so that it can be used in other applications. (Use the Select All command to select the entire document.)

Accessing HTTP /0.9 documents

Some older WWW documents may require you to use an earlier version of the Transfer Protocol, HTTP/0.9, to access them. In most cases, the hyperlinks to those documents will warn you that HTTP /0.9 is required to read them. Check HTTP/0.9 in the Options menu to read these older documents.

12 Network news

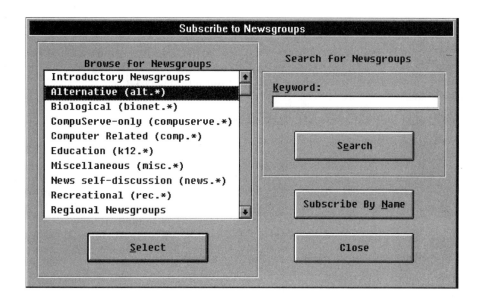

As well as getting textual information from the 'Net via email and mail-lists, you can also fill up your hard disk with information from Usenet. Usenet is really a large virtual bulletin board onto which any Tom, Dick and Harriet can post a message. Messages may cover any topic and be posted onto any message base, but generally speaking messages in any given newsgroup will follow a particular topic. At least that's the theory, although there's much within Usenet topics which is decidedly 'off-topic'. Any message posted into a topic will be trundled around the world in a couple of days, or in some cases, hours.

You get access to Usenet by logging into a News Server with a News software client. CompuServe achieve this from within CIM which logs into their own servers, so you don't need any extra software to use CompuServe's internal news features. If you don't want to use CIM, but wish to access news from outside of the managed news services of CompuServe, you can use the CompuServe Internet Dialler (CID) and any Internet news software to log into any other public news server in the world.

CompuServe and Usenet morality issues

CompuServe provides access to most Usenet groups from within CIM (GO INTERNET), although does not publicize groups containing material likely to be regarded as offensive. What constitutes offensive is up to you; CompuServe doesn't moralize about what you may access - but presumes that you know what you want to access on Usenet, and also know which groups you don't want access to.

As this book went to press, pressure from German legislators forced CompuServe Ohio to remove direct access to some of the more contentious newsgroups from CompuServe. This is possibly a useful benefit for CompuServe as it reinforces the service's appeal to professional, parental, and educational users, although those concerned with Internet issues will see it as a problem of national interference with an International system.

Getting hold of Usenet

If you don't want to use CIM you can use third party Usenet readers programs over the PPP link. These programs vary in their ability to make life difficult for the user. Many of them don't cater for capturing news to disk for perusal at a later date (thus saving on costs of running a dial-up line while you download, sort and read your news). Others have a clunky batch-driven system which attempts to provide off-line facilities of some sort.

Nearly all network news outside of services like CompuServe is delivered using a scheme called NNTP – Network News Transfer Protocol, and consequently you'll need an NNTP-savvy program to collect it from your provider.

Newsgroup contents

Newsgroups are divided into hierarchies and their title is thus supposed to be descriptive of their contents. Anything beginning with SCI should contain topics bearing some resemblance to scientific matters, REC is recreational, SOC is social, and so on. There are any numbers of ALT newsgroups too, where ALT stands for 'alternative'.

You get hold of image files from Usenet groups by using the UUdecode or BinHex decoders already mentioned.

The basic USENET hierarchies include:
comp Computer topics
rec Recreational topics
sci Scientific topics
soc Social issues
talk Conversational topics, often controversial
news Topics related to operating a USENET system
misc Groups which don't fit well elsewhere
alt Alternatives to conventional or standardized thinking

The alternative (alt.*) newsgroups are possibly the most contentious.

Figure 12.2 *Using Usenet from within CIM. Go to the Internet forum, select News, then the graphical browser. First set your options . . .*

FAQ's

Most news groups will contain a 'FAQ' - a list of Frequently Asked Questions. FAQs generally give information about the way the group works, who runs it, what the rules are and so forth. Normally newcomers to a group would look for the FAQ and absorb it before asking the same old newbie questions. The word FAQ has since been usurped to mean any list of Frequently Asked Questions about any topic, and as with everything else Internet based there are people who obsessively compile FAQs as part of some obscure hobby, just as there are endless compilers of lists. Writers of FAQs often add the name of their FAQ to their email signature, just as you'd add VC to your name if you won the Victoria Cross.

Getting your hands dirty with Usenet

The actuality of Usenet is simple – you join a newsgroup and download or read on-line the messages it contains. If you feel sufficiently moved you hit a key, and your computer presents you with a text editor into which you compose your message and then hit the send key. Your witty and brilliant reply then appears in the newsgroup and is there the next time you log on.

Many Usenet messages seem to be entirely constructed of the text from the previous message, preceded by a > sign. This is a function of some message editor programs, where you click an on-screen button marked 'Reply' and the editor constructs the reply message headers but adds in the complete text of the message to which you are replying. This makes it very convenient for you, but a pain in the butt for everyone else who has to read the complete text of a message dozens of times over. The problem gets worse when Internet geeks, intent on making some facile point, will not only copy the entire message, but the ten-line signature of the guy who sent it in the first place. This makes sure that out of the 30 megabytes of Usenet stuff you've downloaded at great cost, only ten bits of it is of any real interest. The rest is repeats of messages and signatures. So, use your editor with care and sense, and watch for that copying facility. It can get out of hand. And keep your signature (called a 'sig' in geek-speak) to three lines or less. It all helps keep the tedium of free speech to a minimum.

Some newsgroups are 'moderated', which means that you can't post to them directly. A 'moderator' is someone who is egocentric enough to believe they should operate a closed newsgroup, and limit or control what appears in it. To send mail to a moderated news group you mail the moderator directly, who then decides whether what you have to say carries any virtue and includes it if it doesn't.

Net etiquette

There is a spurious form of control on the Internet, imposed by cyber-idealists and regulated by its denizens. 'Netiquette' demands that you use lower case for all public mail (upper case is translated as SHOUTING!) and that you shouldn't use more than three lines for your signature as it 'uses up disk space'. These rules (and others) seem extremely petty once you're plugged into the Internet, especially when you see some of the blasphemous and obscene messages posted by users, and mind-blowingly inconsequential stuff posted by religious evangelists. It seems that while you can inform the world that Elvis Presley is not only God, but is alive and well and will be signing books at McDonuts on Thursday, you can't use upper case for the text of a message.

Strange also, that the Internet community which prides itself so much on its supposed freedom should choose to impose any limits at all, but then anarchy can only work properly if it's correctly controlled. Whether you subscribe to Netiquette is up to you. But use upper case incautiously and other users will send you mail grumbling about your wild excursion into the unknown.

Watch out too for Flame Wars as mentioned in the Forums Chapter. They exist in large numbers on Usenet, where there are few moderators to calm things down. Abuse of other users is common place on Usenet, and readers are urged to tread carefully before jumping in, with one foot firmly in place in the mouth.

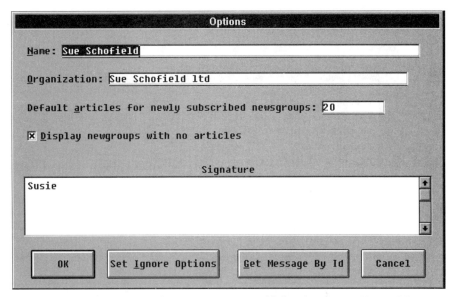

Figure 12.3 *Your Name and Organization are added to headers in Usenet Messages. Make sure they contain information you want made public . . .*

Newsgroup distribution

Remember that whatever you send to a Usenet group is splashed all over the world in a matter of hours, and can be and often is reproduced without permission or payment, so be careful of what you say. However, there are ways you can limit distribution of your postings. If you put a line in your message header thus, you'll limit distribution to the USA only:

Distribution: usa

There are huge numbers of distribution limiters, so most people don't bother with them, mainly because they don't always work. But you can limit your postings to just the UK with the UK suffix, so try that if you don't want the whole world to comment on your writing abilities. If you have a half-decent news editor on your system you'll find that there's a 'distribution' box which pops up with a pick list of all the distribution limiters.

New newsgroups

New groups appear on Usenet almost by the hour. Many of them will have little or no consequence to you (or anyone else) and you won't want them eating up space on your computer. Your news program will either tell you that

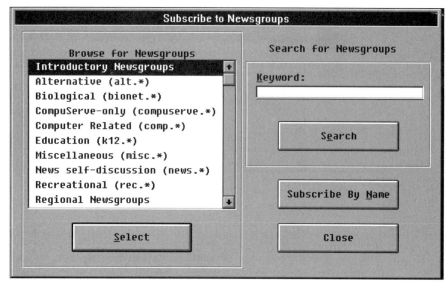

Figure 12.4 *In you go. News Groups in CIM are pre-organized for you. This isn't the case outside CIM. Go to Introductory first . . .*

a new group has been created, or will provide a clicky-button which you can click on to show all the new groups which have sprung up since you last checked.

Every so often, say once a fortnight for newsgroup freaks, you'll want to grab a complete list of all newsgroups, and then spend a week formatting it up as a nice text document which you can pin on the bathroom wall. You've then got a huge list of newsgroups which you can browse through at leisure, selecting target groups to add to your personal list.

Make sure you do it a time when you can afford the resultant phone bill. Many news programs not only download the complete list of newsgroups but sort them alphabetically too, and they will quite happily do this while your modem is sitting on the line eating up your non-disposable income. Despite this warning, most Internet freaks have huge and complete lists of newsgroups lying around like confetti, which shows just why the telecomms providers are starting to get interested in the Internet. In principle you can join and leave newsgroups at will; in reality your ability to do this will be limited or enhanced by the software you're using to provide access. Some providers keep a compressed (zip, tar or hqx) up-to-date list which can be downloaded very quickly but you may or may not be able to use this with your news reader directly.

Yes, but is it art?

Many newsgroups provide binary files of images, artistic or otherwise, and there are a number of techniques used over the Internet to get these files into standard messages. The most common is to encode a binary file such as

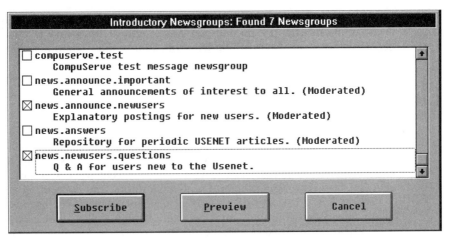

Figure 12.5   *The five groups here are specifically for newbies. Subscribe to add them to yur list, or just popin for a Preview.*

an image file into an ASCII representation of itself with a program called UUencode, and to use UUdecode to bring the file back to binary. It can then be decompressed if need be, and run on your computer. Quite often these files turn out to be compressed archives, which for PC users means that they will be compressed using PKZip or a similar alternative. For Macs they will be archives created using Stuffit or Compactor or similar. In each case you'll need the relevant software to decompress the file.

File segmenting

Because of the file size limits imposed by some servers, or by some news programs, binary files are often stored in 64k chunks as news messages. They have sequential file names such as ODD1.ZIP, ODD2.ZIP, ODD3.ZIP and so on. You download the complete set of files, and your UUdecode program stitches them back together as a complete archive. At least that's the theory, but computer technology being what it is there are a number of UUdecode programs incapable of working with segmented binary files. However a quick hunt around the newsgroup, the Internet Resources Forum, or a word with a close friend will tell you which decoder program works for your particular computer.

File archives

After they have been decoded, some files will turn out to be 'self-extracting compressed archives'. These need no external program to expand them – you just run them if they are DOS EXE files, or click on an icon if they are Mac or

Amiga files. In many cases you'll already have a battery of file decompressors if you've been using a computer for any length of time, and in all cases file decompressors can be downloaded from almost any computer-centric FTP site or from a variety of CompuServe Forums.

Listserv

Listserv groups are slightly different to Usenet groups. (See the Chapter on Email for more details.) You send a mail message to the group's email address, and your message gets sent to everyone on the list, if it's set up that way. Everyone else's mail gets sent to you in return. (On some systems mail only gets sent between originating and replying authors, and consenting adults.)

Listserv is a great way of generating mail to yourself, but beware the cost of downloading a hundred mail messages over a dial-up link. You can get a complete list of listserv servers emailed to you by sending 'list global' to internet:listserv@bitnic.educom.edu. Don't send your signature, and don't expect a rapid reply. (WARNING - the resulting email is over 712,000 bytes long.)

When you find a listserv which you think is worthy of your razor-sharp intellect, you send a subscribe message:

mail to: listserv@ames.arc.nasa.gov
Message Text: subscribe frequent-flyer joe smith

Use your own real name, not your email address after the subscribe command (The listserv picks up your email address from your mail header.) You can abbreviate 'subscribe' to 'sub' if you like beaming non-human-readable messages around the world.

The listserv address here is actually 'frequent-flyer@ames. arc.nasa.gov' but you are sending your request for mail to the listserv computer.

When subscribing to listservs your mail should always be addressed to the group, not to the listserv, although when you've had enough you can mail the listserv with an 'unsubscribe' message:

mail to: listserv@ames.arc.nasa.gov
signoff frequent-flyer

or

unsubscribe frequent-flyer

You can also mail the listserv with a demand for help, and if you send 'info ?' you should get a list of available documentation back. 'Help' will bring you the help files.

Some Listservs use a system called 'majordomo'. Look out for that word in the name of the server. For majordomo servers just do the logical thing and send 'subscribe listname' where listname is the name of the list. It's just a complicated way of making things easy.

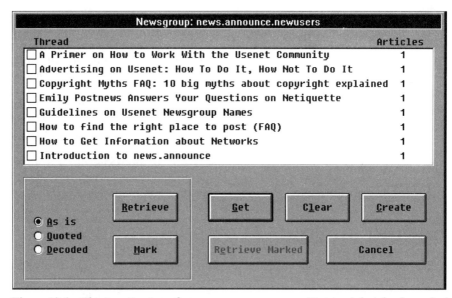

Figure 12.6   *This is a Preview of news.announce.newusers. 'Retrieve' downloads marked texts to your disk. 'Get' lets you read them online. 'Subscribe' adds it to your personal list for direct access.*

Look out too, for the SET commands available on your favourite listserv. 'SET frequent-flyer digest' will bundle all your replies up into a daily report. Not all SET commands are available on all listservs, so check out the help files.

Other useful commands are:

SET xxx NOACK, which stops the blessed thing returning your own mail to you as an acknowledgment.
SET xxx NOMAIL, which stops mail temporarily.
SET xxx MAIL starts it again

where xxx is the name of the list.

Listserv and Usenet mirrors

The listserv system shows up the pitfalls of trying to communicate with three million people from your back bedroom. Listserv is quite a dumb process, and you'll get lots of messages from some servers saying that such-and-such people who were once on the list are no longer reachable. You might also fall unsuspecting into a moderated list, where the moderator used to be a Personnel Manager, and doesn't let your messages into the list until you've been a subscriber for a year, just so you know your place. And some moderators are

Network Nazis, and won't let you into the list unless you agree entirely with what they have to say, and sign a Non Disclosure Agreement (NDA).

To complicate matters some apparently private lists are mirrored in Usenet groups. You then find that, where you mistakenly believed you were replying to just a couple of hundred people, your mother/boss/publisher finds you plastered publicly all over Alt.Hamster.Eating, or worse.

As with everything else on the Internet you can now search for and sign on to Listservs from a World Wide Web browser. You simply search for the topic you're interested in, perhaps using a Boolean construction to overly complicate matters, and the search result should hot-link you to the server of interest. This relatively new fangled way of hooking into Listservs is much easy than the old 'subscribe me' method, but somehow loses the romance of fighting with the tortuous syntax needed to log into listservs by email.

Setting up your own newsgroup

Ever wondered how to set up your own newsgroup? You will when you've read some of the stuff on Usenet. 'Heck' you'll say to yourself, 'this is just the place to set up a group for my Cat Woman fetish'. The first place to look is in the list of all Usenet groups you've got pinned on your bathroom wall for a similar topic. More often than not someone's got there before you. In this case you might find alt.fan.gus-the-cat, alt.tv.eek-the-cat or alt.bbs.wildcat (a bulletin board program). To set up your very own alt.fan.catwoman.grrr group you first have to get the proposal passed by the worthy people in the news.group newsgroup. You'll find all the info you need there to do it but note that it will take some time, and a lot of your patience, to get alt.fan.cat-woman.grrr off the ground. Once there you might fill the group with chatter about Cat Woman (did she really die at the end of Batman Returns?) and so on. The more narrow your choice of subject the more chance there is of getting a special newsgroup set up. Conversely, boring old topics like education, computers, software and television programmes already fill the Usenet groups and you'll have to be wonderfully inventive to avoid crossing the path of an existing group. As you'll see from Usenet, most people aren't.

Censoring Usenet

It's the 'uninhibited' nature of the Internet in general, and the graphics files on Usenet in particular, which is causing the hairs on the necks of UK Government ministers to stand up. Already the media has latched on to the fact that there are images and messages in many of the ALT Usenet groups which are deemed unsuitable for public consumption in this country, and it's very likely that the next few years will bring in some sort of knee-jerk legislation to limit access to these feeds in the UK. The only real way that this can be done is to threaten Internet providers with the crime of distributing pornography, which will result in many of the Usenet groups being pulled from general distribution.

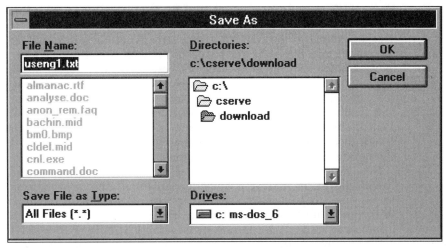

Figure 12.7   *Marked messages are saved as text to disk. You can read them with any text editor. Otherwise use the PPP link and an off-line reader such as Nuntius for Macs or FreeAgent for Windows.*

Some Internet providers censor newsgroups by simply disappearing them from their access lists, while others actively bar them. In all cases censorship of Net topics inevitably fails because if you can't get what you seek in a newsgroup you can get it via listserv, or Gopher, or if all else fails, via CD ROM. And if you can't get it via CD ROM, Kevin next door will certainly sell it to you on a floppy.

Usenet groups for UK newbies

Most of the stuff on Usenet is of limited interest to UK users, simply because the vast part of it originates in the USA, where different value systems apply. You'll doubtless find your own level in these groups but for newcomers there's news.announce.newusers. News.answers is worth looking at (allegedly) although rec.humor.funny, which is mentioned in all the other Internet books as being riotously amusing, is about as funny as Women's Hour, as far as this scribbler is concerned. UK.net carries stuff of interest, as does UK.Media, and a search through newsgroups with the CIM newsreader search facility will find many more.

The CompuServe news FAQ - frequently asked questions

Access to USENET Newsgroups from within CompuServe and CIM was the first of several products and services designed to give CompuServe members access to information which exists on the Internet.

How will CompuServe ensure that its members mesh with the cultural expectations of the Internet?

The sub-culture of the Internet is very strong, and those who fail to abide by the culture are often the recipients of "flames" (an Internet term for hate mail.) CompuServe intends to do its best to ensure that members are not flamed, and are able to participate welcomely in newsgroup discussions. The rules of "netiquette" (Internet etiquette) will be displayed to a member the first time they access USENET newsgroups. In addition, these rules will be available from a menu item for review at any time. You are encouraged to review them. CompuServe reserves the right to disallow access to USENET newsgroups to any user who fails to abide by these rules.

New members may be unaware of CompuServe policies and USENET "netiquette". CompuServe is doing its part to inform new members of proper "netiquette" to help make their experience on the Internet more enjoyable. With this in mind, CompuServe has implemented a policy that allows new members to read but not to post messages in USENET. Full USENET access will be permitted after the new member has received their second password in the mail.

What settings allow for the best use of the USENET Newsgroup CIM interface?

WinCIM: In order to create the largest display area for reading USENET Newsgroups, your video display resolution should be at least 640x480. In addition, the size of the window that displays Newsgroup message text is negotiated between the news server and CIM at the beginning of your USENET session. To take advantage of this you should make your WinCIM window as large as possible prior to entering the CIM interface to USENET. You may resize manually or "maximize" the WinCIM window.

MacCIM: MacCIM automatically negotiates the size of the window for displaying Newsgroup text based on the size of your monitor. You need not do anything except be aware you will see a sub-optimal display if you are using a Classic, Mac Plus or other machine with a 9" diagonal display.

I'm glad to see that CompuServe has implemented the auto-decode feature in USENET. Can I mark multiple articles of different filenames and auto-decode all of them?

The auto-decode feature will only retrieve and decode one filename at a time, though one image file may consist of several files.

For example:

image name.jpg (1/3)
image name.jpg (2/3)
image name.jpg (3/3)

You would mark all three files and decode the one image. If a different file-name is in the file title, it must be decoded separately.

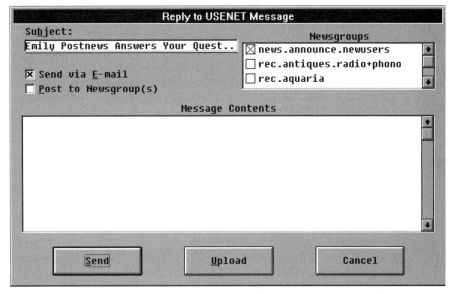

Figure 12.8   *Posting a message. Normally you would respond with the 'Post To Newsgroup' option checked.*

Why do some image files begin with zero (ie 0/3)?

Occasionally, a description of the image will accompany the image files. The standard is to number the description with a zero. This file is not part of the image. However, if you mistakenly include and decode the description with the other image files, the decode process will ignore the description and complete the image decode process successfully.

Can I still use the auto-decode feature of USENET even though I am using the ASCII newsreader and not the CIM newsreader?

Yes, the auto-decode feature will work in the ASCII newsreader. For example, if you would like to download and auto-decode messages 1-10, you would use the following syntax:

down /decode 1-10

You can get additional information on using the ASCII newsreader by typing HELP at the ! prompt while in USENET.

Can I use the CIM USENET Newsreader to read messages offline?

The CIM newsreader allows you to mark articles from multiple newsgroups, place them in a batch download queue and retrieve them using the RETRIEVE MARKED ARTICLES button. After the articles have been retrieved, you can disconnect from CompuServe and read them off-line.

If you would like to use a "non-CIM" based off-line newsreader, you can use CompuServe's Dial PPP access to connect to the news-server at news.compuserve.com. For information on alternative off-line news-readers, visit the Internet Resources Forum (GO INETRES). For information and step-by-step instructions on using CompuServe's Dial PPP access, GO PPP.

When posting a message using the CIM newsreader, my messages keep cutting off after the 25th line. How do I compose larger messages?
Proper USENET netiquette recommends keeping your posts short and to the point, but there may be a time when you need to post longer messages or files. If your posting is longer than 25 lines, you will need to compose your message off-line, and use the UPLOAD button to upload the message file into the USENET window. Not only are you saving time and money by creating your post off-line, but you will also be able to use features of your word processor such as spell-checking and grammar-checking. Please keep in mind that USENET supports ASCII text only. Any messages that are created in word processors, must be saved in ASCII text format.

The newsreader sometimes reports more articles than what is available for me to read. Why does this happen?
The newsreader calculates the total number of articles for each newsgroup every time you enter based on the last time you were in the newsreader. If you have not used USENET for a while, you may notice that the total number of articles accessible is smaller than the amount reported by the newsreader. This is due to the expiration of articles or users cancelling their posts.

Is it OK to disconnect from CompuServe while I'm still in the USENET area?
You should exit completely from USENET and logoff of CompuServe before disconnecting. If you turn off your modem or disconnect from CompuServe while in USENET, your newsgroups will not be updated as being "read".

CompuServe policy on Usenet

If you access USENET Newsgroups from CompuServe you are able to read articles and post articles which are shared among millions of people worldwide connected to the Internet.

This information originates OUTSIDE of CompuServe, and CompuServe therefore claims no responsibility for the content. Newsgroups differ from Forums in that most are not moderated or managed. Therefore, you are viewing uncensored comments directly from the Internet.

Although there are newsgroups which you may find interesting, there are also newsgroups you may find offensive and may wish to avoid. CompuServe has created menus containing newsgroups which are generally regarded as acceptable. Other newsgroups may be accessed only if you enter the exact newsgroup name. You may wish to supervise access by children.

In accordance with USENET standards, any article you post to USENET displays your name and account I.D. in the From field. You have the option of modifying the display of your name, however, the use of alias names are not well accepted on USENET.

Over the last 15 years of the USENET's existence, social customs, habits, and tendencies have developed. These are often referred to as the rules of "netiquette". Specifically note that advertising not only violates USENET netiquette, but also violates CompuServe's Operating Rules. CompuServe is committed to being a good Internet citizen, and it is your responsibility to follow these netiquette guidelines. CompuServe reserves the right to protect members' privilege to access USENET by disallowing access to USENET newsgroups to any user who fails to follow these guidelines.

Since CompuServe exercises no control over the content of the information passing through the USENET interface, please be sensitive to the rights of ownership and assure compliance with copyright law and the CompuServe Agreement and Operating Rules before redistributing any information obtained through USENET.

13 FTP

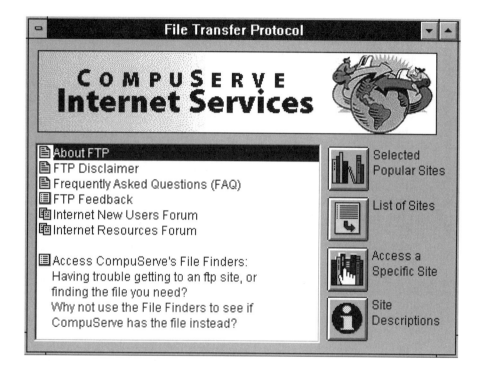

FTP stands for File Transfer Protocol, and it's the single most popular hobby on the 'Net, if the fact that it takes up 48 per cent of all network traffic is anything to go by. FTP is simply the art of transferring files from one place to another, using the 'file transfer protocol', which gives its name to the process. You use FTP to gather files from the Internet, much in the same way as you would grab files from CompuServe's Forum Libraries, except if you grab files from CompuServe you are using an internal transfer protocol called CIS B+ (developed from XMODEM).

The other difference for CompuServe users is that files on remote FTP sites aren't always virus checked, they aren't always vetted for content, and they are rarely indexed. You'll doubtless want to give FTP a go, but remember that remote FTP sites can be exceedingly slow to respond to you (their fault not CompuServe's) and it's almost always quicker to use the CompuServe File Finder to find files you want. If it's not on CompuServe, then go trawling the FTP sites for it, but you might be in for long session if the Internet or the servers you are accessing are busy.

Starting up

You can get to FTP from within CIM (GO INTERNET) or through a CompuServe PPP link, using your own FTP software. The FTP software within CIM is so good you may not want to bother using a PPP link so we'll stick with CIM for the examples here.

To get into an FTP site you fill in an on-screen form containing the information required or click on one of the preconfigured FTP sites on CompuServe. Once you get to the log-in screen you'll be asked for a username and password. Here's your first problem. Unless you work at the site you won't have a login identity. So you use 'anonymous' if you can spell it, and 'ftp' if you can't. Most sites accept either, but for those that don't you'll have to learn to spell, anonymously.

For a password you should type your full email address which makes anonymous FTP rather less anonymous than it would otherwise be. You should then be logged into the system. However, you'll often find that many FTP sites don't like hordes of people logging in during office hours, or that the number of anonymous users is limited for various reasons. The convention is that anonymous users should keep their FTP usage to a minimum during office hours, but that's going to be difficult as it's always office hours somewhere on the Internet. You'll also find that many of the more popular ftp sites are constantly busy and you won't be able to get in.

Once you're in you'll be presented with a welcome message, and then a directory listing of the files on the server, or at least the files in the first directory of the server. If you're familiar with DOS then you'll know of hierarchical directories, which are a bit like nested Russian dolls. You navigate from the top directory downwards, and have to come back up to the top to go down another branch. CIM provides buttons to let you navigate with ease around Unix directories, which is what you're often looking at when you see a remote FTP server displayed on your screen.

FTP demands that you have to remember to ask for your files as either ASCII or binary. ASCII means that you get a plain text file back at the receiving end of things. Binary means you'll receive your file as an executable, or a spreadsheet, or a graphics file – in short as the sort of eight bit data your computer doesn't expect you to read with a plain text editor. You tell the remote server which type of transfer you want before you start, by typing in ASCII or BINARY before the GET or Retrieve command.

If you're in any doubt then try binary – except for files which are obviously text files, such as Read Me files, or LS–LR files which contain the directory listings of the server you're on. Binary is sometimes called Image mode – as it sends a binary image of the file on the server, bit by bit. In ASCII mode it just sends the characters of the ASCII alphabet, so what you get on your computer can be read by a text editor. You can get multiple files with the MGET instruction and if you have write access to the remote server you can leave files on it with the PUT command. Most anonymous users will never bother with either of these instructions.

Generally speaking, all of these commands are used only on servers con-

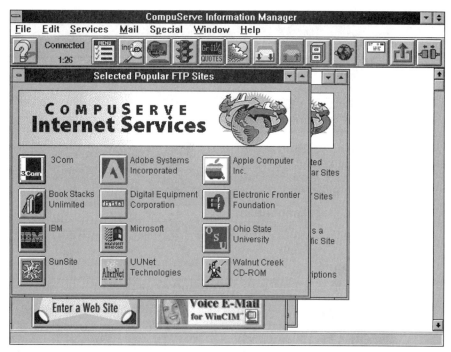

Figure 13.2   *First, select an FTP site from the menu, or go back to Access a Specific Site.*

nected to your computer by terminal emulation – you will have a series of button options to navigate and collect files if you're using CIM. What you may lose with such GUI-based software is the ability to see just how big the remote file is before you start downloading it over a modem link. This can be important, as file transfer speeds over even V32 bis modems can be extremely low due to loading or system usage, and spending half an hour downloading a large file over a modem is quite common. The trick is to look for a file which lists the directory details of the ftp server. This will let you see just how big that file is before you try to download it, and directory listings are often kept in a file called 'Index', or READ.ME or LS LR.

To complicate matters those files can be quite large so you'll still have an expensive download just to pick up the directory listing. Other GUI clients have a Get Info button which hops off to the server and grabs the file size and directory information. GUI clients tend not to download this sort of stuff by default, as it takes up even more modem time to get data which you may not be interested in.

If you're using a terminal to hook into ftp you'll see that each command you type in to the server results in some sort of output, preceded by a three-number digit. This is put there, not so that the guy with the beard and sandals who is looking after the remote site can suss out these diagnostic codes, but so your ftp program can take appropriate action if there's an error. Most ftp programs don't bother with these numbers, because if they did, writers would

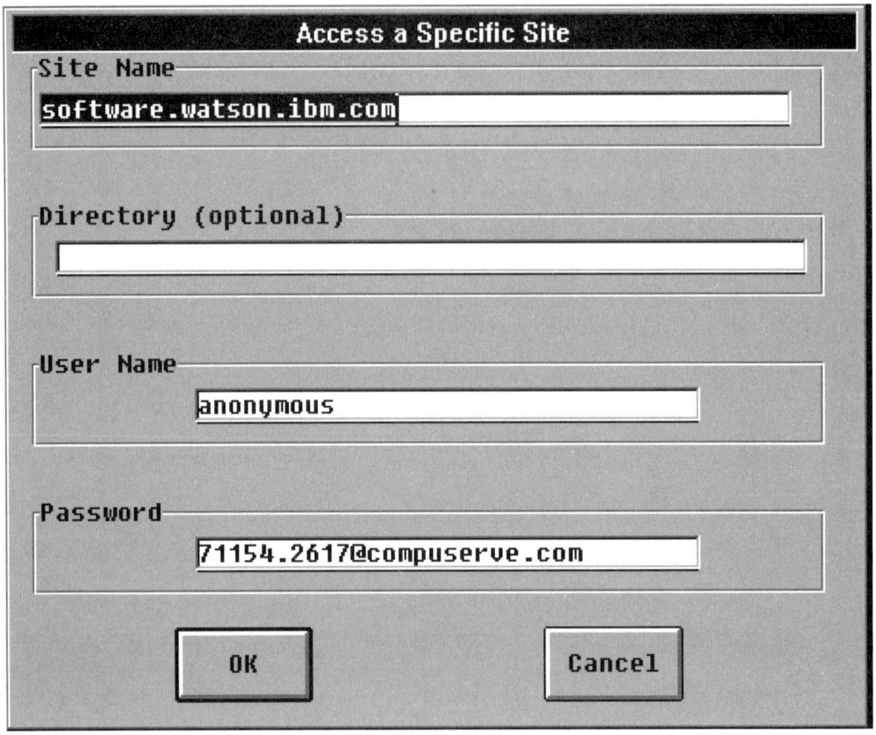

Figure 13.3 *In either case you'll get a login screen, with your ID as password, and Anonymous as your user name. This is Anonymous FTP.*

have to fill up needless pages in books with long and sordid explanations of what they mean.

And what about those codes you see before a file, like -rw- -rw- r- -? These are the attribute settings for the file or directory, and are called 'permission masks'. You only need to know that if you need to know more you should be buying UNIX books, and that 'r' stands for 'read only' and 'w' for 'write'. You shouldn't be able to overwrite a read-only file or change its name or do any of those things which, in the UK, will put you in breach of the Computer Misuse Act. And you won't see those masks under many of the GUI based programs, which is yet another blessing, although a Show File Information or Get Info button should bring them up.

Here are some useful terminal commands for ftp. CIM replaces all of these with a set of buttons for navigation, but one day you'll be using a different program, either by design or by accident.

cd up – goes up one directory
cd /– go to top of tree
cd fred– go down one directory to fred
cd ..– go up one subdirectory

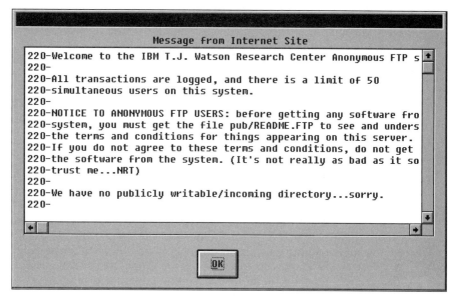

Message from Internet Site

```
220-Welcome to the IBM T.J. Watson Research Center Anonymous FTP s
220-
220-All transactions are logged, and there is a limit of 50
220-simultaneous users on this system.
220-
220-NOTICE TO ANONYMOUS FTP USERS: before getting any software fro
220-system, you must get the file pub/README.FTP to see and unders
220-the terms and conditions for things appearing on this server.
220-If you do not agree to these terms and conditions, do not get
220-the software from the system. (It's not really as bad as it so
220-trust me...NRT)
220-
220-We have no publicly writable/incoming directory...sorry.
220-
```

[OK]

Figure 13.4 *Most sites will send you a log in welcome, or a message saying that the site is too busy to let you in.*

asc– sets file transfers to ASCII
bin– sets file transfer as binary
mget– use for multiple file receives (not with GUIs)
cd / nextdir– changes to a new directory.

Don't forget to leave a space between the / and everything else as you need a space after the first word. And don't forget that these commands may differ from server to server. And UNIX file and directory names are case sensitive. FREd is different from FReD, just to make life as difficult as possible.

The CompuServe FTP FAQ

What is FTP and how does it work?
FTP is an acronym for File Transfer Protocol. CompuServe's FTP interface is a system for locating, and acquiring files from remote computers. We call these remote computers "sites".

In a nutshell, the interface works by telling the FTP software which site you want to go to, gaining access to it by using a private password or logging in as an "anonymous" user, browsing the files available on that system, marking the files you want to download, and downloading the files into your computer.

Do I need special software to use FTP?
The FTP area on CompuServe uses enhanced menus. The use of enhanced menus in FTP helps members find files more easily. A window of icons

representing popular Internet file downloading sites includes logos illustrating each information source. Members looking for files from these popular sites simply click on the icon.

While you may use any version of the CompuServe Information Manager interface to access FTP you will need WinCIM V1.3 or higher, or MacCIM V2.4 or higher to see the iconic buttons.

Be sure that the "show graphic menus" option is enabled in the SPECIAL PREFERENCES menu of your CIM software. This option is enabled by default.

How do I use FTP?

CompuServe has developed an easy to use interface for FTP so that most of these steps are as easy as clicking a mouse! Here's how it works:

* You can select from a list of popular sites, or go directly to the site of your choice (if you know the Internet address of the site). If you choose a site from the menu, the address, user name and password will be automatically supplied. Some sites will allow you to log on as an "anonymous", or guest user. Sites that allow anonymous login require you to enter a password. Although almost any password will work, most sites prefer that you enter your e-mail address so they can track who is accessing their files.

* If the site is very busy, and is unable to give you access, it will let you know with a message to that effect, and ask you to try again later. In some cases, the site may be so overloaded that it can not even respond with the usual "I'm busy" message. In such cases, the FTP interface will inform you that the site is too busy and will give you a chance to quit or try again. In other cases, the site may not be up or may be inaccessible for other reasons.

* Once you have gained access, you will be presented with a list of the directories and files available on the computer at the site you chose. You can move from directory to directory, and see which files are there. You may view GIF (graphics) and TXT (text) on-line so that you can decide whether or not you wish to download the file. Files not in this format may be downloaded and then viewed with the necessary software. Support for JPEG files will be implemented in a future release.

* Once you discover files you want to download, just mark the box next to the file name. When you have marked all the files you want to download, select the download button. You will be prompted for the location on your own computer that the files will be stored to.

* When you are done, you can log out of that site and into another, or you can quit FTP.

May I access all anonymous sites through CompuServe?

Approximately 95% of the FTP sites on the Internet are accessible through the CompuServe FTP interface. Some FTP sites are not compatible with

Figure 13.5   *And then you're in. This is a UNIX server so you must navigate through the directories with the Back and Top buttons. View displays text and GIF files, Retrieve downloads them to your hard disk.*

CompuServe's FTP software. These sites are not compatible because of the host software they are using. This software includes:

Some Windows NT Servers
Macintosh Servers
MVS Servers

If you do find a site that is not compatible, please report this site to FTP Feedback by clicking on the Feedback button.

How can I find files of interest to me?
Millions of files are available for download from the Internet, and finding the one that you want is not always an easy job. A couple of suggestions that might help:

* Ask other users. This is often the most effective way to find things of interest. Others (especially in the Internet forum) may know the exact location of the file for which you are searching.

* Read the Index Files. Many sites maintain index files listing the names of all the files they provide. These are usually in the top level directory for the site, or in the "pub" directory. Sometimes, the files are named "Index" or something similar. More often, they are named something like "ls-lr" (because they are the output of the UNIX command "ls -lr" used to create the file list).

The index files are often compressed, in which case they will have a suffix to indicate the type of compression used (see below). To make use of the index, download it, uncompress it if necessary, view it off-line, and then download the files of interest.

* Read the README file. Most sites have a README file containing important information about that site. Often, these files contain valuable information on where to find files of interest.

Some of the files I want to download end in an extension of tar. What does this mean?

Many of FTP sites you may be visiting run the UNIX operating system. As a result, files may be archived and stored in a UNIX archive format. One common UNIX archive format is "tar". "Tar" stands for "tape archiver," because the tar program was originally used to copy a collection of files to magnetic tape. By convention, files that have been archived using tar usually have an extension of .tar.

How do I unarchive UNIX tar files?

The way in which a "tarred" file is "untarred" depends on the operating system you are using. If you are doing this on a UNIX computer, untarring the files from inside a tar archive requires the use of the UNIX tar program itself. If you are running DOS, you need GZIP, a special DOS executable for "untarring." This file may be found in the UNIX forum of CompuServe (GO UNIXFORUM).

What about compressed files?

Files are often compressed for sake of storage space. You usually can tell these files by their file extension. A file with the extension Z was most likely compressed with the UNIX compress utility. To restore the original file, use the UNIX uncompress program GZIP. GZIP is available in the UNIX Forum (GO UNIXFORUM).

Files ending in .zip were compressed using the utility PKZIP and can be decompressed with PKUNZIP. You can find PKUNZIP in the IBM communications Forum (GO IBMCOM). This compression scheme is the most widely used for PCs.

For Macintosh users, the most common compression programs are BinHex 4.0 (extension hqx) and StuffIt (extension sit). Decompression utilities for these formats can be found in the Macintosh Communications Forum (GO MACCOM).

Why do some files have no size?

Actually, what you are seeing is an alias for the file that is stored at another location on the site. The host gives no information about the actual size of the alias, which is known as a symbolic link on UNIX systems. However, before you download the file, its size is determined so that you can decide whether you want to continue with the download or not.

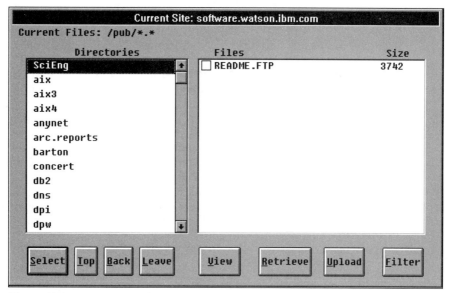

Figure 13.6   *An FTP download via CIM. Files go to your Download directory.*

Why do host sites use aliases, or symbolic links?

The most common reason is that this allows for a single file to be referenced from many different directories. For example, the site may have a README file that it wants to display in every directory. Instead of trying to keep several copies up to date, they simply keep one version of the README file, and place an alias that points to it in each sub-directory.

Sometimes when I retrieve a file, I end up in a different directory. Why is this?

The reason is again an alias or a symbolic link. To retrieve the file it is necessary for the system to change directories to the directory the aliased file resides. Once the retrieve has finished you may find yourself in a different directory than you started. Likewise, directories can be aliased to point to other directories. When you double-click on a directory, the system will take you to the directory to which the alias points.

Sometimes the error box appears when I try to change directories. What does this mean?

The most common reason is that the directory is protected. Most of the time you will probably be logging in anonymously (look at the username field in the connect to site window). Many host sites allow different groups of users to have access to some files but not others. As you can guess, anonymous users typically are not allowed into system directories, the private user directories, and any other directory or file the host site wishes to block from the general public.

Is host site security the reason I can't download certain files?
Usually this is the case. The administrator at the remote host can block anonymous (or any other user for that matter) from both files and directories.

I'm unable to see all of the text in my CIM window. What can I do?
In order to create the largest display area for reading text information in WinCIM your video display resolution should be larger than 640x480. In addition, the size of the window that displays the message text is negotiated between the FTP server and CIM at the beginning of your FTP session. To take advantage of this you should make your WinCIM window as large as possible prior to entering the CIM interface to FTP. You may resize manually or "maximize" the WinCIM window.

MacCIM automatically negotiates the size of the window for displaying text based on the size of your monitor. You need not do anything except be aware you will see a sub-optimal display if you are using a Classic, Mac Plus or other machine with a 9" diagonal display.

14 Telnet

Telnet is yet another bit of client software which you can use to log on to remote computers, and perform tasks as though you are sitting at the remote computer itself. CompuServe supports Telnet as part of its Internet services, so you can use the Telnet terminal software built into CIM. You don't need separate client software to use Telnet from within CompuServe, although you do if you choose to use CompuServe's PPP access.

There are too many telnet sites to list in this section of the book, and you'll have to trust me when I say that telnet is remarkably useful, once you get the hang of all the technical stuff you need to get it going. It's telnet which gives you basic access to many of the Internet's secrets, such as Archie, Internet Relay Chat and live backgammon sessions.

What you need for Telnet

You need a 'terminal emulator' – which is a long word for a piece of software which makes your exotic personal computer look like a boring old character based terminal. A terminal is something which, in its most basic form, takes in and spits out computer information and displays it on a screen or printout. In its most advanced form a terminal can also take in human input and convert it into something computers understand. The earliest terminals were simple solenoid-operated printers, and as electric keyboards became available they were tagged onto printers to give them an input/output capability.

Despite being old technology, terminals are still used in the UNIX world because UNIX was developed to talk to human beings through dumb character based interfaces. Terminals also happen to be cheaper than personal computers, which is why there are still vast numbers of them around in the commercial and academic world.

Like everything else in the computer world, there are various standards for terminals – a standard in this case being something that one manufacturer hopes to foist upon all the others, and the most common standards are Digital Equipment's DEC VT100/ VT102 emulations, and TeleType (TTY). TTY terminal emulation is exceedingly simple, and is the preferred method of getting around, but most UNIX boxes expect to see a slightly more exotic terminal emulation. VT100/102, or derivatives VT220 and VT320, are all used somewhere on the Internet. CIM provides a simulacrum of VT100 which is sufficiently good enough to provide Telnet access to most sites.

Don't forget that your terminal emulation program needs to sit on top of all the other stuff you need for Internet working if you go outside of CIM and CompuServe. You still need your transport system (TCP/IP), your modem handler (PPP) and your telnet client software. You can't just use a terminal emulator on its own to hook into the Internet, unless you are going through a third-party gateway such as a dial-up bulletin board.

Telnet commands

Remote Telnet servers have their own series of commands, even if you're logged in via CompuServe and CIM. Many of them will be running a version of UNIX and will expect you to be able to handle UNIX commands.

Once you're into one you'll need to get out, and the best way to do that is to type 'quit'. If this doesn't terminate your connection to the server then try sending CTRL] (hold down the CTRL key and then press the square bracket sign). This is the telnet escape sequence, and it should drop you back to the telnet> prompt, where you can then type 'quit'. If it doesn't, try CTRL D, or CTRL C. Other logout sequences exist, and the best way to discover them is at first hand. If your terminal has a 'log to disk' facility or a 'scroll-back buffer' then you can use these to grab the data on the screen from the remote service and save it for later perusal.

Other Telnet secrets

Telnet seems impenetrable to users of modern personal computers. No amount of reading books will be a substitute for telnetting around and making a nuisance of yourself. The trick is to log in CompuServe and enter the sitename into the Telnet Dialogue box. Or fire up your telnet client. The CompuServe Telnet client lets you go direct to selected sites, or type in the name of your preferred site.

Telnet ports

If you're using any sort of half-decent terminal emulator you'll find that it lets you connect to different ports on the remote machine. Again there's no widely accepted regime about which port connects you to what, but in many cases logging into one port gives you access to the public service, whilst logging into another gives you access to the most secret inner workings of the System Manager's personal diary. If you see a port number mentioned in listings of telnet addresses then always try that port first – because you will in all probability get thrown off the remote server if you don't.

Slow servers

Like all Internet processes telnet can seem extremely slow at times. You type in a command, the screen starts to display text ... and suddenly stops. The only advice, especially if you're paying on-line or telephone charges, is to log out from slow telnet sessions, and try again later. It's often the case that telnet servers slow down drastically when under load from the other 655,000 users logged in, and your only recourse is to disconnect.

The speed of telnet sessions also depends on the load placed on all the various bits of the routers, cables and other bits of elec-trickery which make up the Internet, so the best advice for maximizing throughput on telnet (or FTP sessions) is to use the Internet during off-peak hours, as far as possible. You can get a fast session to most USA servers from the UK between 7:00–12:00 hrs GMT, as the USA is six or more hours behind us. Some UK Internet users also claim faster results after midnight, UK time.

Telnet file transfers

There are any number of terminal based telnet services around. If you have a CompuServe account you can telnet to compuserve.com from outside of CompuServe over the Internet, instead of through the phone network. You can also use your normal ZMODEM, XMODEM and other file transfer protocols at some telnet sites, because all telnet is doing is providing the link service between you and the remote system.

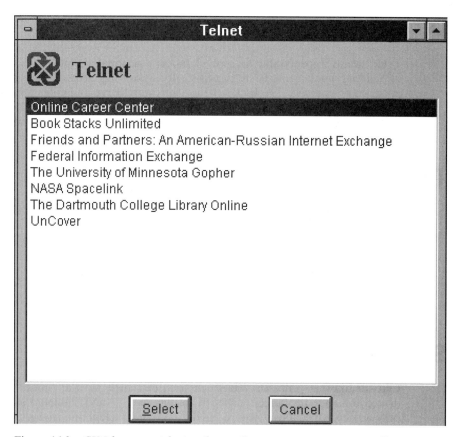

Figure 14.2 *CIM lets you pick sites from a list, or go to your own. In all cases you'll go to terminal emulation . . .*

However, your ordinary terminal software may not be able to communicate over TCP/IP, which is the transport protocol going on underneath telnet. This is because most UK based communications programs like to talk over modems and you'll need a TCP/IP, compliant terminal program to make ZMODEM (or other asynchronous file transfer protocols) work over telnet.

Hytelnet

Hytelnet is an attempt to bring the Graphical User Interface to boring old character based terminals. It's also a neat way to find out about telnet and telnet sites. You log in to a Hytelnet site and follow the prompts. Use the cursor arrows to move up to the <highlighted> options and press Enter. Hytelnet will bring up the page with the information on it. The place to start your search for interesting sites is a Hytelnet server such access.usask.ca. Hytelnet has been overshadowed by recent developments such as the World

Figure 14.3   . . .which looks like this NASA site. You can capture sessions to disk or to printer and configure function keys to do various tricks. What you can't do in CIM Telnet is transfer files with XMODEM. For that you need a telnet software client, and a PPP link. The NASA site sends Shuttle Launch details out by this method, or by FTP.

Wide Web, but is mentioned here for old time's sake. Hardly anyone uses it, but CIM can access Hytelnet sites if you come across one.

Telnet services

Telnet is an important part of the Internet, because it lets you do real work. You can log into the Library of Congress and check out almost any book or author, you can log into the NASA databases and pickup info on Shuttle launches. More than a thousand other databases are available for browsing.

Talk to the world with IRC

IRC stands for "Internet Relay Chat". It was originally written by Jarkko Oikarinen (jto@tolsun.oulu.fi) in 1988. IRC is a multi-user chat system, where people convene on "channels" to talk in groups, or privately. IRC is constantly evolving, so the way things to work one week may not be the way they work the next.

Internet Relay Chat has grown tremendously over the last couple of years and was used by the Labour Party to distribute Conference information. It takes a while to learn how to use IRC - the syntax and commands are arcane and complex and differ from server to server. Nonetheless it can be rewarding; if you have the time to spend on it. IRC servers offer different commands and facilities; try these servers and ask for the help files; often /HELP COMMANDS - or similar. The numbers after the addresses are the Port numbers, used within Telnet clients. There are a number of dedicated IRC clients around in the Internet Resources Forum.

Some UK IRC servers

stork.doc.ic.ac.uk 6667
sun4.bham.ac.uk 6667
shrug.dur.ac.uk 6667

Some IRC commands

"Pub" means public (or "visible") channel. "hack" is the channel name. "#" is the prefix. A "@" before someone's nickname indicates he/she is the "Channel operator" of that channel. A Channel Operator is someone who has control over a specific channel. It can be shared or not as the first Channel Operator sees fit. The first person to join the channel automatically receives Channel Operator status, and can share it with anyone he/she chooses (or not). Another thing you might see is "Prv" which means private. You will only see this if you are on that private channel. No one can see Private channels except those who are on that particular private channel.

To join a channel, type /join #channelname. Once you get to the channel, you will see people talking.

To start talking, just type. And when you're done saying what you have to say, just hit the return key. You can start with something simple like "hello". When you choose to leave a channel, just type /part #channelname

To get a list of channels with their names and topics, do /list -min 30 (on ircII) which will show you channels with 30 or more members. You can also do this for smaller numbers.

Some of the most popular foreign language channels include #42 (which is a Finnish channel), #warung (which is a Malaysian channel. The word "warung" means "coffeehouse" or "small restaurant"), #polska (a Polish channel), #nippon (a Japanese channel, note that "funny" characters are often seen here — this is Kanji. You will need a Kanji-compatible terminal program and Kanji-compatible irc client to converse in Kanji), #espanol (a Spanish channel), #russian (a Russian channel).

These are just examples — a large percentage of languages in the world is spoken on IRC somewhere. If your language/country isn't listed above, ask on #irchelp to see if there is a channel for it.

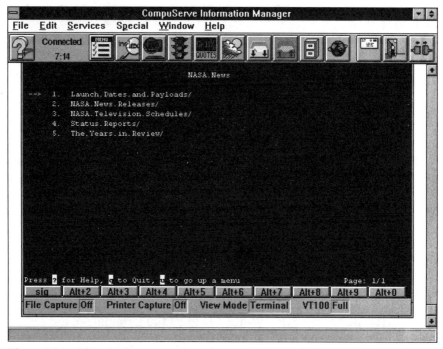

Figure 14.4   *This site lets you navigate between topics with the arrow keys, and go to the next page with the spacebar. Other sites differ.*

Some Internet Relay Chat Networks

Efnet

Undernet

LinuxNet/SysNet

Iaonet Formally Overnet

Chiron

KidLink

DalNet

NetherNet

IdealNet/MTSUnet

Japanese IRC

QuestNet/Taiwan Big-5

ZAnet/South African IRC

Australian IRC

University of Cincinnati

CompuServe Telnet Frequently Asked Questions

What are the advantages of using the CompuServe telnet interface?
CompuServe presents a controlled view of the Internet. Access is gained through a menu system that provides information about a site, as well as seamless menu driven access to a site. In addition, members have the ability to telnet to any site of their choice, even if it is not listed on the menu.

What type of software is recommended for using the CompuServe telnet service?
Telnet sites generally expect that you will be running terminal emulation software that can emulate a VT100 terminal. While VT100 is supported in WinCIM 1.4 and above, WinCIM 1.3 or below may not meet your needs. MacCim 2.4.1 (as well as earlier versions) supports a subset of VT100 capabilities but it is not fully VT100 compliant. MacCim version 3.0 will have full VT100 support. Other terminal emulators that have been used successfully with the CompuServe telnet gateway include Windows Terminal, Procomm, and Dynacomm.

How do I ensure that WinCIM is in VT100 terminal emulation mode?
When using WinCIM to access the telnet service, you will automatically be placed in full VT100 terminal emulation mode. You may notice that your screen changes color as VT100 is turned on. Upon exiting the telnet application, your default terminal emulation settings will be restored.

What do I do if I do not know the user id and password to enter at a site?
Many telnet sites allow people who do not have an account on their computer to login a guest. Just type guest at the user id prompt. In most circumstances you do not have to enter a password if you are a guest. Occasionally, this password is case sensitive. Also, make sure you read the descriptive text issued when logging onto a telnet site. Often, this text indicates the user id and password to be used by visitors. Keep in mind that not all telnet sites allow guest access. You may run across some sites for which a legitimate user id and password are required for access.

What type of performance can I expect when I connect to a telnet site?
Performance at telnet sites is subject not only to usage from the Internet, but also to local demand for resources. If many people access a site at the same time, performance can and will deteriorate quickly. Be prepared to wait for the remote site to respond to your requests if you are using it during periods of peak demand.

How can I change my default telnet options?
There are a number of telnet options you may want to set. To see a listing of these options, type the control key plus the ']' once connected to a telnet site,

and then type HELP SET. A telnet setting may be changed at the same prompt.

Can I telnet to a specific port?

You may now telnet to a specific port. Occasionally, a telnet site will allow you to establish a telnet session to a port so that you may run a specific application such as a Mutli-User Dialogue (MUD), or Internet Relay Chat (IRC).

To indicate that you want to connect to a specific telnet site and a specific port, choose "Access a Specific Site" from the telnet menu, and type the site name followed by a colon and the port number. For example, to telnet to the "alexmud" MUD port, type:

alexmud.stacken.kth.se:4000

By convention, port numbers below 1024 are reserved for predefined uses and those above 1024 are intended for site specific (public) uses. For security purposes, CompuServe will not allow telnet access to ports below 1024.

How do I disconnect from a site?

Typically, a telnet site will provide menu prompts and instructions on how to "quit" or "exit" the site. Once you leave a telnet site, you will be returned to CompuServe. If you have difficulty exiting the site, press the control key plus the "]" key to return to CompuServe.

How can I suggest a site to be included on the telnet sites menu?

If there is a site you think should be added to the menu, just issue your request via Telnet Feedback.

How is access to the telnet service priced?

You may get up to date pricing information by using the GO RATES command or see the Appendices for basic information.

15 Searching the 'Net with Archie, Gopher and WAIS

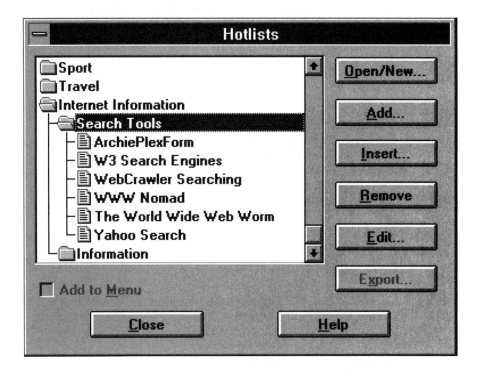

All of the services described here can be accessed either with CompuServe PPP and suitable client software, or more recently, over the World Wide Web. Because sites come and go, use the Web search facilities to look for lists, or use the CompuServe Internet forums for guidance.

Ask Archie

Archie is a tool that helps you find information on the Internet. You tell Archie to go and find a file, and then it comes back with lots of not quite the right information. Archie is only one of the search methods available on the Internet, and like most character based interfaces, it's looking more shabby with each day that passes. Archie is mainly used for searching for generic file types. You might want to search for files for your Amiga, or for Humour, or for Carburettor.

Archie servers can be accessed in three ways; conventionally by telnetting into an Archie server, by sending search requests to the server by email, or by using one of the Archie Web pages now appearing on the Net. The first method is marginally faster than waiting two days or more for an email reply, the third method can be slow as the Web gets clogged with traffic. Probably the best advice for searching for computer files is to use CompuServe's File Finders, but you might want to keep Archie in reserve for a rainy day.

To get into an Archie server you telnet to the Archie server of your choice, and a good start is archie.doc.ic.ac.uk. It's at Imperial College in London, and is fairly fast, if you catch it on a good day when it's working. A number of Archie clients are also starting to appear for Windows and Macintosh computers.

Search me

Archie uses several search methods to locate the data you want, and all of them are command line driven and come in various guises of complexity. You set up which search method you want after login. Here's Archie via Telnet, which is the best way of learning how tedious command line interfaces are.

The search methods are:

exact
sub
subcase
regex

You should try the exact method first, as long as you know what you're looking for. It's faster, allegedly. However, most people start with sub.

You set the search method up with:

set search exact (or sub etc.)

and then type in whatever it is you want to search for:

set search sub
prog amiga

The Archie server will then do its stuff and rummage around the world's databases until it finds a match. In this case Archie will come up with a list of all of the sites which provide Amiga PROGram files, as a scrolling list. In fact it's such a long list that the information will scroll off your screen. You should therefore at least be using a terminal emulator with a scroll-back buffer, which lets you call back the data for display. DOS people, who know little of scroll-back, will find benefit in a terminal emulation package that logs

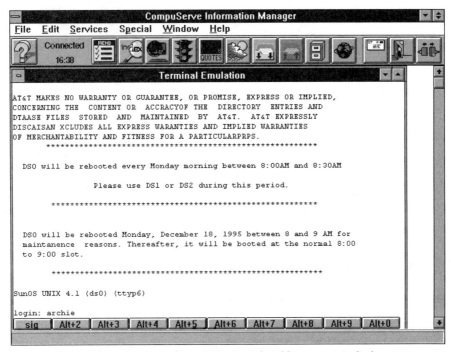

Figure 15.2   *Archie via CIM Telnet. Sometimes the old ways aren't the best . . .*

data to disk. In both cases you'll need to investigate whatever Archie sends you, as you'll get a lot of information back, not all of which will be relevant. You can also use the mail commands to mail the output to yourself.

Archie search methods

The exact method looks for an exact match to the search string you've typed in – but there are other choices. Here they are:

Sub matches the search string anywhere in the text. If you typed:

set search sub
prog amigastuff

Archie should find:

amigastuff.lzh
Amigastuff.faq
amigastuff.txt

Subcase matches the search string for case. If you typed:

set search subcase
prog Amigastuff

Archie should find:

Amigastuff.faq

It won't find:

amigastuff.txt
amigastuff.lzh

Regex stands for 'regular expression' and is a method of using wildcards to limit search matching. Not many PC or Mac users bother with it, because it's about as intuitive as discovering Relativity. Consequently many personal computer users are happy to do sub matching. If you want to get to grips with regex searching then you're recommended to pick up a book on UNIX – because typing long search strings hooked together by regex expressions leads to more errors than success.

Other Archie commands

You should limit Archie's searching, to provide you with a reasonable number of matches. Archie will look for up to 1000 matches before it gives up, which takes time. You can change this limit with the maxhits command:

set maxhits 50

will ensure that you only get the results of 50 matches. A good number is somewhere between 100 and 200.

The pager sets up the number of lines displayed on a page, which is normally 24. You can check with the show command, and reset the pagination with:

set pager 18 (or some such)

Autologout will set the time allowed before throwing you off. Again, check with show before you alter it.

Status (on/off) gets Archie to show you the status of the ongoing search, and sortby sets the way Archie displays the results. You can set sortby to:

hostname/rhostname – which displays the results by alphabetical list of the host on which the search string is found. Rhostname gives a reverse alphabetical search.

time/rtime – newest or oldest modification date.
filename/rfilename – alphabetical filename or reverse alphabetical filename.

The availability of commands can vary, so check before you configure Archie to send you nothing, after a long wait.

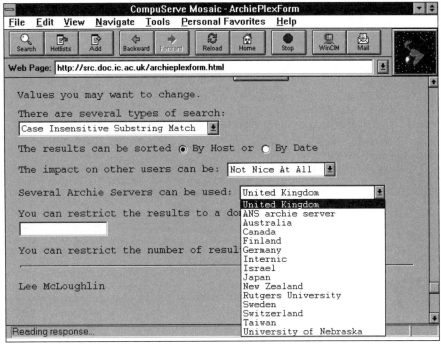

Figure 15.3 *Archie via PPP and the Web. Faster, better, more responsive, and no command line interface.*

Archie also has a whatis function, which is used instead of the prog command. If you type whatis filename you might get a list of descriptions of available files. The whatis command searches these description lists for matches, and is a slightly more intuitive method of fighting with Archie. But don't forget that Archie doesn't do any file transfers for you – you will still have to FTP to the indicated site and directory to get the data. Progressive it ain't. However, some Archie clients can now do this. They remove all the command line stuff and display the results nicely. You then double click on the file to be FTP'd and it's sent to you directly.

Mailing Archie

You can email search requests to Archie, which makes more sense than hanging around an Archie server, consuming telephone time and patience. All the functions mentioned so far will work. You simply send an email to the Archie server of your choice, containing the search requirements, and if you've done everything correctly, you should get a reasonable response. Remember not to send your automatically generated signature to Archie, as it won't appreciate it.

Here's an Archie email request:
Email to archie@archie.doc.ic.ac.uk

set mailto yourname@compuserve.com
(makes sure you get the response mailed to you)
servers
(returns a list of other archie servers)
help
(returns the help file for that server)
set search subcase
prog Amiga
set maxhits 100
quit
(ends the request.)

And that's it. If you've done everything properly you should get a reply, usually within a few hours, although it can take longer, like three days, to arrive.

Other search methods

Archie is, well, kind of quaint. It's a bit like those stodgy computerized indexes they've now put into municipal libraries. It's quicker to search through the shelves by hand than it is to learn the archaic user interface. There's several more forms of search mechanism on the Internet including Gopher, Veronica and World Wide Web. So if Archie doesn't suit you then look at other ways of finding what you're after.

Gopher

Gopher is an information search tool, which originally came from the University of Minnesota, which has a Gopher of the Geomyidae variety as a mascot. You use Gopher to search for things on the 'Net – but unlike Archie, Gopher is menu driven. You could get to like Gophering, whereas the same cannot always be said for Archie-ing.

To set about Gophering you need a Gopher client on your computer at best – or the use of a telnet client over a terminal link at worst. You open your Gopher client (you have already connected to the 'Net by modem or Ethernet) and start clicking on menus, or fighting with typed-in commands. Gopher is client-dependent – that is, some Gopher clients are pretty poor, some are just pretty, and some are just poor. Windows users get a good Gopher client in the Shareware HGopher software. Mac users will love TurboGopher, which is also Shareware and as fast as they come. You'll need to use your gopher Client over the CompuServe PPP link, as CompuServe don't yet provide an internal one as part of the CompuServe service.

The speed of the Gopher client you are using is fairly important, especially so over phone lines where you're paying money not to receive data. And

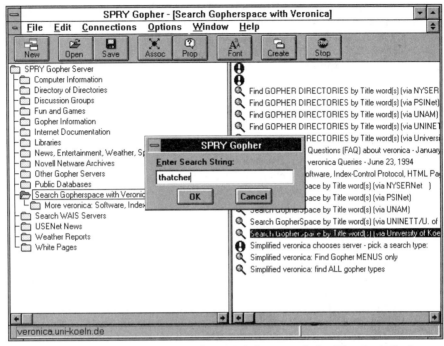

Figure 15.4   *Using a gopher client and a PPP link to search for 'Thatcher'. Gopher can be very fast.*

Gopher likes to pull pictures off the 'Net and show them to you, so a speedy user interface is vital. You can get most of the latest releases of Gopher software from the ftp site at boombox.micro.umn.edu but alas the site is often busy. The Web also supports Gophering as part of its search procedures, so using the search mechanisms on the Web is probably the easiest way to find data. Here's details of the other way of Gophering, for Internet diehards.

I know I want it – but what does it do?

Gopher pulls information off the 'Net. It's a 'document delivery service' which can get you text files, binaries, images, executable and plain old lists. Gopher was originally developed in April 1991 by the University of Minnesota and consequently you'll find that many Gopher clients default to the University of Minnesota on start-up.

Gopher in actuality is a bunch of dedicated computers called Gopher servers. Each Gopher server knows about all the other servers (most of the time), so if a Gopher server doesn't have the info you want it should go and look it up elsewhere at another Gopher server. It presents these searches as a series of menus from which you pick the next item you want. You navigate around between Gopher servers, or you search either a particular server for information, or all of the servers, or just all the menu titles on all the servers (menu titles contain preset pointers to major services like Electronic Books). The All Servers approach means that you have discovered GopherSpace – that hypothetical realm inhabited by those stupid boxes of silicon we are pleased to call computers.

Using GopherSpace

You can access a Gopher server by using your very own Gopher client software. You can also telnet into a Gopher server and do it that way, but running your own client software is faster, and you get a say in what the interface looks like. Most Gopher client software comes ready configured with a 'home' server. This is usually the University of Minnesota, as previously mentioned.

Once you're connected you will be presented with a menu of places to go, things to do, and it's up to you to start exploring. You do this by actioning menu requests and following menu items until you get to where you want to be. This is easier than it sounds but in the early days of your Gophering you will neither know where you want to go, nor recognize where you are once you get there. But it doesn't take long to navigate around the system, and after a while you'll really get the feeling that GopherSpace is a rather good term for the virtual environment you're in whilst Gophering.

Gopher servers will present you with a list of 'hits' on your search string. You then click on each document or file and it's sent to your computer by FTP. Some Gopher Clients also let you read ASCII files on line, although most of them prefer to send the file to you, for storage on your already packed hard disk. You can use Gopher to search for any topic, which makes it useful for tracking down hard-to-find stuff like Great American Novelists or lists of honest British politicians. Gopher searches are generally very rewarding as they cover wide numbers of subjects per search.

Veronica

After a couple of hours of floating around in GopherSpace you are going to ask how to find specific items in such a sea of menus? The answer is the 'Very Easy Rodent-Oriented Net-wide Index to Computerized Archives', or Veronica. Of course it is. (Veronica was a character of the cult American cartoon series The Archies)

You get to Veronica by following Gopher menus to Search topics in GopherSpace using Veronica. You'll get to a further set of menus from where you choose a Gopher server (pick the one nearest to you). Picking one site then lets you type in a search string, and off it goes to get the data. You'll get a response in seconds, or more probably you'll get a message saying that the Gopher you chose as a gateway for searching is too busy to handle your request. You can either try again, or go to another server. If you search

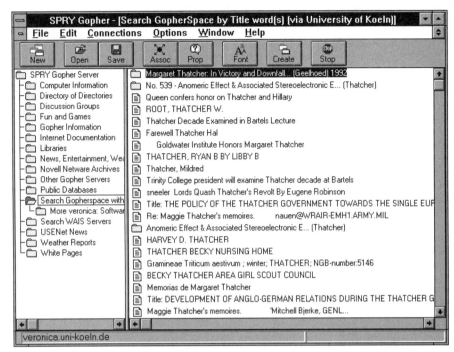

Figure 15.5   *A cabinet full of Gopher Thatcher files from around the world.*

'Gopher directory titles' you'll just be searching the menus available on the Gopher servers, which is useful for those common searches like Lists of Gopher Servers (search on Lists). If you search 'GopherSpace' you'll be looking at all of the indexes, and you'll find many more files that match your search criteria.

If you know where the information is that you want, you can usually go straight to that server and type in your request. This saves network bandwidth and should speed things up a tad, although many Gopher servers seem to be permanently busy these days. In both cases you'll be rewarded with screens full of information which matches the keyword typed in, and your heart will surge with joy.

It's worthwhile remembering that Gopher gets about the Internet by telnet and that if you do find a site you're interested in and want to return to you can telnet there yourself. But it's often quicker to Gopher around, especially if you have a GUI Gopher client, because you don't have to muck around with UNIX's demands for login codes and so forth.

You may also run into the phenomenon of The De-Clienting of GopherSpace – where network administrators remove telnet clients from their Gopher servers on the basis that it's better if you use your own. This is also a great move towards the Coming GUI-ness of GopherSpace and the day may come when you'll never see a command line interface ever again.

Bookmarks

Once you discover bookmarks you'll wonder why the Internet is reputed to be so difficult. The Gopher client lets you navigate back to places you've already been by way of bookmarks. You find a Gopher server which contains, say, the entire text of 'The Big Dummy's Guide to the Hitch-Hikers Guide to the Art of Derivative Book Titles', and you want to go back there when Kevin arrives with the brown ale and the modem. You set a Gopher bookmark (methods vary depending on the access method) which will take you back to the site or archive you were at when you set it. On a Mac or a PC those bookmarks will still be there the next time you use your Gopher client – but alas, if you telnet to a Gopher site you'll lose your bookmarks as soon as you disconnect. But at least it's a great way of justifying an upgrade to a Mac or Windows computer.

Getting files with Gopher

Gopher is user friendly, despite that fact that the server side of things runs under UNIX. The latest Mac and Windows versions of the client software (using something called HGopher) can do as many things at once as you've got the memory for, which rather makes you wonder how DOS ever got to be so popular. You can kick off a search in one window, navigate in another, and download a file in a third – as long as your modem, your service provider and your personal computer can take the strain. Gopher can then download the file to you via FTP or, if you're using a terminal, via one of the asynchronous file transfer protocols like Zmodem or Xmodem.

GUI Gopher software can also be hooked into other programs you've got sitting on your computer, and will display GIF files on-line if it can find a GIF viewer, or pick up and play sound files if you have the matching software and hardware installed. In fact Gopher is the single really neat way of finding files and data on the 'Net, and one can only wonder why it's such a comparatively recent introduction. If you're confused about why you should be using Gopher servers instead of Archie to locate files and data – remember that Archie providers pointers to FTP sites, while Gopher is an archive indexing system in its own right. In many cases you'll be able to find what you need with Gopher – but in some cases you still need Archie. And the astute Internetter will use both methods to find files, and perhaps use Gopher for a bit of recreation.

WAIS

WAIS is Wide Area Information Server. WAIS servers themselves are in a constant state of being rehashed – which means that any examples given may not work – and you may find that you can get all the information you need from the Internet using Gopher. (Gopher can pick up WAIS servers as part of its ferreting.)

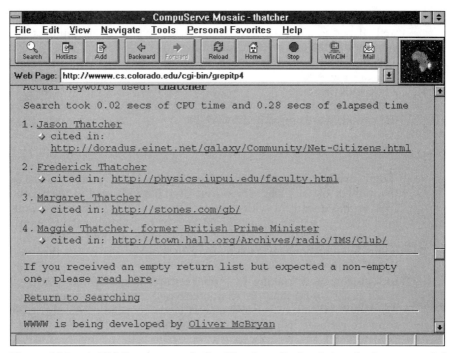

Figure 15.6 *A WebCrawler search for Thatcher. Gopher brings back more varied results.*

The main advantage of WAIS over Gopher is that it will search multiple WAIS servers at one swoop, whereas Gopher takes a peek inside one at a time. WAIS servers also tend to carry a lot of academic files, and it's consequently of great use for scientific or educational research.

You get to a WAIS server by telnetting to one, or by using the WAIS client you almost certainly don't have on your machine. Or you can now get to WAIS via the World Wide Web, which is getting to be the grandaddy of all Internet search mechanisms. Try telnetting to quake.think.com as your first attempt – it was running as this book went to press. Type WAIS at the login prompt, to get to the WAIS front end.

WAIS servers used to present the user with a list of other WAIS servers, but had to stop when the list started to edge up to several hundred sites. So WAIS (at quake.think.com) now presents only the top directory, which might not mean much if you've not WAISed before.

You search through WAIS-space by entering a keyword – you'll be given a prompt – and then picking from a list of databases which contain the keyword you entered. With some WAIS clients you can point the search at a single server or the whole list of WAIS servers, which will provide more results, quantitatively speaking.

Telnet WAIS screens are a bit picky about the sort of terminal emulation you have – you need to be able to select an item from the list by moving up and down, which means your terminal emulation has to work well. If it doesn't work like that then try typing in the number in brackets you'll see at the end of each search item.

The Boolean search mechanism is simple – if you want to refine the search you can use AND, OR, NOT as separators – but not all WAIS servers will work with them.

As an example, if you want to search on 'arabic' and 'grammar' you enter the two keywords separated by AND:

arabic AND grammar

(Don't use 'and' in lower case.) You'll get a list of search results back, with the number of 'hits' per search (out of 1000) indicated in the Score Column. Pick up the document with the space bar and if it's what you want you can mail it to yourself by hitting the M key, or by following the prompt.

If you find WAIS useful then try the Gopher method of accessing it, which might be quicker. And if you get really hooked on WAIS then you can get WAIS client software for your machine from several sites, notably by FTPing to wais.com and looking in /pub/freeware. Some of the WAIS clients are much easier to use than the character based interface you get with telnet, and the MacWAIS client in particular is a joy to behold. As always, the client software varies in its usability, so if you have a choice, shop around.

Which one when?

Despite protestations from Internet geeks armed with Ethernet terminals and UNIX, the best method of searching the Internet is the one you're happiest with. Archie is slow and command line based – which means you can use it from almost any dial-up provider via a terminal connection; WAIS works best with a GUI client and provides a direct link to many academic databases. But Gopher is the easiest of the lot, and the fastest over modem links. It can also hook into those WAIS servers, and so it perhaps offers the best compromise. It's worth spending a little time exploring Gopher client programs too, as they differ in their ability to present information in a coherent manner. And you may have to configure your Gopher client to bring up various file viewers; as an example the Windows Gopher programs tend to bring up 'Write' for text files, Paintbrush for BMP files and so on. You'll need to spend some time fine-tuning this aspect of your Gophering to get the best from it.

Finally, Gophering is one of the nicest ways of giving money to your telecomms provider – it provides a key to many of the doors on the Internet. If you can't find it on CompuServe then go for Gopher.

Enhanced Veronica searching

When you select a query type, your Gopher client will present a dialog box. The search is not case-sensitive. You may get better results by entering a multi-word query rather than a single word. Multi-word queries will find only those items whose titles contain all of the specified words. For instance, 'book' might find 4000 items, but 'Apple PowerBook' will find 2000.

By default, the Veronica servers will deliver only the first 200 items that match your query. You can request any number of items by including the '-mx' command phrase in your query. X is the number of items you wish.

'book -m' will provide all available matching items.
'book -m1000' will provide 1000 items.

You may find a message at the end of your Veronica results menu:

"*** There are 59173 more items matching your query ****"

Use ' book -m' to rerun the search and get all the items.

Boolean Veronica searches

The search understands the logical operators AND, NOT, OR. If you use a simple multi-word query, such as 'mammal whale', it is the same as using AND between the words. For instance 'book electronic' is the same query as 'electronic AND book'. An asterisk ('*') at the end of a query will match anything, so use it as a limited form of wildcard search. The asterisk character may be used only at the end of words as the search will fail if a '*' is placed within a word or at the beginning of a word.

16 Epilogue

Imagine an electronic world, with the population connected to a huge multimedia communications network, where information is fed directly into your computer by a fibre optic cable, and where hard disks and local storage are a thing of the past.

CompuServe offers a glimpse into just such a future, where you'll pull down all the information and applications you need from a central server, rather than from your own internal storage systems. Back in 1994 CompuServe was simply an Information service, albeit a large one. Today it has become a gateway to almost all of the public electronic on-line services available on the planet.

This growth of digital electronics and communications has reshaped a world which we were once able to take for granted. Is the Casio wristwatch on my wrist just there to tell the time, or does it also hold two hundred phone numbers? Does my personal electronic organizer really need a printer to transfer information or can I squirt the data over an invisible infrared link to a colleague? Is CompuServe merely an electronic toy for those we once derided as yuppies, or is it a vital part of the Information Revolution, in which we are all now immersed?

It's not computers which are the building blocks of the Revolution, but digital networked communications. The computer-driven links which form the Internet are merging with telephone and television systems into a digital infrastructure which one day will form a coherent single network. Soon, your computer will be a telephone, answer phone, television, email/fax terminal and a window on the world. We already have the chip technology and CompuServe currently offers most of these options - all we need is the communications infrastructure to link it all together, and the next generation of micro-processor technology.

Al Gore's 'Information Superhighway' is a global data-pipe. Using it, information on a patient in New York would be available in real time to a surgeon in San Francisco, a global television and radio network would become a reality, and the Internet as we see it now would be a laughable anachronism. Gore's vision is quickly coming true. Computer networking technologies can now transfer data faster than your hard disk can store it. Fibre cables are being installed in many UK cities, ready to be lit up by information providers supplying movie and television channels. A Timex wristwatch now works as an on-line data terminal. The infrastructure is going in, and the home terminal with a combined computer/TV and voice mail system will be a reality.

Where does this leave CompuServe and the Internet? Optical transmission systems will use wider bandwidths way beyond the seven and eight bit systems in use today, to give almost instant access across the globe to any system connected to them. Those wider bandwidths will increase data transfer rates beyond that needed for full screen video, and the CompuServe will become almost indistinguishable from broadcast TV - except you'll choose what you want to access. You'll still use a keyboard to compose your email but you'll navigate around the system with a multi-button remote control, not a computer mouse. And you'll also need a Service Provider.

Today you're using a modem to connect to CompuServe. In the next few years you may have a wired ISDN or a direct ATM network connection to a CompuServe hub in your local town. The files you transfer will be larger, but the speed with which they arrive on your screen will be breathtaking.

The commercialization of the Internet is also an indicator of things to come. Once funded entirely by the US government, the Internet is now largely a commercial free-for-all. An Internet with broadcast-quality digital transmission would seriously threaten existing national monopolies. The technology to provide this is here now, and the only weapon governments have to fight it is the continued regulation of cable and Telecomms industries.

If we wait just a few years, CompuServe and the Internet will become just more channels on whatever the Superhighway has become, and accessed by a device which looks not unlike a television set. And a direct link to the brain? A computer manufacturer has just launched a sensor which allows mind control of computer games. Only a few months ago it was science fiction.

Section 4

Appendices

Appendix 1
CompuServe rates

New pricing from February 1st, 1996

CompuServe are removing the communications surcharge from all Mercury and France Telecom nodes across Europe from 1st February. The information in this Appendix is likely to change without notice and is provided for interest only. It applies only to UK pricing. Please GO RATES for up to date pricing information.

How much?

For £6.95, your CompuServe membership entitles you to five free hours on the service. This includes forums, mail, and Internet access. After your first five hours, additional hours are billed at the rate of £1.95 per hour.

For £17.95 a month, the Super Value Plan adds 15 free hours (for a total of 20 hours each month) and each additional hour is just £1.50.

Premium ($) services carry additional surcharges, however, during your free hours, you are not charged for connect-time. Any communications surcharges (such as those incurred for using GNS) apply.

Member service areas are free of connect time charges. These areas include:

Ask Customer Service (GO FEEDBACK) Member Assistance (GO MEMBER) Rates and Pricing Information (GO RATES) Billing Information (GO BILLING) Access Numbers (GO PHONES) Member Directory (GO DIRECTORY) Mail Center (GO MAILCENTER) CompuServe Store (GO ORDER) New Member Welcome Center (GO WELCOME) What's New (GO NEW) Mail Assistance (GO MAILHELP) Financial Services Help Area (GO FINHELP) The WinCIM General Support Forum (GO WCIMGE) The WinCIM Technical Support Forum (GO WCIMTE) The DOSCIM Support Forum (GO DCIMSUP) The CS Navigator Support Forum (CO CSNAVSUP) The Net-Launcher Support Forum (GO NLSUPPORT) The MacCIM Support Forum (GO MCIMSUP) The MacNAV Support Forum (GO MNAVSUP) The CompuServeCD Support Forum (GO CCDSUP) The CIM for OS/2 Support Forum (GO OCIMSUP) The CompuServe Help Forum (GO HELP-FORUM, GO CISHILFE) The New Member Forum (GO NEWMEMBER) The Practice Forum (GO PRACTICE) The CS General Applications Forum (GO CSAPPS) CompuServe Help Database (GO CSHELP)

Additional free services

The following services on-line are also considered free services and will not count toward your free hours each month. These include:

Account/Billing Administration, Special Events/Contests, Find Services Support Directory, Directory of Mall Stores Online, Surveys (GO SURVEY) Missing Childrens Forum (GO MISSING), Forum Upload Credit, CompuServe Visa, CompuServe Upgrade Area, MHS Upgrade, CompuServe Software.

About CompuServe's Family of Software, CompuServe Information Manager Software, CompuServe Navigator, CompuServe Netlauncher for Windows, CompuServe Mail for Microsoft Exchange, CompuServe Mail Driver, CompuServe MS Mail Driver, CompuServe Mail for Powertalk, CompuServe, CD Online, CompuServe for GEOS, CompuServe Scripts/Modem Database, CompuServe FCCopy Utility, CompuServe Support Files, Professional Connection/PC3, German Support Forum, France Support Forum

Internet access

Your CompuServe membership allows you to access the Internet. Currently, you can access the following services on the Internet:

Direct Internet Access (Dial PPP) for use with any stand-alone Internet application, File Transfer Protocol (FTP) Remote Login (Telnet) USENET Newsreader, ASCII USENET, Newsreader CIM, World Wide Web.

For additional information on the listed services, GO INTERNET.

Mail

CompuServe Mail is billed for connect time. This includes reading mail and viewing classified ads. Surcharged areas, such as fax, telex and Congress-Grams carry additional charges. For a complete list of mail services and rates, including hardcopy deliveries through the postal service, GO MAIL-RATES.

Communication surcharges

Communication surcharges are charges that are billed to your account for accessing the Information Service from various networks (such as GNS Dialplus in the UK). Communication surcharges are billed to help cover the cost that it takes to provide access through supplemental networks, and the CompuServe network in certain locations worldwide. Prime and non-prime time rates are determined by the local time at the network location.

Communication charges apply during every session on-line, whether hourly connect-time charges apply or not if you use an additional network to connect to CompuServe. Long distance and other telephone access charges, such as message units, are not included in the surcharge rate.

The CompuServe direct dial network is the most cost effective network to connect to the Information Service and does not incur surcharges. From February 1996 there will be no surcharge for using France Telecom or Mercury 5000 nodes.

CompuServe fax charges for guidance only

Go MAIL/ HELP FAX PRICES for up to date rates.

Europe	Dial	First 1000 char $	Additional 1000 char $
Andorra	33628	.90	.90
Austria	43	.90	.90
Belgium	32	.90	.90
Bulgaria	359	.90	.90
Cyprus	357	.90	.90
Czechoslovakia	42	.90	.90
Denmark	45	.90	.90
Estonia	372	.90	.90
Fed. Rep. of Germany	49	.90	.90
Finland	358	.90	.90
France	33	.90	.90
Georgia	7 *	1.90	.90
Gibraltar	350	.90	.90
Greece	30	.90	.90
Iceland	354	.90	.90
Italy	39	.90	.90
Italy/Vatican City	396	.90	.90
Latvia	371	.90	.90
Liechtenstein	4175	.90	.90
Lithuania	370	.90	.90
Luxembourg	352	.90	.90
Malta	356	.90	.90
Monaco	3393	.90	.90
Netherlands	31	.90	.90
Norway	47	.90	.90
Poland	48	.90	.90
Portugal	351	.90	.90
Rep. of Ireland	353	.90	.90
Romania	40	.90	.90
San Marino	39549	.90	.90
Spain	34	.90	.90
Sweden	46	.90	.90
Switzerland	41	.90	.90
United Kingdom	44	.90	.90
Yugoslavia	38	.90	.90

Appendix 2 European access numbers

If you need more phone nunbers than this GO PHONES. Don't forget you can create a new connection profile for each phone number you need from the Special/Session Settings Menu option.

CompuServe network access numbers

To access CompuServe through the direct-dial CompuServe Network in the United Kingdom, follow the instructions below. GO RATES to view current information on communication surcharges.

LOGON INSTRUCTIONS:

1. Establish a phone connection by dialing a CompuServe (CPS) access number listed under "List Access Numbers" from the previous menu.

2. Once the connection has been made, wait for 3-4 seconds, then press Enter or Carriage Return <CR>.

3. At the "Host Name:" prompt, type CIS and press Carriage Return.

4. At the "User ID:" prompt, enter your User ID number and log on as usual.

  example: CONNECT 2400
        <CR>

        17ACK

        Host Name: CIS <CR>
        User ID:

LOGGING OFF:

To log off from the CompuServe Information Serivce, type OFF at any !

  prompt online.

  ex: ! OFF <CR>

Or, if you are using the Information Manager software, select "Disconnect" from the "File" pull-down menu.

UK-Connect Mercury 5000 network

To access CompuServe through the Mercury 5000 network in the United Kingdom, follow the instructions below. GO RATES to view current information on communication surcharges.

LOGON INSTRUCTIONS:

1. Establish a phone connection by dialing a Mercury 5000 (MER) access number listed under "List Access Numbers" from the previous menu.

2. When the connection has been made, press Enter or Carriage Return <CR> several times until your screen shows:

    *npp=%bsd/pp15 port=1104
    *

        W E L C O M E   T O

        M E R C U R Y   5 0 0 0

    Type M for Menu, or
    ENTER USERNAME,PASSWORD,SERVICE
    *

3. At the * prompt, type ,,UKCNS and press <CR> (two commas followed immediately by UKCNS in all UPPER CASE and a Carriage Return).

    Your screen shows:

        *CONNECTING TO : link=0, nsap=235155200023
        *
        *Connected
        *

        08LXB

        Host Name:
    (The code 08LXB in the example above may be different when you log on.)

4. At the "Host Name:" prompt, type CIS and press <CR>.

5. At the "User ID:" prompt, enter your User ID number and log on as usual.

LOGGING OFF:

To log off from the CompuServe Information Service, type OFF at any ! prompt online.

    ex: ! OFF <CR>

Or, if you are using the Information Manager software, select "Disconnect" from the "File" pull-down menu.

UK-Connect GNS Dialplus network

To access CompuServe through the GNS Dialplus network in the United Kingdom, follow the instructions below. GO RATES to view current information on communication surcharges.

LOGON INSTRUCTIONS:
1. Establish a phone connection by dialing a GNS Dialplus (GNS) access number listed under "List Access Numbers" from the previous menu.

2. After a 3-4 second delay, your screen displays:

CONNECT

       GNS Dialplus   <date>
               British Telecom
        ———————————————————————
                Welcome to

           G N S   D I A L P L U S

       Data communications made easy
      Reliable, cost-effective and error-free

        ———————————————————————

(C) British Telecommunications Plc 1989

To access Dialplus, type your password
and press ENTER:
3. At the ENTER: prompt, type UKCNS and press Enter or Carriage Return <CR>.
(If asterisks [****] appear after the prompt, backspace over them first.)

    Your screen displays:

      Calling UKCNS

      Connected to UKCNS
      Host Name:

4. At the "Host Name:" prompt, type CIS and press <CR>.

5. At the "User ID:" prompt, enter your User ID number and log on as usual.

LOGGING OFF:

To log off from the CompuServe Information Service, type OFF at any !
prompt online.

ex: ! OFF <CR>

Or, if you are using the Information Manager software, select "Disconnect"
from the "File" pull-down menu.

Via France Telecom

LOGON INSTRUCTIONS

1. Connect to France Telecom.

Establish a phone connection by dialing the appropriate access number
listed under "List Access Numbers".

2. Once the phone connection is made your screen will show:

CONNECT XXXX

(i.e. the XXXX indicates your modem's speed)

3. Your screen shows:

Transpac Network Services 98319928

Enter the following number then press <CR> or Enter:
196282595

4. Your screen shows:

COM

xxABC (where xx is a two-digit number and ABC a three-letter
node name)

Host Name:

At this point, enter "CIS" then press Enter <CR>:

5. Your screen shows:

User ID:

At this point, enter your User ID then press Enter <CR> and log on as
usual.

LOGGING OFF:

To log off from the CompuServe Information Service, type OFF at any !
prompt online.

    ex: ! OFF <CR>

Or, if you are using the Information Manager software, select "Disconnect"
from the "File" pull-down menu.

UK access numbers

City	Country Code	STD Code	Phone number	NTW	Baud Rate
Aberdeen	44	01224	210701	GNS	300-2400
Aberdeen	44	01224	840057	MER	300-9600
Aldershot	44	01252	300010	MER	300-9600
Ayr	44	01292	611822	GNS	300-2400
Ayr	44	01292	510010	MER	300-2400
Ballymena	44	01266	654284	GNS	300-2400
Bangor	44	01247	274284	GNS	300-2400
Barnstaple	44	01271	22028	MER	300-2400
Barry	44	01446	430102	MER	300-2400
Belfast	44	01232	778605	FTE	300-14,400
Belfast	44	01232	331284	GNS	300-2400
Belfast	44	01232	550188	MER	300-9600
Benbecula	44	01870	602657	GNS	300-2400
Birmingham	44	0121	742 2200	CPS	1200-28,800
Birmingham	44	0121	633 3474	GNS	300-2400
Birmingham	44	0121	626 0110	MER	300-2400
Birmingham	44	0121	626 0228	MER	9600
Blackburn	44	01254	721000	MER	300-2400
Blandford Forum	44	01258	393205	MER	300-2400
Bradford	44	01274	841001	MER	300-2400
Bradford	44	01274	840034	MER	9600
Brechin	44	013562	5782	GNS	300-2400
Brecon	44	01874	623151	GNS	300-2400
Brighton	44	01273	550045	GNS	300-2400
Brighton	44	01273	860028	MER	300-9600
Bristol	44	0117	930 4351	CPS	1200-14,400
Bristol	44	0117	921 1545	GNS	300-2400
Bristol	44	0117	976 3265	MER	300-2400
Bristol	44	0117	976 3243	MER	9600
Brodick	44	17030	2031	GNS	300-2400
Cambridge	44	01223	352750	FTE	300-14,400
Cambridge	44	01223	460127	GNS	300-2400
Cambridge	44	01223	250014	MER	300-2400
Campbeltown	44	01586	552298	GNS	300-2400
Canterbury	44	01227	762950	GNS	300-2400
Canterbury	44	01227	762462	MER	300-2400
Cardiff	44	01222	344184	GNS	300-2400
Cardiff	44	01222	583201	MER	300-2400
Cardiff	44	01222	583235	MER	9600
Carlisle	44	01228	512621	GNS	300-2400
Carlisle	44	01228	890017	MER	300-2400
Chelmsford	44	01245	491323	GNS	300-2400

City	Country Code	STD Code	Phone number	NTW	Baud Rate
Chelmsford	44	01245	700010	MER	300-9600
Cheltenham	44	01242	227547	GNS	300-2400
Chester	44	01829	771265	FTE	300-14,400
Coleraine	44	01265	56284	GNS	300-2400
Colonsay	44	01951	2351	GNS	300-2400
Colwyn Bay	44	01492	532232	MER	300-2400
Coventry	44	01203	530425	MER	300-2400
Coventry	44	01203	530437	MER	9600
Crawley	44	01293	569610	CPS	1200-14,400
Crawley	44	01293	890102	MER	300-2400
Crewe	44	01270	588531	GNS	300-2400
Crewe	44	01270	410014	MER	300-2400
Dalmally	44	01838	200410	GNS	300-2400
Darlington	44	01325	500016	MER	300-2400
Derby	44	01332	622010	MER	300-2400
Doncaster	44	01302	791000	MER	300-2400
Downpatrick	44	01396	616284	GNS	300-2400
Dundee	44	01382	204682	FTE	300-14,400
Dundee	44	01382	22452	GNS	300-2400
Dundee	44	01382	595061	MER	300-2400
Dundee	44	01382	595090	MER	9600
Dunfermline	44	01383	640010	MER	300-2400
Dunoon	44	01369	2210	GNS	300-2400
Edinburgh	44	0131	557 5888	CPS	1200-14,400
Edinburgh	44	0131	313 2137	GNS	300-2400
Edinburgh	44	0131	459 0251	MER	300-9600
Elgin	44	01343	543890	GNS	300-2400
Enniskillen	44	01365	328284	GNS	300-2400
Exeter	44	01392	493241	FTE	300-14,400
Exeter	44	01392	421565	GNS	300-2400
Exeter	44	01392	310118	MER	300-2400
Fionnphort	44	016817	203	GNS	300-2400
Glasgow	44	0141	840 4494	CPS	1200-9600
Glasgow	44	0141	204 1722	GNS	300-2400
Glasgow	44	0141	307 0352	MER	300-2400
Glasgow	44	0141	307 1058	MER	9600
Gloucester	44	01452	513201	MER	300-2400
Golspie	44	014086	33021	GNS	300-2400
Grange-over-Sands	44	015395	34771	MER	300-2400
Grimsby	44	01472	353550	GNS	300-2400
Guildford	44	01483	38632	GNS	300-2400
Guildford	44	01483	452273	GNS	9600
Halifax	44	01422	349224	GNS	300-2400
Hastings	44	01424	722788	GNS	300-2400
Hull	44	01482	325070	MER	1200-2400
Huntly	44	01466	793653	GNS	300-2400
Invergarry	44	018093	406	GNS	300-2400
Inverness	44	01463	711940	GNS	300-2400
Ipswich	44	01473	210212	GNS	300-2400
Ipswich	44	01473	200010	MER	300-9600
KingsLynn	44	01553	691090	GNS	300-2400
Kingussie	44	01540	66 1078	GNS	300-2400
Kinross	44	01577	863111	GNS	300-2400
Kirkwall	44	01856	876004	GNS	300-2400
Leamington	44	01926	451419	GNS	300-2400
Leeds	44	0113	287 4571	FTE	300-14,400

City	Country Code	STD Code	Phone number	NTW	Baud Rate
Leeds	44	0113	244 0024	GNS	300-2400
Leeds	44	0113	283 0132	MER	300-2400
Leeds	44	0113	283 0156	MER	9600
Leicester	44	0116	262 8092	GNS	300-2400
Leicester	44	0116	265 3730	MER	300-9600
Lerwick	44	01595	6211	GNS	300-2400
Lincoln	44	01522	532398	GNS	300-2400
Liverpool	44	0151	255 0230	GNS	300-2400
Liverpool	44	0151	473 0053	MER	300-2400
Liverpool	44	0151	473 0089	MER	9600
Llandrindod Wells	44	01597	825881	GNS	300-2400
Llandudno	44	01492	860500	GNS	300-2400
Lochcarron	44	015202	598	GNS	300-2400
Lochgilphead	44	01546	603717	GNS	300-2400
Lochinver	44	015714	548	GNS	300-2400
London	44	0171	490 8881	CPS	1200-14,400
London	44	0171	570 5000	CPS	1200-28,800
London	44	0171	490 2200	GNS	300-2400
London	44	0171	827 9778	MER	300-2400
London	44	0171	827 9700	MER	9600
London	44	0181	862 0236	MER	300-2400
Londonderry	44	01504	370284	GNS	300-2400
Luton	44	01582	481818	GNS	300-2400
Luton	44	01582	446061	MER	300-9600
Machynlleth	44	01654	703560	GNS	300-2400
Magherafelt	44	01648	34284	GNS	300-2400
Maidstone	44	01622	610005	MER	300-9600
Mallaig	44	01687	2728	GNS	300-2400
Manchester	44	0161	491 1199	CPS	1200-14,400
Manchester	44	0161	8345533	GNS	300-2400
Manchester	44	0161	9530240	MER	300-2400
Manchester	44	0161	9531824	MER	9600
Melvich	44	016413	364	GNS	300-2400
Middlesbrough	44	01642	245464	GNS	300-2400
Middlesbrough	44	01642	340020	MER	300-2400
Middlesbrough	44	01642	340044	MER	9600
Milton Keynes	44	01908	837026	MER	300-9600
Mintlaw	44	01771	624560	GNS	300-2400
Neath	44	01639	641650	GNS	300-2400
Newcastle	44	0191	265 0481	FTE	300-14,400
Newcastle	44	0191	261 6858	GNS	300-2400
Newcastle	44	0191	401 0100	MER	300-2400
Newcastle	44	0191	401 0160	MER	9600
Newry	44	01693	64284	GNS	300-2400
Northampton	44	01604	33395	GNS	300-2400
Northampton	44	01604	730021	MER	300-2400
Norwich	44	01603	763165	GNS	300-2400
Norwich	44	01603	200011	MER	300-2400
Nottingham	44	0115	986 6640	FTE	300-14,400
Nottingham	44	0115	950 6005	GNS	300-2400
Nottingham	44	0115	935 7036	MER	300-2400
Nottingham	44	0115	935 7012	MER	9600
Oban	44	01631	63111	GNS	300-2400
Omagh	44	01662	240284	GNS	300-2400
Oxford	44	01865	798949	GNS	300-2400
Oxford	44	01865	380016	MER	300-9600

City	Country Code	STD Code	Phone number	NTW	Baud Rate
Peterborough	44	01733	555705	GNS	300-2400
Peterborough	44	01733	280100	MER	300-2400
Petersfield	44	01730	265098	GNS	300-2400
Plymouth	44	01752	603302	GNS	300-2400
Plymouth	44	01752	255912	GNS	9600
Plymouth	44	01752	222454	MER	300-2400
Pontypool	44	01495	330102	MER	300-2400
Poole	44	01202	666461	GNS	300-2400
Port Ellen	44	01496	2143	GNS	300-2400
Portadown	44	01762	351284	GNS	300-2400
Portree	44	01478	613208	GNS	300-2400
Portsmouth	44	01329	828691	FTE	300-14,400
Portsmouth	44	01705	403207	MER	300-2400
Preston	44	01772	204405	GNS	300-2400
Preston	44	01772	830025	MER	300-2400
Preston	44	01772	830058	MER	9600
Reading	44	01734	581818	CPS	1200-14,400
Reading	44	01734	500722	GNS	300-2400
Reading	44	01734	496362	MER	300-9600
Romsey	44	01794	893205	MER	300-2400
Rotherham	44	01709	820402	GNS	300-2400
Rugeley	44	01889	576610	GNS	300-2400
Scarborough	44	01723	353886	MER	300-2400
Sedgewick	44	01539	561263	GNS	300-2400
Sevenoaks	44	01732	740966	GNS	300-2400
Sheffield	44	0114	282 0020	MER	300-2400
Sheffield	44	0114	282 0060	MER	9600
Shrewsbury	44	01743	231027	GNS	300-2400
Southampton	44	01703	634530	GNS	300-2400
Southampton	44	01703	313211	MER	300-2400
Southampton	44	01703	313226	MER	9600
Stoke-on-Trent	44	01782	580102	MER	300-2400
Stornoway	44	01851	706111	GNS	300-2400
Strathdon	44	019756	51396	GNS	300-2400
Swansea	44	01792	350050	MER	300-2400
Swindon	44	01793	541620	GNS	300-2400
Swindon	44	01793	414129	MER	300-9600
Taunton	44	01823	335667	GNS	300-2400
Taunton	44	01823	335114	MER	300-2400
Telford	44	01952	770925	MER	300-2400
Tobermory	44	01688	2060	GNS	300-2400
Truro	44	01872	223864	GNS	300-2400
Truro	44	01872	222836	MER	300-2400
Warminster	44	01985	846091	GNS	300-2400
Wick	44	01955	4537	GNS	300-2400
York	44	01904	625625	GNS	300-2400
York	44	01904	450020	MER	300-2400

France access numbers

City	Country Code	STD Code	Phone number	NTW	Baud Rate
Lille	33		20 91 87 80	CPS	1200-9600
Lyon	33		72 41 97 89	CPS	1200-14,400

City	Country Code	STD Code	Phone number	NTW	Baud Rate
Nice	33		92 29 00 16	CPS	1200-14,400
Outside Paris	33		36 06 24 24	TPC	300-2400
Paris	33	1	47 89 39 40	CPS	1200-14,400
Paris	33	1	47 08 07 08	CPS	1200-14,400
Strasbourg	33		88 79 04 20	CPS	1200-9600
Toulouse	33		61 71 49 55	CPS	1200-9600

Italy access numbers

City	Country Code	STD Code	Phone number	NTW	Baud Rate
Agrigento	39	0922	604199	SEV	2400-9600
Ancona	39	071	2801610	SEV	2400
Arezzo	39	0575	23577	SEV	2400
Bari	39	080	5741033	SEV	2400-9600
Bergamo	39	035	270198	SEV	2400
Bologna-A	39	051	6575037	SEV	2400-9600
Bologna-M	39	051	735665	SEV	2400
Bologna-M	39	051	250004	SEV	2400-9600
Brescia	39	030	2421505	SEV	2400-9600
Cagliari	39	070	655163	SEV	2400-9600
Catania	39	095	204822	SEV	2400-9600
Cesena	39	0547	645350	SEV	2400
Cosenza	39	0984	413320	SEV	2400
Faenza	39	0546	680267	SEV	2400-9600
Fano	39	0721	826803	SEV	2400-9600
Firenze	39	055	5000480	SEV	2400-9600
Firenze	39	055	562001	SEV	2400-9600
Forli	39	0543	739119	SEV	2400
Genova	39	010	5536208	SEV	2400-9600
Ivrea	39	0125	523741	SEV	2400
Ivrea	39	0125	644040	SEV	2400-9600
Mantova	39	0376	223566	SEV	2400
Messina	39	090	674330	SEV	2400-9600
Milan	39	02	22479532	CPS	1200-9600
Milan	39	02	2155072	INF	300-2400
Milan	39	02	2157121	INF	300-2400
Milan	39	02	2157681	INF	300-2400
Milan	39	02	2157814	INF	300-2400
Modena	39	059	589058	SEV	2400-9600
Napoli	39	081	7644326	SEV	2400-9600
Napoli	39	081	7651423	SEV	2400
Padova	39	049	8073160	SEV	2400
Palermo	39	091	6169256	SEV	2400-9600
Parma	39	0521	250023	SEV	2400
Perugia	39	075	5732644	SEV	2400
Pescara	39	085	4215799	SEV	2400-9600
Piacenza	39	0523	453150	SEV	2400-9600
R. Emilia	39	0522	586193	SEV	2400
Ravenna	39	0544	404073	SEV	2400-9600
Rimini	39	0541	785964	SEV	2400-9600
Rome	39	06	51957347	CPS	1200-9600
Rome	39	06	2315728	INF	300-2400
Siena	39	0577	44946	SEV	2400

City	Country Code	STD Code	Phone number	NTW	Baud Rate
Siracusa	39	0931	441892	SEV	2400-9600
Torino	39	011	5612998	SEV	2400-9600
Trapani	39	0923	553222	SEV	2400
Trento	39	0461	932931	SEV	2400-9600
Udine	39	0432	523300	SEV	2400-9600
Venezia	39	041	5312970	SEV	2400
Venezia	39	041	5489255	SEV	2400-9600
Verona	39	045	8010800	SEV	2400
Vicenza	39	0444	320422	SEV	2400

Belgium access numbers

City	Country Code	STD Code	Phone number	NTW	Baud Rate
Brussels	32	02	726-8830	CPS	1200-14,400
Brussels	32	02	647-9847	INF	1200-2400
Brussels	32	02	647-6398	INF	1200-2400
Brussels	32	02	646-9070	INF	9600

Nederlands access numbers

City	Country Code	STD Code	Phone number	NTW	Baud Rate
Alkmaar	31	072	564 5655	FTE	300-28,800
Amstelveen	31	020	647 6171	INF	300-2400
Amstelveen	31	020	640 3331	INF	9600
Amsterdam	31	020	688 0085	CPS	1200-28,800
Arnhem	31	026	327 0280	FTE	300-28,800
Breda	31	076	520 2240	FTE	300-28,800
Eindhoven	31	040	246 7799	FTE	300-28,800
Enschede	31	053	430 6668	FTE	300-28,800
Groningen	31	050	527 8110	FTE	300-28,800
Maastricht	31	043	325 5688	FTE	300-28,800
Nijmegen	31	024	343 0117	FTE	300-28,800
Rotterdam	31	010	466 6767	FTE	300-28,800
Utrecht	31	030	251 4211	FTE	300-28,800
Zwolle	31	038	455 1161	FTE	300-28,800

Spain access numbers

City	Country Code	STD Code	Phone number	NTW	Baud Rate
Barcelona	34	3	487-3888	CPS	1200-9600
Barcelona	34	3	430-0202	INF	300-2400
Barcelona	34	3	410-8773	INF	9600
Madrid	34	1	577-0686	CPS	1200-9600
Madrid	34	1	304-1040	INF	1200-2400
Madrid	34	1	304-7717	INF	9600

Switzerland access numbers

City	Country Code	STD Code	Phone number	NTW	Baud Rate
Basel	41	061	332 1130	CPS	1200-14,400
Bern	41	031	382 6060	CPS	1200-9600
Bern	41	031	382 0931	INF	300
Bern	41	031	382 0787	INF	1200-2400
Bern	41	031	382 9243	INF	9600
Geneva	41	022	738 9740	CPS	1200-9600
Geneva	41	022	798 5756	INF	300
Geneva	41	022	798 6364	INF	1200-2400
Nationwide	41	049	047111	TLP	300-2400
Nationwide	41	049	049111	TLP	9600
Zurich	41	01	273 1028	CPS	1200-14,400

Appendix 3
CompuServe
product index listing

Last Updated: 11/30/1995 14:26 EST

Product Description	GO Word
1-800-FLOWERS	FGS
1995 World Series	WSERIES
3COM Forum	ASKFORUM
4Home "Simply" Forum	SIMPLY
A WinCIM Add-on: VOICE E-MAIL	VOICEMAIL
A WinCIM Spell-Check	ASPELL
A2Z Multimedia SuperShop(FREE)	MMSS
AA Roadwatch	AAROADWATC
AA Travel Services	UKTRAVEL
AARP	AARP
ABC Worldwide Hotel Guide	ABC
Access Numbers(FREE)	PHONES
Access Phone Numbers(FREE)	PHONE
Account/Billing Information(FREE)	MEMBER
Accountants Forum	AICPA
Accounting Vendor Forum	ACCOUNTING
AccuTrade Online(FREE)	ACCUTRADE
ACI US Forum	ACIUS
Action Games Forum	ACTION
Adaptec Forum	ADAPTEC
Administrator's Workstation(FREE)	ADMINI
Adobe Applications Forum	ADOBEA
Adobe Software GmbH Forum	ADOBEGER
Adobe Systems Forum	ADOBESYS
Adobe Systems, Inc.	ADOBE
ADP's Global Report	GRP
Advansys Software Area	ADVANSYS
Adventures In Food(FREE)	AIF
Adventures in Travel	AIT
African American Culture	AFRO
Agriculture Forum	AGFORUM
AI EXPERT Forum	AIEXPERT
Aids News Clips	AIDSNEWS
Air Canada Forum	AIRCANADA
Air France(FREE)	AF

Air Traffic Controller	ATCONTROL
AirData Forum	AIRDATA
Airline Services Unlimited	ASU
Alamo Rent-A-Car(FREE)	AL
Alaska Peddler(FREE)	ALASKA
All Music Guide Classical	AMGCLASSIC
All-Movie Guide	ALLMOVIE
All-Music Guide	ALLMUSIC
All-Music Guide Forum	AMGPOP
ALPA	ALPA
Alpha Software Forum	ALPHAFORUM
ALPS Support+ Forum	ALPS
America's Cup Forum	AMERICASCU
America's Funniest Home Videos	HOMEVIDEOS
American Heritage Dictionary	DICTIONARY
American Nurses Association	NURSE
American Public Power Assoc	APPA
Americana Clothing(FREE)	AC
Amiga Arts Forum	AMIGAARTS
Amiga File Finder	AMIGAFF
Amiga Tech Forum	AMIGATECH
Amiga User's Forum	AMIGAUSER
Amiga Vendor Forum	AMIGAVENDO
Ample Living Forum	AMPLE
Animation Vendor A Forum	ANVENA
ANZ Company Research Centre	ANZCOLIB
AOPA	AOPA
AOPA Online Store(FREE)	AOS
AP France en Ligne	APFRANCE
AP Sports($)	SPORTS
Apogee Forum	APOGEE
APPC Info Exchange Forum	APPCFORUM
Apple Feedback	APLFBK
Apple II Prog. Forum	APPROG
Apple II Users Forum	APPUSER
Apple II Vendor Forum	APIIVEN
Apple News Clips($)	APPLENEWS
Apple Support Forum	APLSUP
Apple Tech Info Library	APLTIL
Apple What's New Library	APLNEW
Apple WW Software Update Forum	APLWW
Aquaria / Fish Forum	FISHNET
Arcada Software Forum	ARCADA
Archive Films Forum	ARCFILM
Archive Photos Forum	ARCHIVE
Arista Records Download A	BARRY
Articulate Systems	MACAVEN
Artisoft Forum	ARTISOFT
Artist Forum	ARTIST
ASCII Developers Forum	ASCIIDEV
ASDA GO PROMOTION	ASDAUK
ASE Technicians Forum	NIASE
Ashmount Research Forum	ASHMOUNT
Ask3Com	THREECOM
ASNA Support Forum	ASNA
ASP CD-ROM Forum	ASPCD
ASP/Shareware Forum	ASPFORUM
Associated Press Online	APONLINE

Associated Press($)	ENS
Association Vendor Forum	AFORUM
AST Forum	ASTFORUM
Astrological Charting	ASTROLOGY
Astronomy Forum	ASTROFORUM
AT&T Home Business Resources(FREE)	ATTHBR
Atari File Finder	ATARIFF
Atari GAMING Forum	ATARIGAMIN
Atari ST Prod. Forum	ATARIPRO
Atari Users Network	ATARINET
Atari Vendor Forum	ATARIVEN
ATT/NCR	NCRATT
Attachmate Corporation	ATTACHMATE
Attachmate Crosstalk Forum	XTALK
Attachmate Forum	ATTM
Attentat a Paris($)	ATTENTAT
Attn. Deficit Disorder Forum	ADD
Audio Book Club(FREE)	AB
Audio Engineering Society	AESNET
Austad's(FREE)	GOLF
Australian Associated Press	AAPONLINE
Authors Forum	TWAUTHORS
Auto-By-Tel(FREE)	AUTOBYTEL
Autodesk AutoCAD Forum	ACAD
Autodesk Multimedia Forum	ASOFT
Autodesk Retail Products Forum	ARETAIL
Autodesk Showcase Forum	ASHOWCASE
Automobile Forum	CARS
Automobile Info Center(FREE)	AI
Automobile Live	AUTOLIVE
Automobile Magazine Forum	AUTOFORUM
Automobile Magazine Store(FREE)	AUTOSTORE
Automotive Information	AUTO
AutoNet New Car Showroom($)	NEWCAR
Autonet Used Car Lot	USEDCAR
AutoVantage OnLine(FREE)	ATV
Aviation Forum (AVSIG)	AVSIG
Aviation Menu	AVIATION
Aviation Safety Institute	ASI
Aviation Support Forum	AVSUP
Aviation Week Group	AWG-1
Aviation Week Group Forum	AWO-4
Bacchus Wine Forum	WINEFORUM
Banyan Forum	BANFORUM
BASIS International Forum	BASIS
Bassett Furniture(FREE)	BASSETT
Bay Networks Forum	BAYNETWORK
Baywatch	BAYWATCH
BBC Music Magazine	BBCM
BBDO Techsetter Hotline	BBDO
BDI German Industry($)	BDIGERIND
Bed & Breakfast Database	INNS
Belgium Forum	BELFORUM
Bellsouth Cellular Corp.(FREE)	BSCC
Benchmark & Standards Forum	BENCHMARK
Bertelsmann Lexikon	BEPLEXIKON
Better Homes Kitchen	KITCHEN
BetterHomes Kitchen Forum	BHKFORUM

Bettmann Archive Forum	BETTMANN
Billing Information(FREE)	BILLING
Biorhythms	BIORHYTHM
Biz*File($)	BIZFILE
BlackDragon	BLACKDRAGO
Block Financial Forum	TAXCUT
Blyth Forum	BLYTH
BMG Compact Disc Club(FREE)	CD
Bonds Listing($)	BONDS
Book Preview Forum	PREVIEW
Book Review Digest($)	BOOKREVIEW
Books in Print($)	BOOKS
Books On Tape(FREE)	BOT-1
BORLAND	BORLAND
Borland Application Forum	BORAPP
Borland C++ for Win/OS2 Forum	BCPPWIN
Borland C++/DOS Forum	BCPPDOS
Borland Connections Forum	BORCONN
Borland DB Products Forum	BORDB
Borland dBASE For Windows	DBASEWIN
Borland dBASE Forum	DBASEDOS
Borland Delphi Forum	DELPHI
Borland Dev. Tools Forum	BDEVTOOLS
Borland Germany	BORGER
Borland GmbH Forum	BORGMBH
Borland Paradox/Dos Forum	PDOXDOS
Borland Paradox/Windows Forum	PDOXWIN
Bosnia Clipping Folder($)	BOSNIA
BR Online Forum	BRFORUM
BR-Online	BR-ONLINE
Breton Harbor Gift Services(FREE)	BH
Bridge Forum	BRIDGE
British Books in Print	BBIP
British Legends	LEGENDS
British Trade Marks($)	UKTRADEMAR
Broadcast Pro Forum	BPFORUM
Broderbund Online Forum	BBFORUM
Broderbund Software(FREE)	BB
Brooks Brothers(FREE)	BR
Btrieve Technologies Foru	BTRIEVE
Bull & Bear(FREE)	BNBG
Business Database Plus($)	BUSDB
Business Dateline($)	BUSDATE
Business Demographics($)	BUSDEM
Business Incorp. Guide(FREE)	INC
CA App. Development Forum	CAIDEV
CA Business Partners Forum	CAPARTNERS
CA Germany Forum	CAGER
CA Pro Solutions Forum	CAIPRO
CA Visual Objects Forum	VOFORUM
CA-Clipper Germany Forum	CLIPGER
CA-Simply Forum	CASIMPLY
Cabletron System, Inc.	CTRON
Cabletron Systems Forum	CTRONFORUM
CADD/CAM/CAE B Vendor Forum	CADDBVEN
CADD/CAM/CAE Vendor Forum	CADDVEN
Cadence Forum	CADENCE
Cadillac(FREE)	CADILLAC

Calculate Net Worth	FINTOL
California Forum	CALFORUM
Campmor(FREE)	CAM
Canada Forum	CDNFORUM
Canada Services Menu	CANADA
Canada's Atlantic Coast(FREE)	ATL
Canadian Business Online Forum	CANBUS
Cancer Forum	CANCER
Canon Support	CANON
Canopus Forum	CANOPUS
Capricorn Download Area	CAPRIVIEW
Career Management Forum	CAREERS
CASE DCI Forum	CASEFORUM
CastleQuest	CQUEST
Catholic Online Forum	CATHOLIC
CB Forum	CBFORUM
CB Handle	HANDLE
CB Profiles	CBPROFILES
CB Simulator	CB
CB Society	CUPCAKE
CBA Administrators Forum(FREE)	CBAFORUM
CCM Forum	CCMUSIC
CCML AIDS Articles($)	CCMLAIDS
CD-ROM A Vendor Forum	CDVEN
CD-ROM B Vendor Forum	CDVENB
CDROM Forum	CDROM
CDROMBase Online	CDROMBASE
CE Audio Forum	CEAUDIO
CE General Forum	CEGENERAL
CE Video Forum	CEVIDEO
CENDATA	CENDATA
CH Music Collections(FREE)	CHM-1
CH TV Classics(FREE)	TVC
Change Your Password Program(FREE)	PASSWORD
Chase Manhattan Home Equity(FREE)	CHASE
CheckFree(FREE)	CF
Chef's Catalog(FREE)	CHEFS
Chess Forum	CHESSFORUM
Cheyenne Software Forum	CHEYENNE
Chicago Spotlight	CHICAGO
CHIP Magazin Forum	CHIP
Christian Children's Fund(FREE)	CCF
Christian City Forum	CCITY
Christian Fellowship Forum	FELLOWSHIP
Christian Interactive Network	CIN-1
Christian Interactive(FREE)	CISN
CIM for OS/2 Information Area(FREE)	OCIMSOFT
CIM for OS/2 Support Forum(FREE)	OCIMSUPPOR
CIM Support Forums(FREE)	CIMSUPPORT
CIS Kundendienst Forum	CISHILFE
CISPPP Utility (Mac)(FREE)	CISPPP
Citrix Systems Forum	CITRIX
CITY STREETS Map Connection	CITYSTREET
Claris France Forum	CLARFR
Claris Information Center	CLARIS
Claris Macintosh Forum	MACCLARIS
Claris TechInfo Database	CLATECH
Claris Windows Forum	WINCLARIS

Classic Adventure	CLADVENT
Classic Quotes	TMC-45
Classifieds(FREE)	CLASSIFIED
Clipper Forum	CLIPPER
CMS Home Mortgage Corp(FREE)	CMS
CNN Forum	CNNFORUM
CNN Online	CNNONLINE
Coffee Anyone???(FREE)	COF
Cognos Forum	COGNOS
Collectibles Forum	COLLECT
College & Adult Student Forum	STUFOB
Collegiate Vendor Forum	COLVEN
Colonel Audio Video(FREE)	CVA
Colonel Video & Audio(FREE)	CVA
Color Computer Forum	COCO
Columbia House CD-ROM Direct(FREE)	CDRD
Columbia House Music Club(FREE)	FREECD
Comedy Central	COMEDY
Comics Publishers Forum	COMICPUB
Comics/Animation Forum	COMIC
Comm. & Networking Forum	INTELFORUM
Commerce Business Daily($)	COMBUS
Commodities	COMMODITIE
Commodity Pricing($)	CPRICE
Commodity Symbol Lookup	CSYMBOL
Commodore Applications Forum	CBMAPP
Commodore Arts/Games Forum	CBMART
Commodore Newsletter	CBMNEWS
Commodore Service Forum	CBMSERVICE
Commodore Users Network	CBMNET
Commonly Asked Questions(FREE)	CSHELP
Company Analyzer($)	ANALYZER
Company Corporation, The(FREE)	CORP
Company Information	MMM-70
Company Screening($)	COSCREEN
Company Snapshot	BASCOMPANY
Compaq Connection	CPQFORUM
Compaq UK Forum	CPQUK
Compu-Cruise by Rosenbluth(FREE)	CRUISE
CompuAdd Forum	COMPUADD
CompuBooks(FREE)	CBK
CompuServe Applications Forum(FREE)	CSAPPS
CompuServe Community Center(FREE)	CISCENTER
CompuServe Convention Center	CONVENTION
CompuServe Espanol	ESPANOL
CompuServe Europe	EUROPE
CompuServe for GEOS Software	CS4GEOS
CompuServe France Forum	FRSUPPORT
CompuServe Help Forum(FREE)	HELPFORUM
CompuServe Home Page Wizard(FREE)	HPWIZ
CompuServe Magazine	OLI
CompuServe Magazine 3-D Image	FREE3D
CompuServe Mail	MAIL
CompuServe Mail Center(FREE)	MAILCENTER
CompuServe Mail for PowerTalk	PTALK
CompuServe Mail Hub	MAILHUB
CompuServe Main Menu	TOP
CompuServe MS Mail Driver	MAPI

CompuServe Navigator, Mac	MACNAV
CompuServe News Forum	CSNEWS
CompuServe Operating Rules(FREE)	RULES
CompuServe Pacific Forum	PACFORUM
CompuServe Pricing Plans(FREE)	CHOICES
CompuServe Product Index(FREE)	QUICK
CompuServe Rates(FREE)	RATES
CompuServe Shareware Service	SHAREWARE
CompuServe Software	CISSOFT
CompuServe T-Shirt Contest	TSHIRT
CompuServe Tax Connection	TAXES
CompuServe Telnet Access	TELNET
CompuServe Visa Card	CARD
CompuServe WinSupport	WINSUP
CompuServeCD Forum(FREE)	CCDSUP
CompuServeCD Online(FREE)	CCD
Computer Animation Forum	COMANIM
Computer Art Forum	COMART
Computer Associates Forums	CAI
Computer Buyers' Guide($)	COMPBG
Computer Club Forum	CLUB
Computer Consult. Forum	CONSULT
Computer Database Plus($)	COMPDB
Computer Express(FREE)	CE
Computer Gaming World	CGWMAGAZIN
Computer Library	COMPLIB
Computer Life Magazine	LIFE
Computer Life UK Forum	CLIFEUK
Computer Peripheral, Inc.	VIVAMODEM
Computer Reseller News Forum	CRN
Computer Shopper (UK) Forum	UKSHOPPER
Computer Shopper Magazine	CSHOPPER
Computer Training Forum	DPTRAIN
Computers on Television Forum	PCTV
Computing Support	COMPUTERS
COMPUTRACE($)	TRACE
Comshare Forum	COMSHARE
Concord Coalition Forum	CONCORD
Congressional Tracking	BUDGET
ConnectSoft(FREE)	CST
Consumer Electronics Forums	CEFORUMS
Consumer Forum	CONFORUM
Consumer Reports	CONSUMER
Consumer Reports Auto.	CRAUTO
Consumer Reports Drug Ref.	DRUGS
Contact Lens Supply(FREE)	CL
Continental Insurance Center(FREE)	CIC-12
Conversion Area	NEWBASIC
Cook's Online Forum	COOKS
Corel Applications Forum 1	CORELAPPS
Corel Applications Forum 2	VENTURA
Corel Corporate Forum	CORELCORP
Corporate Actions Notification	CORPACTION
Corporate Affiliations($)	AFFILIATIO
Court Reporters Forum	CRFORUM
Cowles/SIMBA Media Daily	MEDIADAILY
CP/M Users Group Forum	CPMFORUM
Creative Labs Forum	BLASTER

Creative Solutions/Forth Forum	FORTH
Creditreform Deutsch($)	CREFDEU
Creditreform Oesterreich($)	CREFAUSTRI
Critic's Choice Video(FREE)	CCV
Crutchfield(FREE)	CFD
CS Lotus Notes Information Svc	NOTES
CS Mail for Microsoft Exchange	CSMAIL
CSNav-Win Support Forum(FREE)	WCSNAVSUP
CTOS/Pathway Forum	CTOS
Cuba News Clips($)	CUBA
CupidGrams	GRAMS
Current Market Snapshot	SNAPSHOT
Current Quotes	CQUOTE
Customer Service Help Database(FREE)	CSHELP
Cyber Forum	CYBERFORUM
Cyber Shopping Network(FREE)	NETSHOP
CyberWarehouse(FREE)	CYBERWAREH
Cycling Forum	CYCLING
Da Vinci Forum	DAVINCI
Dalco Computer Electronics(FREE)	DA
Danbury Mint(FREE)	MINT
Dashboard 3.0 for Windows	DASHBOARD
Data Access Corp. Forum	DACCESS
Data Based Advisor Forum	DBADVISOR
Data Based Advisor Mall Store(FREE)	DB
Data-Process. Newsletter($)	DPNEWS
DataEase International Forum	DATAEASE
Dataquest Online	DATAQUEST
DATASTORM Forum	DATASTORM
Day-Timer Forum	DAYTIMER
DBMS Magazine Forum	DBMSFORUM
DeBeers Online	DEBEERS
DEC PC Forum	DECPC
DEC Users Network	DECUNET
DECPCI Forum	DECPCI
Dell Forum	DELL
Delrina Technology Forum	DELRINA
Democratic Forum	DEMOCRATS
Department of State	STATE
Der Spiegel Forum	SPIEGEL
Desktop Publishing Forum	DTPFORUM
Desktop Publishing Vendor A	DTPAVEN
Desktop Publishing Vendor B	DTPBVEN
Desktop Video Forum	DTVFORUM
Desktop/Electronic Publ.	DTP
Detroit Free Press Forum	DETROIT
Detroit Free Press Store(FREE)	DFM
Deutsche Firmendatenbank($)	COGERMAN
Deutsches CA-VO Forum	VOGER
Deutsches Computer Forum	GERNET
Deutsches Film Forum	FILME
Deutsches Funk Forum	DEUFUNK
Deutsches Internet Forum	GERINTERNE
Deutsches MacCIM Forum(FREE)	DMCIMSU
Deutsches PC Direkt Forum	PCDIREKT
Deutsches PCpro-Forum	PCPRO
Deutsches Win95 Forum	DEUWIN95
Deutsches Windows Mag Forum	GERWIN

Deutschland Info	INFOGER
Deutschland Online Forum	GERLINE
Developer Relations Forum	MSDR
Diabetes Forum	DIABETES
DiagSoft Forum	DIAGSOFT
Dial-A-Mattress(FREE)	BEDS
Digital Business Partner	DECNIDEV
Digital Consulting - DCI	DCIEXPO
Digital Equipment Corp.	DEC
Digital's PC Store(FREE)	DD
Digitalk Database	DBDIGITALK
Dinosaur Forum	DINO
Directory of Catalogs(FREE)	DTC
Dirk Jasper's Filmlexikon	JASPER
Disabilities Forum	DISABILITI
Disclosure SEC($)	DISCLOSURE
Dissertation Abstracts($)	DISSERTATI
Dividends and Splits($)	DIVIDENDS
Dixons	DIXONS
DMV Verlag Forum	DMVGER
Document Translation($)	TRANSLATE
Dolls Forum	DOLLS
DOSCIM Information Area(FREE)	DCIMSOFT
DOSCIM Support Forum(FREE)	DCIMSUPPOR
Download Clint Black Single	CLINT
Download Pricing Data	IQINT
DPA-Kurznachrichtendienst	DPANEWS
Dr. Dobb's Journal Forum	DDJFORUM
Dr. Neuhaus Forum	NEUHAUS
Dreyfus Corporation(FREE)	DR
DTP Partner Forum	DTPPARTNER
DTPONLINE	DTPONLINE
Dun&Bradstreet Deutschl.($)	DBDEUTSCH
Dun&Bradstreet France($)	DBFRANCE
Dun&Bradstreet Internat.($)	DBINTL
Dun&Bradstreet UK($)	DUNBUK
Dun's Canadian Mkt. Ident($)	DBCAN
Dun's Elect Business Dir($)	DYP
Dun's Market Identifiers($)	DMI
Dvorak Development Forum	DVORAK
Dwellings Forum	TWDWELLING
E*TRADE Securities	ETRADE
E*TRADE Stock Market Game	ETGAME
E-Span Online Job Listing	ESPAN
Earth Forum	EARTH
easySABRE	SABRE
easySABRE (CIM)	SABRECIM
EDI Forum	EDIFORUM
EDRIVE Limited(FREE)	ESTORE
EDRIVE Movie Viewer	VIEWER
EDRIVE'S Movie Forum	EMOVIES
Education Forum	EDFORUM
Education Product A	EDPROA
Education Product B	EDPROB
Educational Res. Forum	EDRESEARCH
EETnet	EETNET
Ei Compendex Plus($)	COMPENDEX
Eicon Technology Forum	EICON

Electric Soul Forum	SOUL
Electronic Books	EBOOKS
Electronic Filing	TAXRETURN
Electronic Frontier Foundation	EFFSIG
Electronic Gamer(tm)	EGAMER
Electronic Word Forum	EWORD
ELSA GmbH Forum	ELSA
EMI Aviation Services($)	EMI
Encounters Forum	ENCOUNTERS
Engineering Automation Forum	LEAP
Enhanced Adventure	ENADVENT
Entertainment Drive	EDRIVE
Entertainment Drive Forum	EFORUM
Entertainment Multimedia Area	EMEDIA
Entrep. Magazine Subscriptions(FREE)	ENT
Entrep. Small Business Square	BIZSQUARE
Entrepreneur Magazine	ENTMAGAZIN
Epic MegaGames Forum	EPIC
Epson Forum	EPSON
ERIC - Education Research($)	ERIC
eServ Travel Network(FREE)	ESV
Ethel M Chocolates(FREE)	ETHELM
ETV Forum	ETV
Euro-Zugfahrplaene	BAHN
European Co. Reasearch Centre($)	EUROLIB
European Company Library($)	COEURO
European Forum	EURFORUM
European Newspaper Promotion	EUROPROMO
European Rail	RAILWAY
EVIDEO Forum	EVIDEO
Examine Detailed Issue($)	EXAMINE
Executive News Service($)	ENS
Executives Online	EXECONLINE
Familie & Computer Forum	FAMCOM
Family Handyman Forum	HANDYMAN
Family Services Forum	MYFAMILY
Fan Club A Forum	FANACLUB
Fan Club B Club	FANBCLUB
Fantasy Basketball	FASTBREAK
Fantasy Football League	SIFFL
Fantasy/Role-Playing Adv.	ADVENT
FAST Multimedia	FAST
FCC Access Charge Area	FCC
FCCopy Utility Download(FREE)	FCCOPY
Fed. Of Int'l Distributors	FEDERATION
FEDEX Online	FEDEX
Feedback to Customer Service(FREE)	FEEDBACK
Fibercrafts Forum	FIBERCRAFT
File Transfer Protocol	FTP
Finance	MONEY
Financial Documentation	FINHLP
Financial File Transfer	FILTRN
Financial File/MQUOTE II	MQUOTE
Financial Forecasts	EARNINGS
Financial Forums	FINFORUM
Financial Interfaces	INTERFACES
Financial Services Help Area(FREE)	FINHELP
Financial Services Info. Ctr.	INFOCTR

Financial Software Forum	FINVEN
Fine Arts Forum	FINEARTS
Firearms Forum	FIREARMS
First Floor Download	NCENTRAL
Fishing Forum	FISHING
Flight Simulation Forum	FSFORUM
Florida Forum	FLORIDA
Florida Fruit Shippers(FREE)	FFS-1
Florida Today Forum	FLATODAY
Flower Stop(FREE)	FS
FocServices Forum	FOCSERVICE
FocWizard Forum	FOCWIZARD
FontBank Online	FONTBANK
FORBES	FORBES
Ford Credit(FREE)	FC
Ford Motor Company(FREE)	FORD
Ford Stockholders(FREE)	FSH
Foreign Language Forum	FLEFO
FORTUNE	FORTUNE
Fortune 500 Lists	FORT500
FORTUNE Forum	FFORUM
Fortune Personal Investing	FPERINV
Forums	FORUMS
Fragen zur Abrechnung	RECHNUNG
Fragrance Counter	FRAGRANCE
Frame Relay Forum	FRAME
France Cinema Forum	FCINEMA
France Forum	FRFORUM
Free Offer Outlet(FREE)	FOO
French Company Info($)	FRCOMPANIE
FTC FREE Downloads	FTCFILES
FTD Online(FREE)	FTD
FTM AirMax	AIRMAX
Fuji Photo Film USA Forum	FUJI
FundWatch by Money Magazine	FUNDWATCH
Funnies Forum	FUNFOR
Fuse Forum	FUSE
Game Developers Forum	GAMDEV
Game Forums and News	GAMECON
Game Publisher Beta Forum	GAMBETA
Game Publishers A Forum	GAMAPUB
Game Publishers B Forum	GAMBPUB
Game Publishers C Forum	GAMCPUB
Game Publishers D Forum	GAMDPUB
Game Publishers Forums	GAMPUB
Gamers Forum	GAMERS
Games File Finder	GAMEFF
Gardening Forum	GARDENING
Garth Brooks Spotlight	GARTH
Gateway 2000 Forum	GATEWAY
Genealogy Forum	ROOTS
Genealogy Support Forum	GENSUP
General Accident Assurance(FREE)	GA
General Computing Forum	GENCOM
General Magic Forum	MAGIC
General Services	BASIC
German Company Research Center($)	GERLIB
Getting Through Customs	GTC-1

Gfx User Group A Forum	GUGRPA
Gimmee Jimmy's Cookies(FREE)	GIM
Glamour Graphics Forum	GLAMOUR
Global Crises Forum	CRISIS
Global Quotes	GQUOTES
Global Report($)	GLOREP
Golden CommPass Support	GCPSUPPORT
Goldmine Forum	GOLDMINE
Goodyear Online(FREE)	GOODYEAR
Government Giveaways Forum	INFOUSA
Government Publications	GPO
Graphics B Vendor Forum	GRAPHBVEN
Graphics Corner Forum	CORNER
Graphics Developers Forum	GRAPHDEV
Graphics File Finder	GRAPHFF
Graphics Forums	GRAPHICS
Graphics Gallery Forum	GALLERY
Graphics Plus Forum	GRAPHPLUS
Graphics Showcase Forum	GRFSHOW
Graphics Support Forum	GRAPHSUPPO
Graphics Vendor Forum	GRAPHVEN
Graphics Vendors C Forum	GRVENC
Graphics Visual Index Forum	GRFINDEX
Graphics Welcome Center Forum	GRFWELCOME
Green Mountain Coffee Roasters(FREE)	GMR
Grolier Encyclopedia	ENCYCLOPED
GroupWare Files Forum	NGWFILES
GTE Phone Mart(FREE)	GTE
Guardian newspaper	GUARDIAN
Gupta Forum	GUPTAFORUM
H&R Block(FREE)	HRB
Haiti News Clips($)	HAITI
Hallmark Connections(FREE)	HAL
Hammacher Schlemmer(FREE)	HS
Hamnet Forum	HAMNET
Handcrafts Forum	HANDCRAFTS
Handicapped User's Data	HANDICAPPE
Hangman	HANGMAN
Hardware Forums	HARDWARE
Hawaii Forum	HAWAII
Hayes	HAYES
Hayes Online	HAYFORUM
Health & Fitness Forum	GOODHEALTH
Health & Vitamin Express(FREE)	HVE
Health Database Plus($)	HLTDB
Health/Fitness	FITNESS
HealthNet	HNT
Hollywood Hotline	HOLLYWOOD
Hollywood Online DL Area	HOLFILE
Hollywood Online Forum	FLICKS
Home Forum	HOMEFORUM
HOMEFINDER BY AMS	HF
HoneyBaked Ham(FREE)	HAM
Hong Kong Forum	HKFORUM
Hoover Company Database	HOOVER
Hoppenstedt Benelux($)	HOPPBEN
Hoppenstedt Deutschland($)	HOPPDEU
Hoppenstedt Oesterreich($)	HOPPAUS

Hoppenstedt Wirtschaftsvl($)	HOPPWIRT
Hot Games Download Area	HOTGAMES
Hot News Online	HOTNEWS
HP Handheld Forum	HPHAND
HP OmniBook Forum	HPOMNIBOOK
HP OmniGo Showcase	OMNIGO
HP Peripherals Forum	HPPER
HP Specials	HPSPEC
HP Systems Forum	HPSYS
HSX Adult Forum	HSX200
HSX Open Forum	HSX100
Hubble Uranus Images	URANUS
Human Sexuality Databank	HUMAN
Hungary Forum	HUNGARY
Hunting Forum	HUNTING
Huntington Clothiers(FREE)	HC-1
Hyatt Hotels & Resorts(FREE)	HYA
IBES Earnings Est Rpts($)	IBES
IBM Aptiva & PS/1 Forum	IBMPS1
IBM CAD/CAM Forum	IBMENG
IBM CICS Forum	CICS
IBM Clinton Health Plan	IBMHEALTH
IBM COS Network Solution Forum	IBMCOS
IBM DB2 Database Forum	IBMDB2
IBM Desktop Forum	IBMDESK
IBM ImagePlus Forum	IBMIMAGE
IBM INTERACTIVE FORUM	INTERACTIV
IBM Internet Forum	IBMINET
IBM Languages Forum	IBMLANG
IBM LMU2 Forum	LMUFORUM
IBM MQSeries	MQSERIES
IBM Netview Family Forum	NETVIEW
IBM Object Technology Forum	IBMOBJ
IBM Online	IBM
IBM OS/2 B Vendors Forum	OS2BVEN
IBM OS/2 Developer 1 Forum	OS2DF1
IBM OS/2 Developer 2 Forum	OS2DF2
IBM OS/2 Help Database	OS2HELP
IBM OS/2 Support Forum	OS2SUPPORT
IBM OS/2 Users Forum	OS2USER
IBM OS/2 Vendor Forum	OS2AVEN
IBM PC Direct(FREE)	BUYIBM
IBM PC Server Forum	IBMSVR
IBM Personal Software Products(FREE)	IBMPSP
IBM Power Personal Series	IBMPPS
IBM PowerPC Forum	POWERPC
IBM PS2 Forum	IBMPS2
IBM PSM Deutschland Forum	OS2UGER
IBM PSP A Products Forum	PSPAPROD
IBM Software Solutions Forum	SOFSOL
IBM Special Needs Forum	IBMSPEC
IBM Storage Systems Forum	IBMSTORAGE
IBM ThinkPad Forum	THINKPAD
IBM ValuePoint Forum	VALUEPOINT
IBM VoiceType Forum	VOICETYPE
IBM WRAD Support Forum	VISUAL
ICAA Forum	ICAA
ICC Directory of UK Comp.($)	ICCDIR

Ideas & Inventions Forum	INNOVATION
Il Sole 24 Ore($)	ILSOLE
Imaging Vendor A Forum	IMAGAVEN
Incue Online	INCUE
IndustryWeek Forum	IWFOR
IndustryWeek Interactive	INDWEEK
IndustryWeek Management Centre(FREE)	IW
Info-Please Business Almanac	BIZALMANAC
Info. Please Sports Almanac	SPORTALMAN
Infocheck($)	INFOCHECK
Informant Forum	ICGFORUM
Information Almanac	GENALMANAC
Information Management Forum	INFOMANAGE
Information USA	LESKO
Information USA Mall(FREE)	IUM
Informatique France Forum	INFOFR
Informix Forum	GERINFORMI
Inn and Lodging Forum	INNFORUM
Int'l Dun's Mkt Identifier($)	DBINT
Intel Architecture Labs Forum	INTELARCH
Intel Components/Embedded	INTELCORP
Intel Corporation	INTEL
Intelligence Test	TMC-101
Inter@ctive Week Magazine	INTWEEK
Interflora	UKINTERFLO
International Trade Forum	TRADE
Internet Commerce Forum	INETCOMMER
Internet France Forum	INETFR
Internet New Users Forum	INETNEW
Internet Publishing Forum	INETPUBLIS
Internet Resources Forum	INETRESOUR
Internet Services	INTERNET
Internet WebMasters Forum	INETWEB
Internet World Forum	IWORLD
Intersolv Forum	INTERSOLV
Intuit Forum	INTUIT
Investext	INV
InvesText($)	INVTEXT
Investor's Business Daily(FREE)	IB
Investors Forum	INVFORUM
Iowa State Forum	IOWASTATE
IQUEST Business InfoCenter	IQBUSINESS
IQUEST Education InfoCenter	IQEDUCATIO
IQUEST Engineering InfoCenter	IQENGINEER
IQUEST Medical InfoCenter	IQMEDICAL
IQUEST Technology InfoCenter	IQTECHNOLO
IQuest($)	IQUEST
IRI Software Forum	IRIFORUM
IRL Wireless Vendor Forum	WVENDOR
IRS Tax Forms/Documents	TAXFORMS
ISDN Forum	ISDN
Island of Kesmai	ISLAND
Israel Forum	ISRAEL
Issue Pricing Interface($)	MQINT
Issues Forum	ISSUESFORU
Isuzu(FREE)	ISUZU
Italian Forum	ITALFOR
J.C. Whitney & Co.(FREE)	JCW

Jaguar(FREE)	UKJAGUAR
Japan Forum	JAPAN
Jazz Beat Forum	JAZZ
JCPenney(FREE)	JCPENNEY
JDR Microdevices(FREE)	JDR
Jensen-Jones Forum	JJSUPPORT
Jeppesen Aviation Weather	JEPPESEN
Jerry's World	JERRY
Jerry's World Forum	JWORLD
Jerusalem Post($)	JERUSALEM
John Wiley Publishing Online(FREE)	WILEY
JordanWatch($)	JORDANS
Journalism Forum	JFORUM
Journalist Download Area	JOURNALIST
JP Morgan	JPMORGAN
Jurassic Park	SCENE
Just For Friends Download($)	JUSTFRIEND
Kachelmanns Wetter Forum	KACHELMANN
KAOS AntiVirus	ANTIVIRUS
Key British Enterprises($)	KEYBRIT
KHK Euro Line Forum	EUROGER
KHK Office Line Forum	KHKOL
KHK Software E-Menu	KHKSOFT
Kids & Teens Student Forum	STUFOA
Kids Students Forum	STUFOC
Knowledge Index($)	KI
Kodak CD Forum	KODAK
Kreditschutzver. Oesterr.($)	KREDVER
L'Express Forum	FOREXPRESS
L'Express Online	LEXPRESS
LACE BBS	GGG-102
LAN B Vendor Forum	LANBVEN
Lan Magazine Forum	LANMAG
Lan Vendor Forum	LANVEN
Lands' End(FREE)	LA
Lanier Golf Database	GOLF
Laptop Vendor Forum	LAPTOP
Law Enforcement Forum	POLICE
LDC Spreadsheets Forum	LOTUSA
LDC Word Processing Forum	LOTUSWP
Le Monde($)	LEMONDE
Le Tour de France($)	TOURFRANCE
Legal Forum	LAWSIG
Legal Research Center($)	LEGALRC
Lens Express(FREE)	LENS
Lexmark Forum	LEXMARK
Library Of Science Book Club(FREE)	LOS
Lincoln Showroom(FREE)	LINCOLN
Lion King Download Area	LionKing
Liquor By Wire(FREE)	LBW
Literary Forum	LITFORUM
Living History Forum	LIVING
Loan Analyzer	LOAN
Logitech Forum	LOGITECH
LOGO Forum	LOGOFORUM
LOGOS Online(FREE)	LOGOS
London Film Festival	FILMONLINE
Lotus 123 For Windows Upgrade	LOTUS123W

Lotus cc:Mail Forum	LOTUSM
Lotus Communications Forum	LOTUSCOMM
Lotus GmbH Forum	LOTGER
Lotus Graphics/Info Mgmt Forum	LOTUSB
Lotus Press Release Forum	LOTUSNEWS
Lotus WordPro Forum	WORDPRO
Mac A Vendor Forum	MACAVEN
Mac Applications Forum	MACAP
Mac B Vendor Forum	MACBVEN
Mac C Vendor Forum	MACCVEN
Mac Communications Forum	MACCOMM
Mac Community/Club Forum	MACCLUB
Mac D Vendor Forum	MACDVEN
Mac Developers Forum	MACDEV
Mac Entertainment Forum	MACFUN
Mac Hypertext Forum	MACHYPER
Mac New Users Help Forum	MACNEW
MacCIM en Francais Forum(FREE)	FMCIMSU
MacCIM Information Area(FREE)	MCIMSOFT
MacCIM Support Forum(FREE)	MCIMSUP
Macintosh File Finder	MACFF
Macintosh Forums	MACINTOSH
Macintosh Hardware Forum	MACHW
Macintosh Multimedia Forum	MACMULTI
Macintosh O/S Forum	MACSYS
Maclean's Online	MACLEANS
Maclean's Online Forum	MCFORUM
Macmillan Publishing Forum	MACMILLAN
MacNav Support Forum(FREE)	MNAVSUPPOR
Macromedia Forum	MACROMEDIA
MACup Verlag Forum	MACUP
MacUser Forum	MACUSER
MacWAREHOUSE(FREE)	MW
MacWEEK Forum	MACWEEK
Magazine Database Plus($)	MAGDB
MAGELLAN Geographix Maps	MAGELLAN
Magic Link CS Companion(FREE)	CS4MAGIC
Magill's Survey of Cinema($)	MAGILL
MagnaMedia Forum	MAGNA
Marilyn Beck/Smith Hollywood	BECK
Market Highlights($)	MARKET
Market/Index Lookup	INDICATORS
Market/Mgt Research Cent.($)	MKTGRC
Markt & Technik	MTFORUM
Markt & Technik Online	GERMUT
Marquis Who's Who($)	BIOGRAPHY
Masonry Forum	MASONRY
Max Ule's Tickerscreen	TKR
McAfee Virus Forum	VIRUSFORUM
McGraw-Hill Book Company(FREE)	MH
me2 Promotional Offer(FREE)	ME2OFFER
MECA Software Forum	MECA
MechWarrior 2 Online	MECHWAR
Media Newsletters($)	MEDIANEWS
Media Vision Forum	MEDIAVISIO
Medsig Forum	MEDSIG
MegaWars I	MEGA1
MegaWars III	MEGA3

Member Directory(FREE)	DIRECTORY
Member Information Questions(FREE)	MEMINFO
Member Recommendation Program(FREE)	FRIEND
Member Services(FREE)	HELP
Members of Congress	FCC
Mensa Forum	MENSA
Mentor Technologies	MENTOR
Mercury Showroom(FREE)	MERCURY
Merian Online	MERIAN
Message Handling Service Hub	MHSADMIN
Metroplex	METROPLEX
Metropolitan Museum of Art(FREE)	MMA
Mexico Forum	MEXICO
Michelangelo Anti-Virus Area	MICHELANGE
Micro Focus Forum	MICROFOCUS
Micrografx Forum	MICROGRAFX
MicroHelp Support Forum	MICROHELP
Microprocessors & News Forum	INTELP
Microrim Forum	MICRORIM
Microsoft File Finder	MSFF
Microsoft Mac Office Forum	MACOFFICE
Microsoft Office other Co	MSOFORUM
Microsoft Windows Intl. D	WINTLDEV
MicroStation Forum	MSTATION
Microtest Inc. Forum	MICROTEST
MicroWarehouse(FREE)	MCW
MIDI A Vendor Forum	MIDIAVEN
MIDI B Vendor Forum	MIDIBVEN
MIDI C Vendor Forum	MIDICVEN
MIDI D Vendor Forum	MIDIDVEN
MIDI/Music Forum	MIDIFORUM
Military Display	MILITARY
Military Forum	MILFORUM
Military Multimedia Forum	MILGRAPHIC
Military Organizations Forum	MILORGAN
Mind/Body Sciences Forum	MIND
Mirror Technologies	MACCVEN
Miss Spider Contest	SPIDER
Missing Children Forum(FREE)	MISSING
Mission Control Software(FREE)	MCS
MMS International	MMS
MMS/Daily Comment($)	DC
MMS/Fedwatch Newsletter($)	FW
Mobile Computing	MOBILE
Model Aviation Forum	MODELNET
Modem Games Forum	MODEMGAMES
Modem Vendor Forum	MODEMVENDO
Modem/Modem Game Support	MTMGAMES
Mondo Economico/L'Impresa($)	MONDOECO
Money Book Club(FREE)	MONEYCLUB
Money Magazine	MONEY
Motor Sports Forum	RACING
Motorcycle Forum	RIDE
MotorWeek Online	MOTORWEEK
Movie Reviews	MOVIES
MQDATA($)	MQDATA
MS 32bit Languages Forum	MSLNG32
MS Access Forum	MSACCESS

MS BASIC Forum	MSBASIC
MS Benelux Forum	MSBF
MS Benelux Services	MSBEN
MS Beta CD Forum	BETAEVAL
MS Biz Computing Forum	BIZSOLN
MS CE Systems Forum	MSCESYSTEM
MS Central Europe Forum	MSCE
MS Central Europe Services	MSEURO
MS Client	MSCLIENT
MS Client Server Comp. Forum	MSNETWORKS
MS Connection	MICROSOFT
MS Desktop Forum	MSDESKTOP
MS DEV Network Forum	MSDNLIB
MS DOS 6.2 DLOAD (Microsoft)	MSDOS62
MS DOS 6.2 DOWNLOAD (PCWORLD)	PCWDOS62
MS DOS 6.2 STEPUP (GERMAN)	DMSDOS
MS DOS Forum	MSDOS
MS Education & CP Forum	MSEDCERT
MS Excel Forum	MSEXCEL
MS Foundation Classes Forum	MSMFC
MS Fox Software Forum	FOXFORUM
MS Fox Users Forum	FOXUSER
MS French Forum	MSFR
MS French Services	MSFRANCE
MS Home Products Forum	MSHOME
MS Hong Kong Forum	MSHK
MS Italian Forum	MSITALY
MS Italian Services	MSITA
MS Knowledge Base	MSKB
MS Language Forum	MSLANG
MS Mail and Workgroups Forum	MSWGA
MS Networks Forum	MSNETWORKS
MS Office Forum	MSOFFICE
MS OLE Solutions Forum	OLESOLNS
MS Personal Operating Systems	MSPEROP
MS Plus Services	PLUS
MS Press(FREE)	MSP
MS Sales & Information Forum	MSIC
MS Software Library	MSL
MS Spanish Forum	MSSP
MS Spanish Services	MSSPAIN
MS SQL Server Forum	MSSQL
MS Sweden Forum	MSSWE
MS Sweden Services	MSSWEDEN
MS TechNet Forum	TNFORUM
MS TechNet Services	TECHNET
MS TV Forum	DEVCAST
MS Visual FoxPro Forum	VFOX
MS Win Multimedia Forum	WINMM
MS WIN32 Forum	MSWIN32
MS Windows AV Forum	WINAV
MS Windows Extensions Forum	WINEXT
MS Windows Forum	MSWIN
MS Windows News Forum	WINNEWS
MS Windows Objects Forum	WINOBJECTS
MS Windows Productivity	WINPROD
MS Windows SDK Forum	WINSDK
MS Windows Shareware Forum	WINSHARE

MS Windows Workgroups Forum	MSWFWG
MS WINFUN Forum	WINFUN
MS WinNT Forum	WINNT
MS WinNT SNA Forum	MSSNA
MS Word Forum	MSWORD
MTM Challenge Board	MTMCHALLEN
Multi Issue Price History($)	QSHEET
Multi-Player Games Forum	MPGAMES
Multimedia A Vendor Forum	MULTIVEN
Multimedia B Vendor Forum	MULTIBVEN
Multimedia C Vendor Forum	MULTICVEN
Multimedia Enhanced Menu	MULTIMEDIA
Multimedia Forum	MMFORUM
Multiple Sclerosis Forum	MULTSCLER
Municipal Bond Notification	MUNINOTE
Muscular Dystrophy Association	MDA-1
Muscular Dystrophy MDA Forum	MDAFORUM
Music Hall	MUSIC
Music In(tr)Action Forum	IMUSIC
Music Industry Forum	INMUSIC
Music Place, The(FREE)	THEPLACE
Music/Arts Forum	MUSICARTS
Musik Forum	MUSIK
NAIC Invest. Ed. Forum	NAIC
Nat. Computer Security Assoc.	NCSA
National Public Radio	NPR
Natural Medicine Forum	HOLISTIC
NavCIS Download Area	WNAVCIS
NBA Jam Tournament Promotion	NBAJAM
NCAA Collegiate Sports Network	NCAA
NCHELP	NCHELP
NCSA Anti-Virus Vendor Forum	NCSAVEN
NCSA InfoSecurity Forum	NCSAFORUM
NCSA Security Vendor Forum	NCSAVENDOR
Neighborhood Demographics($)	NEIGHBOR
NetGuide Magazine(FREE)	NETGUIDE
Netherlands Forum	NLFORUM
NetLauncher Support Forum(FREE)	NLSUPPORT
NetLauncher(FREE)	NETLAUNCHE
NetManage ECCO Forum	ECCO
Netware General Files Forum	NWGENFILES
NetWare OS Files Forum	NWOSFILES
NetWare Solutions	NWSOLUTION
Network Computing Forum	NWCMAG
Network Professional Assoc.	NPA-1
Network VAR Forum	STACKS
Neue Zuercher Zeitung($)	ZUERCHER
New Age A Forum	NEWAAGE
New Age B Forum	NEWBAGE
New Age Forum	NEWAGE
New Consumer Service	WOW
New Member Forum(FREE)	NEWMEMBER
New Member Welcome Center(FREE)	WELCOME
New York Magazine Online	NYMAG
New York Magazine Store(FREE)	SHOPNY
New York Newslink Forum	NEWYORK
Newbridge Book Clubs(FREE)	NEWBRIDGE
NewMedia 1995 Invision Aw(FREE)	INVISION

News Source USA($)	NEWSLIB
News-A-Tron($)	NAT
NEWS/400 Forum	NEWS3X400
NewsGrid	NEWSGRID
Newspaper Archives($)	NEWSARCHIV
Newton Developers Forum	NEWTDEV
Newton Vendor Forum	NEWTVEN
Newton/PIE Forum	NEWTON
NeXT Forum	NEXTFORUM
Nifty-Serve	NIF-5
Ninety Nines Forum	NINETYNINE
Nintendo's Donkey Kong Country	NINTENDO
Nissan Online(FREE)	NI
NL Computing Forum	NLCOMP
Nominate Image of the Month(FREE)	GRFMONTH
NonProfit Forum	NONPROFIT
NonProfit Forum	NONPROFIT
NORD Services/Rare Disease DB	NORD
Northern Ireland News Clips($)	NIRELAND
Novell AppTID	APPTID
Novell Client Forum	NOVCLIENT
Novell Connectivity Forum	NCONNECT
Novell Dev Support ForuM	NDEVSUPPOR
Novell Dev. Info. Forum	NDEVINFO
Novell DSG Forum	DRFORUM
Novell Files Database	NOVFILES
Novell GroupWise Forum	GROUPWISE
Novell Hardware Forum	NOVHW
Novell Information Forum	NGENERAL
Novell InForms Forum	NINFORMS
Novell Library Forum	NOVLIB
Novell Net. Management Forum	NOVMAN
Novell NetWare 2.X Forum	NETW2X
Novell NetWare 3.X Forum	NETW3X
Novell Netware 4X Forum	NETW4X
Novell NetWire	NOVELL
Novell OS/2 Forum	NOVOS2
Novell PerfectFit Partners	PERFECT
Novell PerfectHome Forum	MAINST
Novell PerfectOffice Forum	PEROFF
Novell Presentation Forum	WPPR
Novell Press Forum	NOVBOOKS
Novell Publishing Forum	ELECPUB
Novell Quattro Pro Forum	QUATTROPRO
Novell SoftSolutions Foru	SOFTSOLUTI
Novell Tech Bullet. Dbase	NTB
Novell User Library	NOVUSER
Novell Vendor A Forum	NVENA
Novell Vendor B Forum	NVENB
Novell WordPerfect DOS Forum	WPDOS
Novell WordPerfect Unix Forum	WPUNIX
Novell WP Macintosh Forum	WPMAC
Novell WP Windows Forum	WPWIN
NT Workstation Forum	NTWORK
NTIS - Gov't Sponsored($)	NTIS
NTSERVER Forum	NTSERVER
NW Solutions Mag Forum	NWSFORUM
NWS Aviation Weather	AWX

O. J. Simpson News Clips($)	OJNEWS
O.J. Simpson Forum	OJFORUM
Objects, Inc. Forum	OBJECTS
Office Auto. Vendor Forum	OAVENDOR
Office Automation Forum	OAFORUM
Office World(FREE)	OFFWORLD
OfficeMax OnLine(FREE)	OM
Official Airline Guide EE($)	OAG
Ohio Travel Forum	OHIO
Oklahoma City Explosion	OKCITY
Oldies Diner Forum	OLDIES
Omaha Steaks Intl.(FREE)	OS
One Hanes Place(FREE)	LEGGS
Online Inquiry	OLN
OnLine Issues Forum	OLISSUES
Online Services Survey(FREE)	OLSURVEY
Online Surveys	SURVEY
Online Today Daily Edition	OLT
OnTime for Windows Offer	OTOFFER
OpenDoc Forum	OPENDOC
Options by IBM	IBMOBI
Options Profile($)	OPRICE
Oracle Software Download	ORASOFT
Oracle User Group Forum	ORAUSER
Order From CompuServe(FREE)	ORDER
OS-9 Forum	OS9
OS/2 Warp Kit	ADDWARP
OTC NewsAlert($)	ENS
Other Ban Patchware Forum	BANPATCH
Outdoors Library	OUTLIB
Outdoors Network Enhanced Menu	OUTDOORS
Outdoors News Clips($)	OUTNEWS
Overview of IBMNET	OVERVIEW
OZCIS Support Forum	OZCIS
PA Financial News	CITYNEWS
PA News	PAO
Pacific Vendor Forum	PACVEN
Packard Bell Forum	PACKARDBEL
Palmtop B Forum	PALMB
Palmtop Forum	PALMTOP
PaperChase-MEDLINE($)	PAPERCHASE
ParcPlace-Digitalk Forum	PPDFORUM
Parlor and Trivia Games	TTGAMES
Parsons Technology Forum	PTFORUM
Parsons Technology(FREE)	PA
Participate	PARTI
Past Times	PASTTIMES
Pat Metheny Spotlight	METHENY
Patent Research Center($)	PATENT
Paul Fredrick Shirts(FREE)	PFS
PBM/Board/Card Game Forum	PBMGAMES
PC Applications Forum	PCAPP
PC Bulletin Board Forum	PCBBS
PC Communications Forum	PCCOM
PC Computing Magazine	PCCOMPUTIN
PC Contact Forum	PCCONTACT
PC Direct En Ligne	PCDFRANCE
PC Direct France	PCDIRF

PC Direct UK Forum	PCDUK
PC Expert En-ligne	PCEXPERT
PC Expert Forum francais	PCEFORUM
PC File Finder	PCFF
PC Fun Forum	PCFUN
PC Hardware Forum	PCHW
PC Industrie Forum	PCINDF
PC Magazine	PCMAGAZINE
PC Magazine UK Online	PCUKONLINE
PC MagNet	PCMAGNET
PC New User's Forum	PCNEW
PC Plug and Play Forum	PLUGPLAY
PC Plus / PC Answers	PCPLUS
PC Programming Forum	PCPROG
PC Publications(FREE)	PCB
PC Sports	PCSPORTS
PC Today(FREE)	PCA
PC Utilities/Systems Forum	PCUTIL
PC Vendor A Forum	PCVENA
PC Vendor B Forum	PCVENB
PC Vendor C Forum	PCVENC
PC Vendor D Forum	PCVEND
PC Vendor E Forum	PCVENE
PC Vendor F Forum	PCVENF
PC Vendor G Forum	PCVENG
PC Vendor H Forum	PCVENH
PC Vendor I Forum	PCVENI
PC Vendor J Forum	PCVENJ
PC Vendor K Forum	PCVENK
PC Week Extra Forum	PCWEEK
PC Week Magazine	PCWONLINE
PC World	UKPCWORLD
PC World 3D Gaming Forum	GAME3D
PC World Entertainment Forum	GAMING
PC World Online	PCWORLD
PC World Online Forum	PWOFORUM
PC World Online Store(FREE)	PWM
PC World SOHO Forum	SOHO
PC-ONLINE Magazin Forum	PCONLINE
PC/Contact Polls	PCCPOLL
PCNet Online	PCNET
PCNet Online Trivia Contest	PCTRIVIA
PDP-11 Forum	PDP11
Peachtree Software Forum	PEACHTREE
PEARL Forum	PEARL
Pen Technology Forum	PENFORUM
PEOPLE Halloween Quiz	PEOQUIZ
People Magazine	PEOPLE
People Magazine Forum	PEOFRM
PerfectOffice Files Forum	NPOFILES
Personal File Area	FILES
Personal Menu	MENU
Personality Profile	TMC-90
Pet Products A Forum	PFVENA
Pet Products B Forum	HOM-174
Peterson's College Database	PETERSONS
Pets News Clips($)	PETSNEWS
Pets One	PETSFORUM

Pets Two	PETSTWO
Phone*File($)	PHONEFILE
Photo Gallery Forum	PHOTOGALLE
Photo Professionals Forum	PROPHOTO
Photodex Forum	PHOTODEX
Photography Forum	PHOTOFORUM
Photos To Go	PHOTOSTOGO
Physicians Data Query($)	PDQ
Playbill On-Line Forum	PLAYBILL
PLAYBOY	PLAYTV
Polaris Software Forum	POLARIS
Political Debate Forum	POLITICS
Pontiac Showroom(FREE)	Pontiac
Pope	POPE
Portable Prog. Forum	CODEPORT
Portfolio Valuation($)	PORT
PowerBuilder Forum	PBFORUM
Powersoft Forum	PSFORUM
Powersoft Support	POWERSOFT
PR and Marketing Forum	PRSIG
PR Newswire Today	PRNEWS
Practical Periph. Forum	PPIFORUM
Practice Forum(FREE)	PRACTICE
PRC Publishing	PRC
Premier Dining(FREE)	DINE
Price/Vol Graph($)	TREND
Pricing Statistics($)	PRISTATS
Prisma Deutschland Forum	PRISMA
Programming MS APPS	PROGMSA
Project & Cost Management	TCMFORUM
Project & Cost Mgt Forum	TCMVEN
ProPublishing Forum	PROPUB
ProTRADE Forum	PROTRADE
PSP BETA FORUM	PSPBETA
PsychINFO Abstracts($)	PSYCINFO
Publications Online($)	PUBONL
Quality Paperbacks(FREE)	QPB
Quark Forum	QUARK
Quarterdeck Forum	QUARTERDEC
Quick & Reilly($)	QWK
Quick Picture Forum	QPICS
QuickTime 2.0 Download Ar	QTIME
RateGram Fed Insured CDs	RATEGRAM
Recording Industry Forums	RECORD
Recovery Forum	RECOVERY
Recreation Vehicle Forum	RVFORUM
Rehabilitation Database	REHAB
Religion Forum	RELIGION
Religious Issues Forum	RELISSUES
RELO(FREE)	RELO
Republican Forum	REPUBLICAN
Retirement Living Forum	RETIREMENT
Return Analysis($)	RETURN
Reuter News Pictures Forum	NEWSPI
Reuters Canadian News Clips	RTCANADA
Reuters Financial Report($)	ENS
Reuters UK News Clips	UKREUTERS
Reuters/Variety Entertainment	RTVARIETY

Reveal Forum	REVEAL
Revelation Tech Forum	REVELATION
Review My Charges(FREE)	CHARGES
Rock 'n Roll Hall of Fame	ROCKNROLL
Rock Online Forum	ROCKONLINE
Rock Video Monthly	ROCKVID
Rocknet Forum	ROCKNET
Roger Ebert's Movie Reviews	EBERT
Role-Playing Games Forum	RPGAMES
Rolling Stone Forum	RSFORUM
Rolling Stone Online	RSONLINE
Rolling Stone Online Store(FREE)	RSSTORE
Rosebud Software	ROSEBUD
Rotarians Online Forum	ROTARY
Rox	ISDSUP
Rubbermaid Commercial(FREE)	RUBBERMAID
Rural Living Forum	RURAL
Rush Limbaugh's Download Area	RUSHDL
Rwanda News Clips($)	RWANDA
S&P Online($)	S&P
Safetynet Forum	SAFETYNET
SAFEWARE Computer Insure(FREE)	SAF
Sailing Forum	SAILING
Sailing Reception Area	SAIL
Santa Cruz Operation Forum	SCOFORUM
Santagrams	SANTAGRAM
SAP AG	SAPAG
SBCNet	SBCNET
Schmoozing Forum	PREFORUM
Schweizer Fernsehen	SFDRS
Science Museum	SCMUSEUM
Science Trivia Quiz	SCITRIVIA
Science/Math Ed. Forum	SCIENCE
Scouting Forum	SCOUTING
ScreenScene	SCENE
Scuba Forum	DIVING
Scuba Survey	SCUBASURVE
SDA - Deutsch($)	SDADEU
SDA - Francais($)	ATSFRA
SDA - Italiano($)	AGZITAL
SDA - Sportinfo($)	SDASPORT
Seagate Forum	SEAGATE
Sears(FREE)	SEARS
Seattle Film Works(FREE)	SFW
Securities Screening($)	SCREEN
Securities Symbols Lookup	SYMBOLS
Sega Forum	SEGA
Sega Mall Store(FREE)	SGM
Selfridges(FREE)	SELFRIDGES
Selling Online	SELLING
Selling Online Forum	SELLING
Service Merchandise(FREE)	SVCMER
SF/Fantasy Literature Forum	SFLIT
SF/Fantasy Media Forum	SFMEDIA
Shareware Beta Forum	SWBETA
Shareware Depot(FREE)	SD
Shareware Registration	SWREG
Shop-at-home	SHOPPING

Shoppers Advantage(FREE)	SAC
SHOWBIZ Quiz	SBQ
ShowbizMedia Forum	SHOWBIZ
SI Insider Authentics(FREE)	SISTORE
SI News, Scores, & Stats	SISTATS
SI Photo Gallery	SIIMAGES
SI Subscription Services(FREE)	SIMAG
Siemens Automation	SIEAUT
Siemens Automatisierungs Forum	AUTFORUM
Siemens Nixdorf Forum	SNIPC
Sierra Online	SIERRA
Sight And Sound Forum	SSFORUM
Single Issue Price Hist.($)	PRICES
Skiing Forum	SKIING
Sky & Telescope Online	SKYTEL
Small Computer Book Club(FREE)	BK
SmartCard Forum	SMARTCARD
Smith Micro Forum	SMITHMICRO
SnapGraphics Download Area	SNAPGRAPHI
SNIPER!	SNIPER
Snoopy	SNOOPY
Soap Opera Forum	SOAPFORUM
Soap Opera Summaries	SOAPS
Society of Broadcast Eng.	SBENET
Softdisk Downloads	SPDL
SOFTEX	SOFTEX
SoftKey Forum	SOFTKEY
Software Development Forum	SDFORUM
Software Forums	SOFTWARE
Software Marketing Forum	SWSHOP
Software Pub. Assoc. Forum	SPAFORUM
Software Publisher Online	SPCONLINE
Software Publishing Forum	SPCFORUM
Sound.WAV '95 Contest	SOUNDWAV
Space Exploration Forum	SPACEX
Space Flight Forum	SPACEFLIGH
Space/Astronomy Forum	SPACE
Spanish Forum	SPFORUM
SPEA Forum	SPEA
Speakeasy Forum	SPEAKEASY
Specials/Contests Menu(FREE)	SPECIAL
SPORTRONIC	FUSSBALL
Sports Challenge	SICHALLENG
Sports Forum	FANS
Sports Illustrated Mag	SIMAGAZINE
Sports Illustrated Online	SPORTS
Sports Simulation Forum	SPRTSIMS
Stac Electronics Forum	STACKER
STAGEII	STAGEII
Standard Indus. Class.	SICCODE
Standard Microsystems Forum	SMC
STAR DIVISION GmbH Forum	STARDIVISI
STARBASE PUBLIC FORUM	STR-4
Starfish Software	SIMPLIFY
Starfish Software Forum	STARFISH
STARPIX Download Area	STARPIX
Starplay Productions	STARPLAY
State Bar of Texas (BARLINK)	BARLINK

State Capitol Quiz	TMC-89
State Travel Tourism Forum	USTOUR
State-County Demographics($)	DEMOGRAPHI
Stein Online	STEIN
StockTracker Download($)	STOCKTRACK
Sueddeutsche Zeitung($)	SUEDDEUT
Summer Blockbuster	EDE-41
Sundown Vitamins(FREE)	SDV
SunSoft Forum	SUNSOFT
SUPERSITE Demographics($)	SUPERSITE
Support Directory	SUPPORT
Support On Site	ONSITE
Support Tech Vendor Forum	CSTECH
Supra Forum	SUPRA
Sutherland's HouseMart(FREE)	HM
Sybase Forum	SYBASE
SYBEX Publishing Forum	SYBEX
Symantec AntiVirus Prod. Forum	SYMVIRUS
Symantec Applications Forum	SYMAPPS
Symantec CPS DOS Forum	SYMCPDOS
Symantec CPS WinMac Forum	SYMCPWIN
Symantec Dev. Tools Forum	SYMDEVTOOL
Symantec DOS & OS/2 Forum	SYMDOS
Symantec Europe Forum	SYMEUR
Symantec FGS Forum	SYMFGS
Symantec Forums	SYMANTEC
Symantec Macintosh Forum	SYMMAC
Symantec Norton Util Forum	SYMUTIL
Symantec Ntwrk Products Forum	SYMNET
Symantec Windows 3.1 Forum	SYMWIN
Symantec Windows 95 & NT Forum	SYMNEW
Syndicated Columns	COLUMNS
TalkBack Live Forum	TALKBACK
Tandy Model 100 Forum	TANDYLAPTO
Tandy Newsletter	TANDY
Tandy Professional Forum	TANDYPRO
TAPCIS Forum	TAPCIS
TaxCut Download Area	MECATAXCUT
Tektronix Forum	TEKTRONIX
Telecom Support Forum	TELECOM
Telefirm Directory($)	TELEFIRM
Telework Europa Forum	TWEUROPA
Tennis Forum	TENNIS
Tesco	TESCO
Texas Instruments Forum	TIFORUM
Texas Instruments News	TINEWS
Thanksgiving Online	THANKSGIVI
The 'GO GRAPHICS' Tutorial	PIC
The Absolut Museum(FREE)	ABS
The Academy Awards	OSCARS
The Beatles Anthology	ANTHOLOGY
The Bob Dylan Spotlight	DYLAN
The Business Wire	TBW
The CompuServe Auditorium	AUDITORIUM
The Computer Expo(FREE)	CPE
The Electronic Mall Elite(FREE)	ELITE
The Electronic MALL(FREE)	MALL
The Entrepreneur's Forum	SMALLBIZ

The Escort Store(FREE)	ESCORT
The Focus Connection	FOCUS
The FORTUNE Store(FREE)	FMALL
The Gift Sender(FREE)	GS
The Good Pub Guide	UKPUBS
The Great Outdoors Forum	OUTFORUM
The Gutenburg Collection	GUTENBURG
The Hutchinson Encyclopedia	HUTCHINSON
The International Forum	EETINTFRM
The Laser's Edge(FREE)	LE
The Lotus Organizer Store(FREE)	ORGANIZER
The Mac Zone/PC Zone(FREE)	MZ
The Mask Unix Download Area	MASK
The MBA Forum	MBAFORUM
The Movie Zone Store(FREE)	ZONESTORE
The Multiple Choice	MULTIPLE
The PEOPLE Magazine Store(FREE)	PMSTORE
The Property Forum	REALPRO
The Tandy Users Network	TANDYNET
The Weather Channel Forum	TWCFORUM
The Week's Issue	NEWPEO
The Whiz Quiz	WHIZ
The World of Lotus	LOTUS
The Worship Center	WORSHIP
The ZD Mall	ZD
The ZD Store($)	STORE
Thomas Register Online($)	THOMAS
Thomas-Conrad Forum	TCCFORUM
TICFIL	TICFIL
Ticker/Symbol Lookup	LOOKUP
Time Warner Bookstore(FREE)	TWEPB
Time Warner Crime Forum	TWCRIME
Time Warner Elect. Publishing	TWEP
Time Warner Lifestyles Forum	TWLIFE
Time Warner-Dogs & Cats Forum	TWPETS
Timescape Library Forum	ENERGY
TIMESLIPS Forum	TIMESLIPS
Tips/Tricks From PC/Computing	TNT
TopSpeed Corporation Forum	CLARION
Toshiba Forum	TOSHIBA
Toshiba GmbH Forum	TOSHGER
Town Hall	TOWNHALL
Toyota Interactive(FREE)	TOYOTA
TRADEMARKSCAN($)	TRADERC
Trading Card Forum	CARDS
Trainers & Training Forum	TRAINERS
TrainNet Forum	TRAINNET
Travel Britain Online	TBONLINE
Travel Forum	TRAVSIG
Travel Software Support Forum	TSSFORUM
Travelers Advantage(FREE)	TRAVAD
Trinity Delta Forum	TDELTA
TRW Bus. Credit Reports($)	TRWREPORT
TurboTax Support Forum	CHIPSOFT
TV Zone Forum	TVZONE
TV1	TVONE
Twentieth Century(FREE)	TC
U. S. News Women's Forum	WOMEN

U.S. News & World Report	USNEWS
U.S. News & World Report Store(FREE)	USM
U.S. News College Fair Forum	USNCOLLEGE
U.S. News Forum	USNFORUM
UFO Forum	UFOFORUM
UK Company Information($)	COUK
UK Company Library($)	UKLIB
UK Entertainment Reviews	UKREVIEWS
UK Forum	UKFORUM
UK Historical Stock Pricing	UKPRICE
UK Information Tech Forum	UKIT
UK Newspaper Library($)	UKPAPERS
UK Politics Forum	UKPOLITICS
UK Professionals Forum	UKPROF
UK Recreation Forum	UKREC
UK Travel Forum	UKTF
UK Vendor A Forum	UKVENA
UK What's On Guide	UKWO
UKSHAREWARE Forum	UKSHARE
Ultimate Sample Site(FREE)	SAMPLE
Unabomber Manifesto Files	UNABOMBER
United Connection	UNITED
United Press Int'l($)	ENS
United Way(FREE)	UW
Univ of Phoenix(FREE)	UP
UNIX Forum	UNIXFORUM
UNIX Vendor A Forum	UNIXAVEN
UnixWare Forum	UNIXWARE
UPS Online Air Service Center(FREE)	UPS
USENET Newsgroups	USENET
User Profile Program(FREE)	TERMINAL
UserLand Forum	USERLAND
VARBusiness Forum	VARBUSINES
VAX Forum	VAXFORUM
VBPJ Forum	VBPJFORUM
Vegetarian Forum	VEGETARIAN
Vektron Online(FREE)	VEK
Veranstaltungskalender	VERANSTALT
Vestor Stock Recommendation	VESTOR
Video Games Forum	VIDGAM
Video Gaming Central	VGCENTRAL
Viewer's Edge(FREE)	VID
Vines 4.x Patchware Forum	VINES4
Vines 5.x Patchware Forum	VINES5
Virgin Megastore	MEGASTORE
VISA Advisors	VISA
Visio	SHAPEWARE
Vobis AG Computer Forum	VOBIS
Vogel Online	VOGEL
Walter Knoll Florist(FREE)	WK
Wang Support Area	WANG
War Games	WARGAMES
Warner Bros. Song Preview	WBPREVIEW
Watcom Forum	WATFORUM
Way to Go CompuServe	WAYTOGO
Weather Maps	MAPS
Weather Reports	WEATHER
Wer Gehoert zu Wem($)	WERZUWEM

West Coast Travel	WESTCOAST
WH Smith	WHSMITH
What's New	NEW
White House Forum	WHITEHOUSE
White House Mail	PRESMAIL
WIN Magazin Forum	WINGER
WinCIM FT-Connect Script:NL	NLLOKAAL
WinCIM General Forum(FREE)	WCIMGENERA
WinCIM Information(FREE)	WINCIM
WinCIM Technical Forum(FREE)	WCIMTECH
Windows 3rd Party A Forum	WINAPA
Windows 3rd Party App. D Forum	WINAPD
Windows 3rd Party App. F Forum	WINAPF
Windows 3rd Party App. G Forum	WINAPG
Windows 3rd Party App. H	WINAPH
Windows 3rd Party B Forum	WINAPB
Windows 3rd Party C Forum	WINAPC
Windows 3rd Party E Forum	WINAPE
Windows 3rd Party I Forum	WINAPI
Windows Business Applicat	WINBIZ
Windows Components A Forum	COMPA
Windows Components B Forum	COMPB
Windows Components C Forum	COMPC
Windows Connectivity Foru	WINCON
Windows Games Forum	WINGAME
Windows Magazine Forum	WINMAG
Windows Networking A Forum	WINETA
Windows News Clips($)	WINCLIPS
Windows Sources Forum	WINSOURCES
Windows Sources Magazine	WSOURCES
Windows Utility Forum	WINUTIL
Windows Utility Vendor A Forum	WINUTA
WindowShare France Forum	WSHARE
WinNav Information	WINNAV
WinSupport 95	WIN95
winTV Download Area($)	WINTV
Wired on Country	COUNTRY
Wireless Comms. Forum	WIRELESS
Wireless Communication Survey	WIRELESS
Wolfram Research Forum	WOLFRAM
Women in Aviation Forum	WIAONLINE
Women's Wire	WOMEN
WordPerfect Corporation	WORDPERFEC
WordPerfect GmbH Forum	WPGER
WordPerfect Magazine	WPMAG
WordPerfect Users Forum	WPUSER
Working-From-Home Forum	WORK
World Community Forum	WCOMMUNITY
World Motoring News Forum	MOTORING
WorldsAway	AWAY
WORLDSPAN Travelshopper (CIM)	WORLDCIM
Worldwide Car Network	WWCAR
WP Magazine Forum	WPMAGFORUM
WPCorp Files Forum	WPFILES
Writers Forum	WRITER
WRQ/Reflection Forum	WRQFORUM
WUGNET Forum	WUGNET
Xerox Office Solutions Forum	XRXOFFICE

XEROX PROD. PRINTING FORUM	XRXPRINT
Xerox Software Forum	XRXSW
Xircom Forum	XIRCOM
Y. Rabin Assassination	HOTNEWS
You Guessed It!	YGI
Youth Drive Forum	YDRIVE
Zagat Restaurant Guide	ZAGAT
ZD Benchmark Forum	ZDBENCHMAR
ZD Net	ZDNET
ZD Net Computing News	NEWREFEREN
ZD Net Membership & Benefits	ZDMEM
ZD Net Software Center	CENTER
ZD Net Support Forum	ZDHELP
ZD Net/Mac	ZMAC
ZD University	ZDUNIVERSI
Zenith Data Systems Forum	ZENITH
ZMac Arts & Fun Forum	ZMACARTS
ZMac Tech & Business Forum	ZMACTECH
Zugangsnummern(FREE)	ZUGANG

Appendix 4
Using the
CompuServe Home
Page Wizard

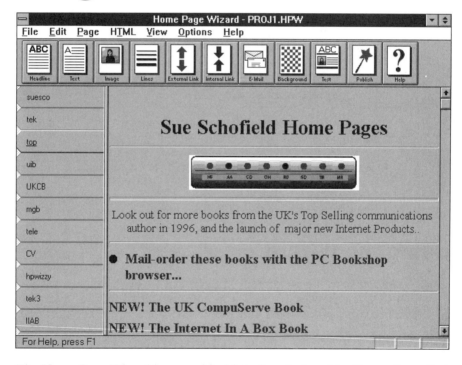

The Home Page Wizard is a graphical interface designed by CompuServe that makes it easy for users to submit their Personal Home pages on-line. The Wizard allows a user to create a Web page, view it within a browser, and submit it to CompuServe to be placed on the Internet. You can check out the Author's Home Page on the Web at:

http://ourworld.compuserve.com/homepages/suesco

for a small example of what can be achieved with the Home Page Wizard.

HyperText Markup Language (HTML) is the "programming language" that Web pages are created in. Since the Wizard provides a graphical interface that uses drag-and-drop buttons on the Toolbar, it requires no knowledge of HTML.

Not only is the Wizard easy to install, it is easy to use too! If by chance you run into problems, CompuServe provide context-sensitive help from the HELP pull-down menu, and a "Tip of the Day" that is displayed when the program starts.

Home Page Wizard 1.0 equipment requirements

* An IBM or compatible personal computer.

* An 80386 processor (or higher) and, at least 4MB of RAM.

* Microsoft Windows Version 3.1, Win95 or WinNT.

* An IBM VGA or higher resolution monitor compatible with the Microsoft Windows graphical environment.

* One hard disk (at least 2 megabytes available - with Windows installed) and one high-density floppy drive.

* A WINSOCK.DLL and an Internet dialer (CompuServe Internet Dialer (CID) included with NetLauncher and WinCIM v2.0).

* A mouse (or pointing device) that is compatible with Microsoft Windows.

Using the Wizard

When creating a new "project" in the Home Page Wizard, you will be presented with a few choices that will help you get started creating your home page. Choose one of the styles you would like to start with and fill in each of the fields. These templates are created as starting points and can be edited or changed. If you prefer to use your own style, begin with a blank template and build your page from scratch.

The Home Page Wizard lets you create your own Home World Wide Web page on the Internet. It can show who you are, where your interests lie, what you like and dislike, or where you stand on the issues of the day. Use the Home Page Wizard to create your own personal home page, and then use Publishing Wizard to put it on the Web for everyone to see.

It's your home page, and it can be whatever you want it to be. Words, pictures, partitions - you choose the size, choose the shape, choose the colour, and put them all together any way you want. You can even choose a colour or a graphic image as a background for your presentation.

You don't have to be satisfied with a single page. You can create other pages and link them to your main home page and to each other. You could use your home page to introduce yourself, and other pages to explore the many facets of you in depth.

CompuServe offers you a megabyte of space to hold your Home Page. This may seem quite a lot, but space does get eaten up by large graphic files. Where possible keep your graphic files small. Don't forget that you can use an 'external link' to hop to another page anywhere on the Web. This is useful if two or more members want to get together to share their one megabyte of space, say for club use. Just include a link to the other members page. However you must get the permission of the owners of other Web pages before you include links to their pages.

Hardware/software

You don't need any extra hardware or software to create your Web pages with Home Page Wizard. If you're a CompuServe member and your computer runs Windows 3.1 or Windows 95 in enhanced mode, you've got the basics.

You need software that can convert your own photos to GIF, JPEG, PNG, or some other graphics format that can be read by Web browsers. Home Page Wizard comes with an image library of graphics files, but you'll probably want to personalize it by adding others of your own. See Chapter 5 Email, for descriptions of graphics file formats. If you want to use a 35mm camera to take photo's for use in your home page you can have films processed onto CD ROM at most large photo chains. These photos can then be converted into GIF or JPEGS using programs such as Graphics Workshop found on CompuServe. Use the Graphics File Finder (GO GRAPHFF) to hunt them down.

To view your pages when they're on the Web (and to test your pages before you publish them), you also need a Web browser. CompuServe Mosaic which comes free with the CompuServe Information Manager, Windows version, Release 2.0 or later works well, but you can use any browser you like.

How to install Home Page Wizard and Publishing Wizard

Home Page Wizard and Publishing Wizard are both on the same disk. To install the programs:

1. Insert the disk in the floppy disk drive.
2. Choose Run the Program Manager's File menu, or choose Run from the Windows 95 Start menu.
3. Type A:SETUP (or B:SETUP if you are installing from Drive B) and click the OK button.

The Set-up program installs both Home Page Wizard and Publishing Wizard, notifying you of its progress. When set-up is complete, you'll see two new icons in your CompuServe program group.

How to start a home page project

To begin creating your personal home page, double-click the Home Page Wizard icon in the CompuServe program group window. The first time you start the program, you provide a home page title and a name for your home page project. You also tell Home Page Wizard whether to use a template.

Home Page Wizard needs a project name so that it can keep this group of Web pages separate from any other groups you create. You can have any number of projects, although you can only publish one at a time on the Web.

Home Page Wizard comes with a number of templates, which can help you get started . A template is only a pattern; once you pick it, you can make any changes you like.

Once you provide this information, you move on to the main Home Page Wizard window. This is where you create your home page.

Creating Your Home Page

You can add a variety of elements to your home page using the toolbar icon. When you want to insert something, just drag and drop the toolbar icon to wherever you want to put it. When you drop the icon, a window opens where you compose text, select a picture, or whatever else you need to do to tell Home Page Wizard what goes in that location.

Headline
Use a headline for a section title or anything else you want to emphasize. Headlines come in six different sizes, and you can centre them on the page.

Text
Use a text block to provide details and express yourself to the fullest. You can centre any given text block on the page, put a bullet in front of it, or pre-format it to preserve line breaks and columns.

Image
Use an image when a picture is better than a thousand words. You can put a graphic image in the centre of the page, expand or shrink it proportionally, or stretch or squeeze it in just one dimension to create your own personal special effects.

Line
Use a horizontal line to create a partition between one text block and another, or between a text block and a headline, or just for decoration. A line can be as thin or as wide as you want to make it, and it can cross just a little of the page or a lot.

Internal Link
Use an internal link to connect your home page to an associated Web page in your project.

Background

Use Home Page Wizard's background facility to change the background colour for your page, or to select a graphic image that will become the page's wallpaper.

External Links

Use an external link to help your visitors jump to a Web page outside your project. You'll need to supply the other page's Internet address or URL (Uniform Resource Locator). Before you create a link to someone else's home page, it's only polite to get the other party's approval. Also, it's a good idea to review outside pages frequently, because their content may change or they may disappear entirely. If your external links are out of date, you may end up with puzzled or disgruntled visitors to your page.

E-mail link

You can put your pages up on the Web and just leave them out there as your statement to humanity. But wouldn't it be more fun to give humanity a chance to respond? You might even get fan letters. Use an email link to help your visitors communicate with you. You'll need to supply your Internet or CompuServe email address.

Test

To check the look and feel of your Web pages before you actually put them up for everyone's perusal, click the Test Pages icon. Home Page Wizard first shows you which files will be used to create your pages and how many bytes they have altogether. Then it shows you what your home page looks like. To view your other pages, if you have any, just click their internal links.

If you haven't already specified a Web browser, you'll need to do so before the test can take place. Home Page Wizard can test your pages with any Web browser that you have on your computer.

Publishing Your Web Page

When you're ready to put your pages on the Web, click the Publish pages icon. This starts up Publishing Wizard. All you have to do now is provide some required information (most of it will be filled in for you from Home Page Wizard) and then confirm that you are ready to go. Within minutes, your pages will be available on the World Wide Web.

CompuServe maintains a directory of the home pages set up for CompuServe members. If you want other members to be able to look up your home page by city of residence, occupation, and hobbies, then you should supply this information to Publishing Wizard.

Note: You have to establish a 'Winsock' connection to CompuServe - this can easily be achieved using WinCIM 2.0. See Chapter 9 if you're unsure what this means.

Updating your pages

Once you have your pages on the Web, you can make improve them, or update them at any time. Home Page Wizard makes it easy to update your Web pages or create new ones from scratch, and Publishing Wizard makes it easy to replace your old Web pages with the new ones.

Here are some ways to learn more about Home Page Wizard and Publishing Wizard:

* To find out about the window you're currently using, click the Help button or press the F1 key.

* To learn more about Home Page Wizard while you're using it, try the Help pull-down menu.

* To get tips, news, and any changes to the software, visit CompuServe on-line support service (Go HPWIZ)

* To see what kinds of things other CompuServe members are doing, visit their home pages on the Web. The Web address for CompuServe members' home pages is http://ourworld.compuserve.com/.

If you need additional help, please call CompuServe Customer Service 0800 000 400.

Home Page Wizard FAQ

How long will it take for my page to be "on the net"?
Moments after the publishing process, you and everyone else using the WWW (World Wide Web) will be able to access your home page.

What information am I allowed to post on my Personal Home Page?
Any content on your home page must abide by CompuServe's Operating Rules and Service Agreement Terms. Use of "inappropriate material" such as profanity, pornography, illegal or copyright material on any home page, will result in removal of your home page; and flagrant or repeated violations may lead to termination of membership. If you need to review any of the Rules or Service Agreement Terms please use the GO RULES command on-line.

How much does it cost to download the Home Page Wizard and setup my Personal Home Page?
The download of the Wizard is free. Members may also place their Personal Home Pages on-line free of charge. Please note, standard connect time charges and any supplemental network surcharges do apply during the publishing process.

How often can I submit updates for my Web page?
You may update your Personal Home Page as often as you feel necessary. You will not be charged for any changes or updates made to your Web page.

Once again, standard connect time charges and any supplemental network surcharges do apply during the submission process.

How much storage space do I have available for my page?
CompuServe is allowing a maximum of one megabyte of storage space for each member publishing a home page.

I've published my web page, but how do I view it? What is the address?
During the publishing process, you are prompted for the address you would like to use for your home page. Be sure to write this address down so you do not forget it. The address that you choose for your web page will also pre-register you for a mail alias. In the future, mail aliases will allow you to use a name instead of your User ID number for a mail address. For example, if you choose JOE, your web address or URL (Uniform Resource Locator) will be:

http://ourworld.compuserve.com/homepages/joe

and your mail alias would be: joe and your Internet mail address would be: joe@compuserve.com
If you forget your URL, you can find your page by searching through the OurWorld Home Page database (http://ourworld.compuserve.com/) or you can submit your page again and the same URL will be displayed.

Can I use other HTML authoring tools and HTML documents to create my home page, or do I have to create a new page with the Wizard?
Any HTML file can be published on CompuServe by using the Publishing Wizard. Be sure to include all the HTML documents and any .gif,.jpg files that are "called" within your home page.

Is there a Mac version of the Home Page Wizard?
At this time, there is only a Windows version of the Wizard, although we do plan to release a Macintosh version in the future.

If I cancel my account or if my account is deactivated, what will happen to my home page?
If your account is deactivated/cancelled, your home page will be deleted. Since the Home Page Wizard stores the project on the your machine, you could simply re-publish your home page by opening your project and choosing PUBLISH.

What do the tabs on the left-hand side of the Home Page Wizard do? How do I use them?
The Home Page Wizard allows you to create multiple pages in your project. This allows you to have a "theme" or style for each page. The tabs simply give you a way to see and access all the pages in your project. For example:
One person may have the main page (or index) that gives a short description about themselves and a overview of the contents on their home page. Then they may have a page created of their favorite hot links, a page of their

favorite restaurants, a page of their Top Ten reasons to have a home page on CompuServe, etc. with all of them linked together with Internal Links. With this type of design, it is easy to keep home pages organized and easy to follow.

How do I get assistance if I'm having difficulties with the Wizard?

The Wizard was designed with the novice user in mind. If you run into problems while building your Personal Home Page, please choose the HELP pull-down menu, and you will receive context-sensitive help that will guide you through virtually any problem you may have.

If you continue to have problems, you may receive further assistance by using the NetLauncher Support Forum. Please read/search the messages that are posted in the forum, as someone may be having the same problem. If you do not see a message that relates to your problem, post a message to SYSOP. When posting a message to SYSOP, please compose a clear and concise message that states background information about your machine, the software and version number you are using, and the problems/questions you may have. If you are getting any error messages, please include the EXACT error message and the steps you used to produce the error.

Appendix 5
Glossary of
technical and
Internet terms

acoustic coupler - Means of connecting external devices to a telephone handset avoiding direct electrical connection; most commonly used for low-speed mode access.

address - There are three types of addresses in common use within the Internet. They are email address; IP, internet or Internet address; and hardware or MAC address.

Advanced Research Projects Agency Network (ARPANET) - A pioneering longhaul network funded by ARPA (now DARPA). It served as the basis for early networking research, as well as a central backbone during the development of the Internet. The ARPANET consisted of individual packet switching computers interconnected by leased lines.

ASCII- American Standard Code for Information Interchange (ASCII) A standard character-to-number encoding widely used in the computer industry. ASCII is the standard used for sending non-binary messages over the Internet.

anonymous FTP - Anonymous FTP allows a user to retrieve documents, files, programs, and other archived data from anywhere in the Internet without having to establish a user-id and password. By using the special user-id of "anonymous" the network user will bypass local security checks and will have access to publicly accessible files on the remote system.

archie - A system to automatically gather, index and serve information on the Internet. The initial implementation of archie provided an indexed directory of filenames from all anonymous FTP archives on the Internet. Later versions provide other collections of information.

archive site - A machine that provides access to a collection of files across the Internet. An "anonymous FTP archive site", for example, provides access to this material via the FTP protocol.

BABT - British Approvals board for Telecommunications. An independent body responsible for approval procedures for UK telecomms equipment. Only BABT approved equipment may be connected to UK services, regardless of the supplier of these services.

baud - A unit of signalling speed. The speed in Baud is the number of discrete conditions or signal elements per second. If each signal event represents only one bit condition, then Baud is the same as bits per second. Baud does not otherwise equal bits per second.

BAUD rate - After BAUDOT, who invented time division multiplexing in 1874. Baud rate is not applicable to contemporary modems equipped with data compression. Use BPS.

bis - 'Second Working' or Second Implementation' as used in CCITT recommendations.

BinHex - Program for the Macintosh computer which translates binary files into ASCII representations. Converted binary files can then be transferred as electronic mail. Used to get over the 7 bit limitations of the Internet.

Bitnet - An academic computer network that provides interactive electronic mail and file transfer services, using a store-and-forward protocol, based on IBM Network Job Entry protocols. Bitnet-II encapsulates the Bitnet protocol within IP packets and depends on the Internet to route them.

bounce - The return of a piece of mail because of an error in its delivery.

Bulletin Board System (BBS) - A computer, and associated software, which typically provides electronic messaging services, archives of files, and any other services or activities of interest to the bulletin board system's operator. Although BBS's have traditionally been the domain of hobbyists, an increasing number of BBS's are connected directly to the Internet, and many BBS's are currently operated by government, educational, and research institutions.

client - A computer system or process that requests a service of another computer system or process. A workstation requesting the contents of a file from a file server is a client of the file server.

client-server model - A common way to describe the paradigm of many network protocols. Examples include the name-server/name-resolver relationship in DNS and the file-server/file-client relationship in NFS.

Computer Emergency Response Team (CERT) - The CERT was formed by DARPA in November 1988 in response to the needs exhibited during the Internet worm incident. The CERT charter is to work with the Internet community to facilitate its response to computer security events involving Internet hosts, to take pro-active steps to raise the community's awareness of computer security issues, and to conduct research targeted at improving the security of existing systems.

cracker (USA) - A cracker is an individual who attempts to access computer systems without authorization. These individuals are often malicious, as opposed to 'hackers', and have many means at their disposal for breaking into a system.

CR (carriage return) - A control character causing the print or display position to move to the first position on the line, drawn from the typewriter and teleprinter function with similar action.

Cyberspace - A term coined by William Gibson in his fantasy novel 'Neuromancer' to describe the "world" of computers, and the society that gathers around them.

Data Encryption Key (DEK) - Used for the encryption of message text and for the computation of message integrity checks (signatures).

Data Encryption Standard (DES) - A popular, standard encryption scheme.

Defense Advanced Research Projects Agency (DARPA) - An agency of the U.S. Department of Defense responsible for the development of new technology for use by the military. DARPA (formerly known as ARPA) was responsible for funding much of the development of the Internet we know today, including the Berkeley version of Unix and TCP/IP.

dialup - A temporary, as opposed to dedicated, connection between machines established over a standard phone line.

Digest - Instead of getting email messages from your listserv subscription one at a time as they are posted, the digest format gives you a compilation of the day's (week's, month's) messages. Some folks prefer this format since it helps to manage a large influx of mail and helps hold discussion on a certain topic together. Others prefer the more immediate and spontaneous 'heat' of receiving messages as they are posted. Note: not all listservs offer this distribution option.

dweeb - Slang (USA) Derogatory term for an unliked person, often young and unknowlegable. Dweebs sometimes mature into Nerds, and then into Geeks.

E-journal (Electronic Journal) - Newsletters, zines, periodicals, scholarly journals same as the hard copy, except available over the net. You can access e-journals two ways: 1) a subscription will have the journal delivered to your email box, or 2) you can look up the journal at its host site (via WAIS or GOPHER) and if you want a copy you can have it delivered via FTP.

Electronic Frontier Foundation (EFF) - A foundation established to address social and legal issues arising from the impact on society of the increasingly pervasive use of computers as a means of communication and information distribution.

Electronic Mail (email) - A system whereby a computer user can exchange messages with other computer users (or groups of users) via a communications network. Electronic mail is one of the most popular uses of the Internet.

email address - The domain-based or UUCP address that is used to send electronic mail to a specified destination. On CompuServe the email address is also the same as the membership number, as in 100113,2132.

email address aliasing - The addition of text based pointers to a numerical email address. On CompuServe this takes the form of username@compuserve.com and is used in addition to the numerical address which is retained for billing and administrative purposes.

emulate/emulation - Imitating a system or device such that a connected device accepts the same information, executes the same computer programs and achieves the same results as if the emulator were one of its own kind. Most often, emulation is a downward step in capability of the device being used, as when a personal computer is used to emulate a mechanical teleprinter or a "dumb" terminal on a computer network. While some degree of upward emulation is possible, it is less prevalent in the broad view of computer communications.

FAQ - Frequently Asked Question - Either a frequently-asked question, or a list of frequently asked questions and their answers. Many USENET news groups, and some non-USENET mailing lists, maintain FAQ lists (FAQS) so that participants won't spend lots of time answering the same set of questions.

file transfer - The copying of a file from one computer to another over a computer network.

File Transfer Protocol (FTP) - A protocol which allows a user on one host to access, and transfer files to and from, another host over a network. Also, FTP is usually the name of the program the user invokes to execute the protocol.

finger - A program that displays information about a particular user, or all users, logged on the local system or on a remote system. It typically shows full name, last login time, idle time, terminal line, and terminal location (where applicable). It may also display plan and project files left by the user.

flame - A strong opinion and/or criticism of something, usually as a frank inflammatory statement, in an electronic mail message. It is common to precede a flame with an indication of pending fire (i.e., FLAME ON!). Flame Wars occur when people start flaming other people for flaming when they shouldn't have.

Forum - on CompuServe an area reserved for public messaging, conferencing, and file service provision

For Your Information (FYI) - A subseries of RFCs that are not technical standards or descriptions of protocols. FYIs convey general information about topics related to TCP/IP or the Internet.

Geek - Slang (USA). Derogatory term for computer user or enthusiast of some sort.

Gopher - A distributed information service that makes available hierarchical collections of information across the Internet. Gopher uses a simple protocol that allows a single Gopher client to access information from any accessible Gopher server, providing the user with a single "Gopher space" of information. Public domain versions of the client and server are available.

hacker - A person who delights in having an intimate understanding of the internal workings of a system, computers and computer networks in particular. The term is often misused in a pejorative context, where 'cracker' would be the correct term. In the UK the terms Hacker and Cracker are used indiscriminately.

header - The part of an electronic mail message that precedes the body of a message and contains, among other things, the message originator, date and time.

HTML - Hypertext Markup Language - the script programming code used to generate World Wide Web pages

HTTP - The Hypertext Transmission Protocol used to connect Web Client software with Web Servers. Used as a header in URL's to indicate server types, as in http//www.compuserve.com/

Integrated Services Digital Network (ISDN) - An emerging technology which is beginning to be offered by the telephone carriers of the world. ISDN combines voice and digital network services in a single medium, making it possible to offer customers digital data services as well as voice connections through a single "wire".

internet address - An IP address that uniquely identifies a node on an internet. An Internet address (capital "I"), uniquely identifies a node on the Internet.

Internet Protocol (IP) - The Internet Protocol, defined in STD 5, RFC 791, is the network layer for the TCP/IP Protocol Suite. It is a connectionless, best-effort packet switching protocol.

Internet Relay Chat (IRC) A world-wide "party line" protocol that allows one to converse with others in real time. IRC is structured as a network of servers, each of which accepts connections from client programs, one per user.

KA9Q - A popular implementation of TCP/IP and associated protocols for amateur packet radio systems.

Kermit - A popular file transfer protocol developed by Columbia University. Because Kermit runs in most operating environments, it provides an easy method of file transfer. Kermit is NOT the same as FTP.

listserv - An automated mailing list distribution system originally designed for the Bitnet/EARN network.

mail gateway - A machine that connects two or more electronic mail systems (including dissimilar mail systems) and transfers messages between them. Sometimes the mapping and translation can be quite complex, and it generally requires a store-and-forward scheme whereby the message is received from one system completely before it is transmitted to the next system, after suitable translations.

mailing list - A list of email addresses, used to forward messages to groups of people. Generally, a mailing list is used to discuss certain set of topics, and different mailing lists discuss different topics. A mailing list may be moderated. This means that messages sent to the list are actually sent to a moderator who determines whether or not to send the messages on to everyone else.

moderator - A person, or small group of people, who manage moderated mailing lists and newsgroups. Moderators are responsible for determining which email submissions are passed on to list.

Modem - modulator/demodulator - A piece of equipment that connects a computer to a data transmission line (typically a telephone line of some sort). Modems transfer data at speeds ranging from 300 bits per second (bps) to 32 K bps.

Multipurpose Internet Mail Extensions (MIME) - An extension to Internet email which provides the ability to transfer non-textual data, such as graphics, audio and fax. It is defined in RFC 1341.

Multi-User Dungeon (MUD) Adventure - role playing games, or simulations played on the Internet. Devotees call them "text-based virtual reality adventures". The games can feature fantasy combat, booby traps and magic. Players interact in real time and can change the "world" in the game as they play it. Most MUDs are based on the Telnet protocol.

Nerd - Slang (USA) see 'Dweeb'.

netiquette - A pun on "etiquette" referring to proper behavior on a network.

network - A computer network is a data communications system which interconnects computer systems at various different sites. A network may be composed of any combination of LANs, MANs or WANs.

Network News Transfer Protocol - (NNTP) A protocol, defined in RFC 977, for the distribution, inquiry, retrieval, and posting of news articles.

Packet InterNet Groper (PING) - A program used to test reachability of destinations by sending them an ICMP echo request and waiting for a reply. The term is used as a verb: "Ping host X to see if it is up!"

packet switching - The technique in which a stream of data is broken into standardized units called "packets," each of which contains address, sequence, control, size and error checking information in addition to the user data. Specialized packet switches operate on this added information to move the packets to their destination in the proper sequence and again present them in a contiguous stream.

parity - a constant state of equality; one of the oldest and simplest methods of error checking data transmission. Characters are forced into parity (total number of marking bits odd or even as selected by choice) by adding a one or zero bit as appropriate when transmitted; parity is then checked as odd or even at the receiver.

parity bit - a check bit appended to an array of binary digits to make the sum of all the digits always odd or always even.

Point Of Presence (POP) - A site where there exists a collection of tele-communications equipment, usually digital leased lines and multi-protocol routers.

Point-to-Point Protocol (PPP) - The Point-to-Point Protocol, defined in RFC 1171, provides a method for transmitting packets over serial point-to-point links. An older less sophisticated method is SLIP serial line interface protocol. CompuServe uses PPP.

Post Office Protocol (POP) - A protocol designed to allow single user hosts to read mail from a server. There are three versions: POP, POP2, and POP3. Latter versions are NOT compatible with earlier versions.

postmaster - The person responsible for taking care of electronic mail problems, answering queries about users, and other related work at a site.

Privacy Enhanced Mail (PEM) - Internet email which provides confidentiality, authentication and message integrity using various encryption methods.

quad standard - Modem providing four CCITT modes, usually V21, V22/V22Bis, V23.

quin standard - Modem providing five CCITT modes, usually V21, V22/V22Bis, V23, V32.

remote login - Operating on a remote computer, using a protocol over a computer network, as though locally attached, as with telnet.

Request For Comments (RFC) - The document series, begun in 1969, which describes the Internet suite of protocols and related experiments. Not all (in fact very few) RFCs describe Internet standards, but all Internet standards are written up as RFCs. The RFC series of documents is unusual in that the proposed protocols are forwarded by the Internet research and development community, acting on their own behalf, as opposed to the formally reviewed and standardized protocols that are promoted by organizations such as CCITT and ANSI.

server - A provider of resources (e.g., file servers and name servers).

SIG - Special Interest Group - called a forum on some systems, notably CompuServe.

signature - The three or four line message at the bottom of a piece of email or a Usenet article which identifies the sender. Large signatures (over five lines) are generally frowned upon.

Simple Mail Transfer Protocol (SMTP) - A protocol, defined in STD 10, RFC 821, used to transfer electronic mail between computers. It is a server to server protocol, so other protocols are used to access the messages.

Simple Network Management Protocol (SNMP) The Internet standard protocol, defined in STD 15, RFC 1157, developed to manage nodes on an IP network. It is currently possible to manage wiring hubs, toasters, jukeboxes, etc.

Sysop - SYSTEM OPerator, used on CompuServe and elsewhere to indicate the super-user in charge or partial charge of a Forum. There are hierarchies of Sysops on CompuServe - those with the most powers are called Wizard Operators - WIZOps.

TCP/IP Protocol Suite Transmission Control Protocol over Internet Protocol. This is a common shorthand which refers to the suite of transport and application protocols which runs over IP.

ter - Means 'third working' or third implementation, as used in CCITT recommendations.

terminal equipment - Devices, apparatus and their associated interfaces used to forward information to a local customer or distant terminal.

TTY (Teletype) - 1.) The registered trade name for teleprinters and data terminals of the Teletype Corporation; 2.) Used generically in the tele-communications industry for teleprinters or data terminals that emulate teleprinter operations.

Telnet - Telnet is the Internet standard protocol for remote terminal connection service. It is defined in STD 8, RFC 854 and extended with options by many other RFCs.

terminal emulator - A program that allows a computer to emulate a terminal. The workstation thus appears as a terminal to the remote host. Used on CompuServe to attach users to remote services.

Trojan Horse - A computer program which carries within itself a means to allow the creator of the program access to the system using it.

UNIX-to-UNIX CoPy (UUCP) - This was initially a program run under the UNIX operating system that allowed one UNIX system to send files to another UNIX system via dial-up phone lines. Today, the term is more commonly used to describe the large international network which uses the UUCP protocol to pass news and electronic mail.

UUEncode - Program for personal computers, which translates binary files into ASCII representations. Converted binary files can then be transferred as electronic mail. Used to get over the 7 bit limitations of the Internet. UUDecode is used to effect the reverse transformation

URL - Uniform Resource Locator - a textual address which lets Web Client software locate and log into a remote server.

Usenet - A collection of thousands of topically named newsgroups, the computers which run the protocols, and the people who read and submit Usenet news. Not all Internet hosts subscribe to Usenet and not all Usenet hosts are on the Internet.

Vendor Forum - used on CompuServe to provide marketing and or support. Vendor Forums are flagged as such, as in MacVendor A, Mac Vendor B, and so on.

virus - A program which replicates itself on computer systems by incorporating itself into other programs which are shared among computer systems.

WHOIS - An Internet program which allows users to query a database of people and other Internet entities, such as domains, networks, and hosts, kept at the DDN NIC. The information for people shows a person's company name, address, phone number and email address.

Wide Area Information Servers (WAIS) - A distributed information service which offers simple natural language input, indexed searching for fast retrieval, and a "relevance feedback" mechanism which allows the results of initial searches to influence future searches. Public domain implementations are available.

World Wide Web (WWW or W3) - A hypertext-based, distributed information system created by researchers at CERN in Switzerland. Users may create, edit or browse hypertext documents using Web 'Browser' client software. The clients and servers are freely available.

worm - A computer program which replicates itself and is self-propagating. Worms, as opposed to viruses, are meant to spawn in network environments. Network worms were first defined by Shoch & Hupp of Xerox in ACM Communications (March 1982). The Internet worm of November 1988 is perhaps the most famous; it successfully propagated itself on over 6,000 systems across the Internet.

X.400 - The CCITT and ISO standard for electronic mail. It is widely used in Europe and Canada.

X.500 - The CCITT and ISO standard for electronic directory services.

Index

A

Access Points 17
Account Set-up 24
Advanced CIM Setup 31
Agreement Number 24
Alternate Price Plan 21
Archie 145
Archie By Email 261
Archie Commands 260
Archie Searches 257,258,259
ARPANET 138
ATH 28
ATH0 26
ATM 143,144
AutoPilot 15

B

Backups 76
Baud Rate 38
Bell 103 44
Billing Errors 26
Binary Mail 10
Binhex 4 70, 71
Bounced Mail 62
BT 'Option 15' 20

C

CC:Mail 58
CID 155, 156
CIM Add Ons 15
CIM Mail 64
CIM Menus 33 -42
CIM Setup 31
CIM Upgrading 29
CIM Walkabout 30
CIS B+ 22
CIS B+ 49
CIS Navigator 13
Client Software 156

Compact Pro 74
CompuServe Index 291
CompuServe Internet Dialler 155
ConfigPPP 154
Connection Elapsed Time 40
Cookie Hoax 144
CPS Nodes 18

D

Data Compression 45
Disconnecting 26
Disk Errors/Mac 42
DiskCopy 75
Dun & Bradstreet 113

E

Email see Mail
Email Encryption 78
Email, Internet 146
ENS 116
EPS Files 77
Error Correction 45
Eudora 70
Executive News 116
Explore 114

F

Fax Rates 277
Fax Sending 82
Fax Standards 44
FIFO 51
File
  Compression 74
  Credenza 34
  Decompress 34
  Finders 37
  Finders 95
  Segmenting 227

Filing Cabinet 58
Find Option 35
Finding A Forum 92,94
Finger 150
Flame Wars 102
Forums
  Conference Room 94
  Conferencing 106,107
  FAQ 108
  File Abstract 104
  File Downloads 104
  File Libraries 93,96
  Find/Files 104
  Flame Wars 102
  File Uploading 106
  Index 291
  Joining 96
  Leaving 98
  Message Etiquette
  Message Scroll 102
  Sections 92
  Messages Posting 97
  Messages Waiting 102
  Newsflashes 98
  Nicknames 97
  Notices 98
  Off-line Messaging 101
  Resigning 98
  Topics 91
  Find 92, 95
Forums.Lst 95
France Telecom 18
FTP
  Archives 244
  Chapter 237
  Directories 238
  Downloads 239
  FAQ 241
  File Types 238
  Index 239
  Permission Masks 240
  With CIM 238
  With Mosaic 202

G

GIF 78
Glossary 329
GNS Dialplus 18
GO Command 35, 36
Gopher Bookmarks 266
Golden Compass 14
Golden Life Insurance 3

Gopher
  Downloads 266
  Searching 262,,263
  With Mosaic 203
  GopherSpace 264
Graphic Menus 41
Graphics Files 76
GZ 75

H

Help Forum 96
HMI Time Out 26, 30
HR Block 3
HTML Documentation 176
HTML Writing In 172
HTTP Address 172
Hypertext Transport Protocol 172
Hytelnet 250

I

Inbasket 57
Internet
  Archie 145
  Email 146
  Intro 137
  Mac Set Up 162
  MacCIM Setup 163
  Origins 138
  Relay Chat 251
  Search Intro 169
  Service Provider 153
  Internet Software 156
  Q&A 157
IRC 149
IRC Commands 252
IRC Networks 253
ISDN 143

J

Javascript 175
JPEG 76

L

LHA 74
Library Searches 104
Listserv 149
Listserv Mirrors 220
Listservs 228
Lost Mail 62

M

Mac CIM 25
Mac Classic 154
Mac Ports 38
Mac PPP 156
Mac SE 154
MacPPP Script 161
MacPPP Set Up 159
MacTCP Setup 158
MacTCP 154
Mail
  Address 59
  Address Type 66
  Alias 59
  ASCII Messages 63
  Attachment 70
  BC 66
  Binary Files 61
  Binary Files 63
  Bounced 62
  Caveats 61
  Carbon Copy 66
  Creating 32
  Confirmation 67
  CSI 60
  Directory 66
  Enclosure 69
  Mail Expiration 67
  Fax 58
  File Compression 74
  Forwarding 58
  Get All 67
  Groups 62
  Help 58
  Hubs 58
  Inbasket 57
  Internet Binary 69
  Mail List Digest 78
  Lists 80
  Lost Mail 62
  Member Search 81
  Message Options 66
  Nickname 60
  Outbasket 57
  Passwords 78
  Personal Area 63/64
  Postal 59, 83
  Preferences 33, 65
  Quick Start 57
  Receive Telex 88
  Receiving 57
  Mail Receipt 58
  Saving 65

Mail—*contd.*
  Security 73
  Send Fax 82
  Send File 69
  Send/Receive All 68
  Sending 57, 65
  Settings 60
  Show Recipients 66
  Size Limits 62,63
  Storage Limits 63
  Telex 58, 86
  Test 67
  UUCODE 70
  WHOIS 81
  With Mosaic 208
  WP Files 72
Mercury 132 21
Mercury Nodes 18
MIME 70, 71
MIME Types In Mosaic 216,217
MNP5 44
Modems
  Buying Checklist 46
  Error Correction 58
  Speed Buffering 48
  Speeds 44
  Troubleshooting 50
  Types 38
  RPI 45/46
  Modems INIT String 47
  Network 52
Mosaic
  Bookmarks 186
  Configuring 210
  FTP 202
  Helper Apps 186
  Hotlists 194, 195
  Image Handling 192
  Intro 171
  Local Documents 199
  Mail 208
  MIME 216, 217
  Obtaining 164
  Options 211
  Proxies 185
  Quick Menu 191
  Searching 194
  URL's 200
  Using 184
  Viewers 215
  Gopher 203
  News 204, 205
MountImage 75

N

NaVCIS 14
Net Etiquette 224
Netlauncher 1.0 160
Netlauncher Move Util. 161
Netscape 138
Netscape Navigator, Obtaining 163
Network News 221
Network Settings 38
News With Mosaic 204
News
  Contents 222
  Distribution 225
  FAQs 223
  File Segmenting 227
  Listserv 228
  Setting Up 230
  In Mosaic 207
  New 225
  NFSNET 140

O

OLR's 13
OS/2 Set Up 264
Other Services 113
Outbasket 57
OzCIS 14

P

Passwords 31
PC Connector 38
PCMCIA Modem 43
PGP 78, 79
Phone Numbers
  Spain 288
  Belgium 288
  France 266
  Italy 267
  Nederlands 288
  Switzerland
  UK 283
  Ping 150
PKarc 74
PKzip 74
PNG 77
POP3 Mail 153
Port, Telnet 249
Posting News With Mosaic 205
Postscript Files 78
PPP 153

Practice Forum 95
Preferences/Settings 40
Price Plans 21
Python, Monty 147,

Q

QuickCIS 15

R

Rates 275
Rebuild Indexes 42
Receive A Telex 88
Redial Attempt 39
Ribbon 41
ROT13 78
RTF Files 70, 72

S

SEA Files 75
Searching Forums 35
  Searching With Archie 257
  Searching With Gopher 263
  Searching With Veronica 264, 268,269
  Searching With WAIS 266
Send A Fax 82
Send A Telex 86
Serial Number 24
Serial Ports - Macs 48
Serial Ports - Windows 48
Services/Find 35
SIT Files 74
Special Prefs 37
Special Settings 37
Splodge Key, Mac, 36
Standard Plan 21
Start-up Pack 23
Stuffit 74
Super Value Plan 22
SYS.INI Updating 51

T

TapCis 14
TAR FILES 244
TAR Files 75
TCP/IP Connecting With 155
TCP/IP History 139
TCP/IP Software 154
TCP/IP Software 6
TCP/IP Stack 154

TeePee 14
Telefast Kit 53
Telephone Nodes 279
Telex 86
Telnet 148
Telnet Chapter 247
Telnet Commands 248
Telnet FAQ 254
Telnet Ports 249
Telnet Terminals 248
Telnet, IRC 251
Terminal Access 12
Terminal Emulation 49
Terminal Services 115
Terminal Use 22
TIFF 76,77

U

UART Ports 50
UK IRC Servers 252
UNIX Compressors 75
UNIX Invention Of 140
URLs, Understanding 200
Usenet 148
Usenet CIS Policy On 234
Usenet Mirrors 229
Usenet, Censoring 230
Using Mosaic 184
Usenet FAQ 231
Usenet News 221

V

V21/V34bis 44
V42 Bis 45
Veronica Searches 264

VersaTerm 23
Viruses 76
VT100/102 248

W

WAIS 147
WAIS 266
WAIS Advantages 267
Whois 151
WinCIM 2.0 155
Windows 95 Conflicts 160
Winsock 40
Word 6 76
World Wide Web Chapter 167
WWW
    Business 170
    Bibliography 176
    Home Page Setup 172
    HTML Tag 173
    Intro 150
    Mosaic 183
    Origins 168
    Site List 179
    Writing HTML 172

X

XMODEM 22
Xmodem In Telnet 249

Z

Zipit 75
ZMODEM 23
Zmodem, In Telnet 249
ZOO Files 76